GANGS IN AMERICA

GANGS IN AMERICA

Edited by
C. Ronald Huff

 SAGE Publications
International Educational and Professional Publisher
Newbury Park   London   New Delhi

For information address:

SAGE Publications, Inc.
2455 Teller Road
Newbury Park, California 91320
E-mail: order@sagepub.com

SAGE Publications Ltd.
6 Bonhill Street
London EC2A 4PU
United Kingdom

SAGE Publications India Pvt. Ltd.
M-32 Market
Greater Kailash I
New Delhi 110 048 India

Printed in the United States of America

Library of Congress Cataloging-in-Publication Data

Main entry under title:

Gangs in America / edited by
    C. Ronald Huff.
        p. cm.
    Includes bibliographical references and index.
    ISBN 0-8039-3828-4 (C). — ISBN 0-8039-3829-2 (P)
    1. Gangs—United States. I. Huff, C. Ronald.
HV6439.U5G36 1990
364.1'.06'0973—dc20   90-39608
                                                            CIP

96 97 98 99 00 01 15 14 13 12 11 10 9 8

Sage Production Editor: Diane S. Foster

Contents

Foreword and Overview

ALBERT K. COHEN

In 1955 I wrote a book, *Delinquent Boys: The Culture of the Gang.* This was probably the first scholarly monograph after the Second World War with the word *gang* in its title. A long-delayed and unanticipated consequence of that obscure event was an invitation, 35 years later, to comment on this collection of papers on gangs in the United States. On the score of antiquity, my qualifications for this task are only marginally superior to those of some of the authors of the chapters themselves, but—unlike them—I am not currently active in research and writing on gangs and am therefore fit only to comment on what others have written.

I think it is fair to say that the authors of this collection include most, although not all, of the leading scholars in the field. They report on aspects of their own research; they comment critically and hopefully on what we know and what we don't know, on techniques and strategy of research, on questions of policy. They sometimes disagree. I think therefore that the collection can be said to represent "the state of the art." I do not intend to summarize or assess the individual chapters, but I shall offer some impressions and elaborate on two main themes in the study of gangs.

What Is a Gang and
What Difference Does It Make?

Delinquent Boys: The Culture of the Gang was mostly about the delinquent subculture: what it is, where it is, and what it is about the structure and the culture of American society that can explain why we have a delinquent subculture. It really had very little to say about gangs, or rather it did not see as problematic the question of how gangs differ from other forms of sociation or relational structures. *Groups* of "similarly circumstanced" individuals provided the settings for the production, maintenance, and transmission of the delinquent subculture and physical and moral support to their members in carrying out delinquent activities. It did not strike me as important to consider by what criteria gangs might be distinguished from other kinds of groups and what difference the different forms of sociation might make to the delinquent conduct of their participants.

The authors of these chapters believe that the gangs they have been studying are not just groups or networks of delinquent friends but that they are different and special. More than that, I think they will agree most of the time that *this* group is a gang, that *that* group is not, and that most of the time "people in general" will agree with them. But this approach to consensus on the use of the word is not reflected in the multitudinous attempts at formal definitions. The expression *gang-related*— that is, when is an assault or a robbery a "gang thing" and when is it not?—is even more troublesome.

The chapter by Maxson and Klein is concerned with the generalizability of research findings. Because attempts to measure the prevalence of gangs and the rates and characteristics of gang-related crime are based on data recorded by police and other criminal justice agencies, the picture that we get for a given city depends very much on the criteria that these agencies use in deciding what a gang is and what is gang-related. If they use different criteria in different cities—and they do— how can we compare different cities? How can we estimate the magnitude of "the problem" and formulate policies of intervention appropriate to the character of the problem if different measures yield different descriptions of the problem? Maxson and Klein report on their investigations into the differences these differences might make, and their results (which I will not summarize here) provide some grounds for cautious optimism.

But the question, What is a gang? also has to do with understanding and explaining. When, in doing science, we propose that some set of objects or events be divided into categories on the basis of some criterion, we are implying that categories that are distinguished in this way behave differently in important ways. In short, to propose a definition is to propose a hypothesis, that drawing the line in this particular way is important for theoretical purposes.

The definitions of *gang* are legion. Ruth Horowitz's chapter has an extended and thoughtful discussion of attempts to define the word and, contrary to what one might expect, suggests that we should not be in a hurry to reach consensus on a definition and to standardize its use for research purposes. Her argument is precisely that each definition directs our attention to certain properties of things and away from others. In an early stage of research and theory in a given area, early closure of the definitional question may lead to the neglect or oversight of properties of things that are important to understanding and explanation.

A good point! We should avoid premature closure, but it does not follow that we should not continue to explore definitions and consider their implications. In this spirit, I propose that gangs—in contrast to other forms of sociation—are collectivities. They may be other things as well, but they are at least this. The word *collectivity* occurs frequently in the literature on gangs, and especially in Ruth Horowitz's work. I have defined *collectivities* as those actors to which individual human beings or "natural persons" are related as "members"; the members are seen to "belong to" the collectivities. Like other actors, collectivities have names and reputations. We love them, hate them, admire them, and resent them. They range from families and ball teams to nation-states.

The essential thing is that they are actors: They are seen to *do things*, including deviant and criminal things. Whether some set of persons constitutes a collectivity of a certain sort—a family, a corporation, a ball team—depends on the criteria embedded in the popular culture or the legal system for constituting that sort of an entity. Whether something a member does is seen to be simply that—something he or she did—or is seen to warrant an attribution of agency to the collectivity itself is likewise a matter of criteria embedded in the culture. I have dealt with these matters and their implications for criminological theory at some length in another paper (Cohen, 1990). Here I will deal briefly with their implications for the matter at hand.

I believe that when ordinary people or extraordinary people like criminologists speak of gangs, they usually are thinking of collectivities. Although the definitions they offer may emphasize size, organizational complexity, urban location, hierarchy, leadership, territoriality, and so on, I think the criterion they are operating with intuitively is collectivity, plus some propensity to disruptive, "antisocial," or criminal behavior. As the reader of this volume will see, all of these properties are variable; they may be present in various degrees or not at all in entities that lay and professional people will agree are gangs. On the other hand, most groups—including groups of delinquent or criminal youth—are not full-blown collectivities, although some of them may be embryonic (and even vestigial) collectivities. What their members do is seen to be theirs alone, although they may be seen to have been influenced by others; it is not a basis for the attribution of action or character to some inclusive entity of which the actors are "members." "Nongang" does not mean "nongroup." As Fagan says in his chapter on drug use, "Gangs are only one of several deviant peer groups in inner cities." Vigil, in his chapter on *cholos* and gangs, traces the evolution of Mexican-American gangs historically through different forms of sociation—from the Mexican *palomilla*, or "male cohorting tradition," to the gangs we know today. In April of 1989 the country was shocked by the brutal rape of a 28-year-old investment banker while she was jogging in Central Park, New York City, and at least eight other persons reported being assaulted that night by members of the same group, numbering between 32 and 41. I have seen no description of this group—its organization, the relationships among its members, its duration, or whether its members saw themselves as some kind of entity. The *New York Times* of April 25, 1989, referred to this group as a "pack" and "wolf pack." It does not seem likely that it fits any of the definitions of *gang* that the authors of this book work with, nor, on the other hand, does it seem likely that it is just a bunch of guys who hang on the same corner.

None of the chapters in this volume, however, describes the alternate forms of sociation that make up the category *non-gang*. After all, this is a book about gangs, but if we are interested in the larger problem of youth crime it would be well to remember that if all the gangs were suddenly to vanish, we would still have a plethora of youth crime and most of that crime would (in one way or another) be morally and materially supported by some kind of system of relationships in which the actor is embedded. What are the other relational contexts of youth crime and delinquency? What do they have to offer, and to what kinds of youths do they appeal? What affinities do they have for different kinds of community settings? In what specific ways do variations in relational contexts facilitate—or perhaps inhibit—this or that kind of deviance? For that matter, how might the study of the full spectrum of alternative relational contexts and structures and what they have to offer their participants illuminate what is special or distinctive about the collectivity form, what it has to offer its members, and the conditions that call it forth? Is there not, perhaps, some disproportion in the concentration of our scholarly energies and resources on the collectivity form, which happens to be the most colorful, the most fascinating, and perhaps the most frightening member of this class of social forms?

The starting point for the understanding of collectivities, including gangs, is that membership in collectivities is part of the identities of its members—that is to say, that who we are as individuals (the kinds of objects we are to others and, for that matter, to ourselves) is constituted in part by the fact that we "belong to" and are "a part of" this or that collectivity. This means that the identity of the collectivity—its reputation, its character and accomplishments, its rank or standing among other collective actors of the same class—becomes part of the identity of its members. For some, this may be a minor and peripheral part. For others, that they are members of this or that collectivity is one of the few claims (and perhaps the proudest claim) they can make for themselves. That membership in gangs confers identity is no secret; it could be the single most common proposition encountered in the literature on gangs.

But this, in turn, has other implications. It implies, for example, that members have a stake in the conduct of other members of the collectivity. What people think of *us*, our collectivity, is a result of what we do—what we do collectively and what we do as individuals, insofar as we are seen to be acting in behalf of or as representatives of our collectivity. If what our fellow members do adds luster or does damage to the good name of the collectivity, and if the value of our personal identity in the marketplace of identities reflects that of the collectivity's identity, our fellow members have to that extent given us or deprived us of something of value. Sometimes the mechanism is more direct: If we are seen to act as representatives of our collectivity, what one of us does may be seen to be done by each of us severally. That is to say we may, to a certain extent, be treated as interchangeable and therefore accountable for one another's conduct. For purposes of retribution, any one of us may do as well as the original author of the offending act.

It is not, then, enough to say that belonging to a collectivity confers identity. Because they confer identity, collectivities function differently from other relational systems. Members tend to become their brothers' keepers or—to circumvent the sexism in this time-honored expression—their confederates' custodians. They cannot lightly say, "No skin off my ass." The extent to which they will monitor, discipline, and control one another will depend on various circumstances. For example, members of a college fraternity may exercise intrusive and effective control over their "brothers." A residence hall on the same campus that may have a name and may function as a collectivity in a limited way may, in the main, provide its members with not much more than a place to sleep, three meals a day, and an address. It is only a rudimentary collectivity, where students have little incentive to exercise control over one another. I cannot here elaborate on the many dimensions along which collectivities may vary and that may affect the way they function.

Now let us take a look at some of the material on gangs in this volume in light of these remarks on collectivity. Maxson and Klein were interested in the difference between gang and nongang violent incidents, homicides, and others. Their findings have been detailed in another publication (Maxson, Gordon, & Klein, 1985). (In the present volume they are interested primarily in how the findings are affected by using different definitions or indicators of "gang-related" offenses, and they discuss their findings only from that standpoint.) They found that, among other differences, gang incidents involved more participants, a lesser likelihood that suspects and victims knew one another, and more fear of retaliation. Violence—including homicide—can take many forms and serve many different purposes, but there are some general remarks we can make about the relationship between gang violence and the fact that gangs are collectivities. In the first place a group does not have to be large in order to be a full-fledged gang, but it is not likely to be large unless it is a gang, and this is related to the fact that gangs are collectivities. Because members' identities are bound up with that of the collectivity, they have a common interest and a large stake in the success of the collectivity in all its activities, but especially the kinds of activities on which the collectivity seeks to build its reputation. The common interest in the survival and success of the group and the rewards that the members administer to one another for their contributions to the common cause make it possible for more people to work together, in some measure subordinating their private inclinations to a common discipline. There are such things as "private fights" in gangs—that is to say, fights that individual members get into "on their own," that other members will not recognize as gang matters and therefore as creating an obligation for them to join in. To the degree, however, that gangs are ranked in the larger community of gangs on their fighting prowess, fighting is everybody's business and such conflicts are less likely to be private affairs than are fights in a nongang—that is, noncollectivity—context.

Most violent altercations and homicides occur between husbands and wives, relatives, friends, neighbors, and others who are relatively "close" to one another; they are ways of venting passions and settling grievances that grow out of such relationships. The parties to the violent episodes necessarily know one another, although other persons may sometimes get involved because of special ties to one or the other party. Gang violence, however, is much more likely to grow out of perceptions that one *gang* has been challenged, insulted, offended, or injured by another gang. In a sense, it is "nothing personal." As in war, the soldiers of opposing armies need not know one another. *Any* enemy soldier is a surrogate for the army whose uniform he or she wears. It is not remarkable that suspects and victims are less likely to know one another in gang than in nongang violence.

For much the same reason, there is more fear of retaliation in gang than in nongang violence. The fear is realistic; the essence of collectivity is a community of identity. An injury inflicted by A upon B may count as revenge for a prior injury inflicted by C upon D because, in the algebra of collectivity, A equals D and B equals C.

Consider now a finding from Jeffrey Fagan's chapter in this volume. He found that the "prevalence of self-reported delinquency and substance use was far greater for gang youths compared with nongang youths" for 12 categories of behavior ranging from alcohol use to felony assault. Prevalence is the percentage who reported at least one incident of the specific behavior measured. The participation rate is the mean number of offenses in the past year for those who reported at least one incident. "Significant differences in participation rates between gang and nongang youths were found for all behaviors except FELONY AND MINOR ASSAULT, ROBBERY, and EXTORTION. . . . Evidently, the frequency of violence for those involved at least once is independent of gang involvement." In other words, if you are in a gang, the probability that you will commit violent acts at all is much greater than if you are not in a gang. Looking only at all youths who commit violent acts, however—even just one—those who are not in gangs will on the average commit just as many violent acts as those who are in gangs. Fagan offers some suggestions about why this is so. Let me suggest another: If you join a gang, it need not necessarily mean that you have some special proclivity or commitment to violence. You are in a gang mainly because you want to be known as a member of the gang, because membership confers on you a kind of identity that you would like to display. You value that identity, however, because it suggests power, fearlessness, and domination. To keep it that way—to ensure that it will continue to inspire fear and awe and deference—members of the gang must be prepared to engage in acts of violence, sometimes in collective violence, as in fights with other gangs. There only rarely—perhaps never—will be occasions when all members of the gang, like all members of a military unit when the trumpet calls, will have to assemble and face the enemy. Most members of the gang (maybe all), however, will find it hard to avoid *some* occasions when they will feel that they must join in acts of violence. Again like soldiers, they may just be doing their job, harboring no particular ill will or murderous intent toward the adversaries or victims. The result will be statistics like those in Fagan's chapter showing widespread prevalence, in a gang population, of youths who have committed at least one act of violence.

Outside the gang, there will also be youths (although relatively few as a percentage of the nongang population) who commit acts of violence. They may commit them for a variety of reasons. They may commit robberies, alone or with one or two friends, to get money. Or they may commit acts of violence to validate or to revalidate an identity: as someone who is "bad" or "crazy" and dangerous to mess with, or as a "real man" who does not seek trouble but who will not back down when pushed around. The identity, however, is personal in a way that the gang member's identity is not. It is not a sharing in the identity of a collectivity, which can be validated or vindicated by violent acts of *others* who share that identity. To maintain the credibility of the claimed identity as a nongang youth, that youth must *personally* exhibit, from time to time, the kind of conduct that exemplifies that identity. In either case, whether the violence serves the desire for monetary gain or the demonstration of some kind of macho identity, there is a likelihood that the need to display that violence will recur. There is, then, reason to expect that the prevalence of violence will be greater among gang than among nongang youth, and that in both populations those who commit violent acts have a certain likelihood of doing so again. But there is no clear reason for expecting that, among those who have committed one offense, the likelihood of committing a second, third, or fourth offense is any greater in the one population than in the other. This explanation does not preclude that Fagan's suggestions may also help to explain the data, but I think that it has a certain plausibility that derives from the nature of the relational context within which the violence occurs or, to put it more bluntly, from the fact that a gang is a gang—that is, a collectivity.

To the extent that people join gangs in order to find a worthwhile identity, gangs may be said to have been created and maintained by their members because of the dividends they yield by way of identity. Of course, people are drawn to gangs for other reasons as well: Gang membership can provide the relational rewards and security that we associate with family, and some gangs can facilitate financially rewarding criminal activity. There may be gangs in which the rewards of enhanced identity are secondary in the psychic economies of their members to the relational rewards or the pursuit of money. But the ability of gangs to provide their members with enhanced identity is always part of the explanation of gangs. It is also the case, however, that there are other gratifying identities to be found outside the gang, identities resting on personal qualities or performance or affiliation with other persons ("a good friend of so-and-so") rather than with a gang. This suggests that, in seeking to explain gangs by their ability to confer the identity of collectivity member, we must ask: What is the special attraction of this kind of identity? In a given population, what other roads to identity are there? What kinds of people are drawn to this or that kind of identity? What are the opportunities for the achievement of various identities and what are the costs and gratifications of each?

Parenthetically, it may be observed that once gangs of a certain sort are established in a community, the possibility of realizing certain kinds of identity outside the gang may be altered. For instance, some person who might like to be credited with a tough persona "in his own right" and not by virtue of membership in a gang may find that the gangs won't let him act out this role. They may insist that he join a gang, on pain of being beat up. For that matter, the principle may extend to pursuits other than the pursuit of identity. The quest for money through the sale of drugs by independent entrepreneurs may become dangerous and unhealthy after gangs enter this line of business, and the entrepreneur may find it expedient and prudent to continue his or her quest by joining a gang.

This little essay on collectivity is not just being fussy about definition. I suggest that the property of being a collectivity is the *differentium specificum* that laypeople and professionals alike usually go by when they intuitively say of this or that formation that it is a gang. And finally, with a couple of examples based on data in this volume, I have tried to show how analysis of the implications of collectivity may help to enhance our understanding of gangs.

The Diversity of Gangs

In the study of gangs, collectivity is the place to start because that is what they have in common, more or less. This volume, however, is more of a celebration of diversity, and what gangs have in common will not of itself explain their differences. The authors talk about differences between gangs today and gangs back in the days of Thrasher and Shaw and McKay, or in the 1950s and 1960s. They talk about differences in the age, sex, ethnic, and racial composition of their memberships, about differences by region, by city, and by neighborhoods within cities. They talk also about differences among different members of the same gang. They talk about differences in gang subculture and social organization. And they talk about the differences in what gangs do: the use of drugs and the sale of drugs, stealing, robbery, extortion, fighting.

For example, Campbell's review of what we know about female participation in gangs is largely new and recent knowledge, much of which refutes the received wisdom. I thought I had a pretty good chapter on girls in *Delinquent Boys*, and I still think it contains some important truths, but I now know that it was incomplete and distorted in important ways. Vigil and Yun's Vietnamese gangs are into armed robbery in a big way, but in important ways they don't behave as gangs are supposed to behave: "Fights are few and usually the last alternative in resolving a dispute." They have no sense of turf and think that fighting for neighborhood is stupid. They have apparently not read the manual on How to Be a Gang. Chin describes Chinese gangs in New York City whose main business is making a lot of money through extortion, and who are unlike Chinese gangs in Vancouver and even Chinese gangs in New York in the early 1960s. They are very different again from Vigil and Long's Chicano gangs, whose main activities are fighting and frequent partying. And they are different again from Taylor's "corporate" gangs, highly organized with a division of labor resembling a business firm or military outfit, employing violence ruthlessly but rationally to maintain control over the drug traffic in their territories.

I am awed by how much more we know about gangs than we did 50 years ago. When I read the extant literature in the 1940s and early 1950s there were only a handful of studies, and they were mostly about gangs in Chicago. We did not dream of all this diversity. (Some of this, of course, is a product of social change and did not exist to be known back then.) We have learned a lot and yet, I suppose that from another perspective Hagedorn is right when he says: "What do we know about modern gangs? I don't think we know that much. We simply haven't done the research." Most of the studies, however rich and revealing, illuminate small patches of a vast terrain. The research makes it clear that variations in gang subculture, social organization, and activities are manifold, but we know little about the way gangs are distributed in the social system or, for that matter, what other permutations there are that have not yet been observed. How do we explain the different kinds of gangs and their distribution? What is the relevance of differences in racial and ethnic culture, stages of assimilation and integration into the dominant culture and the social class system, of poverty and powerlessness, hope and despair? What are the relevant aspects of the structure of neighborhood and community, and how exactly do they exert their effect? To answer questions like these we need not only knowledge about gangs but knowledge about these associated, "background," and "contextual" variables. The descriptions of the gangs and of their contextual variables must permit comparability—that is to say, they must provide the information that will make possible the discovery of concomitant variation as clues to or evidence for causal connections.

Walter Miller's strategy for a solution to the gang problem envisions a national, centrally coordinated research enterprise designed to yield a kind of descriptive atlas of gangdom and whatever else we need to know in order to develop theory that would account for variation and provide a rational basis for schemes for intervention. The emphasis in Hagedorn's own advice lies less in a strategic plan and more in improving the quality and depth of our understanding of gangs through skillful, tactful, and sophisticated but also devoted, patient, prolonged, and committed direct observation and participation. He is skeptical of research based on information provided by criminal justice and other agencies that work with gang members or even by interviews with informants who are gang members but in settings still once removed from the action that constitutes the life of the gang.

The differences between Hagedorn's and Miller's emphases are related to the distinction in Vigil and Long's chapter, "Emic and Etic Perspectives on Gang Culture." The first has to do with grasping the underlying rules and assumptions that give meaning to objects and events as they are experienced by the participants in a culture. The latter has to do with translating what participants in different cultures experience as subjective, idiosyncratic, and concrete into a common language, into particular values of a set of abstract variables. This in turn makes it possible to compare and contrast the seemingly unique and incommensurable, and to formulate theoretical propositions that claim that differences among cultures (or other social objects, such as class systems or types of solidarity) with respect to this or that variable are related, as cause or effect, to differences among those cultures (or other social objects) with respect to certain other variables.

There is no explaining differences without a theory. Indeed, an explanation is precisely an attempt to demonstrate that the way that something turned out (or the different ways that two somethings turned out) is what you would have expected according to some theory. I agree with Hagedorn that we need more first-class ethnographies, but we do have some very good ones, some of them summarized in this volume. But the state of theory—and correspondingly our ability to account for variation—is not that impressive. Particularly striking is the recurrent sameness of explanations but the differences among the *explicanda*. You cannot explain variable outcomes with a constant. Short and several others are impressed by underclass theory: The conditions and characteristics of the underclass produce gangs. Several of the authors are impressed by the weakening of community social controls resulting from high rates of mobility. Writers on gangs generally are impressed by the explanatory power of the gang's ability to provide identities. I am impressed by these things too, but the same explanations are offered for very different kinds of gangs. There are some references to special factors associated with particular kinds of gangs. Chin, for example, and Vigil and Yun suggest how special kinds of opportunities help explain Chinese gangs in New York's Chinatown and Vietnamese gangs in California. When you read these two fascinating chapters—I imply no invidious comparisons to the other chapters—you will agree that you can't understand these gangs unless you understand how they represent adaptations to the very special opportunities implicit in the social organization of New York's Chinatown (and possibly other Chinatowns) and the rather peculiar savings habits of Vietnamese immigrants. The concept of differences in the structure of opportunity was offered by Cloward and Ohlin (1960) to account for differences among subcultures, and it remains one of the leading ideas of criminological theory, but it occurs in this volume only here and there in the context of focused discussions of particular kinds of gangs. It does not appear in the context of some kind of effort—however groping and tentative—toward some set of variables or dimensions of variation that an explanation of observed differences might have to take into account, and a set of propositions about how different combinations or configurations of the values of these variables lead to differences among gangs. Our authors are eloquent and convincing in their insistence on the part played by ethnic cultures in shaping the meaning to gang members of what they do, and therefore in accounting for the differences in what they do. But each culture is more or less unique. Is it possible to formulate *general rules*—that is, theoretical propositions—about the ways in which the uniqueness of individual cultures translates into the variables of a general theory of intergang differences?

It is important to build up a solid corpus of focused studies of individual gangs and gang types before rushing prematurely into the construction of "grand theory," but I think we have such a solid corpus, and that it is time to press ahead with the arduous task of explaining not only why we have gangs but why we have the different sorts of gangs that we do.

Acknowledgments

The publication of an edited book of scholarly papers is a complex undertaking, as any editor will attest. The success of such a project is dependent on three key factors: encouragement, support, and cooperation. Encouragement from colleagues is important, because one's peers constitute an important reference group whose opinion concerning the *need for the book*, the *timeliness of the project*, and the *existence of a critical mass of research* is crucial in making the decision to undertake such an effort. Also, encouragement from a publisher's representative provides an important catalyst to get the project moving. In these respects, I've enjoyed a great deal of encouragement on this project. Many colleagues who knew that I was engaged in research on gangs encouraged me to produce a book that would "update our knowledge of this important subject." Perhaps most notable, and most persistent in his encouragement, was my good friend Jeff Fagan at Rutgers. At Sage Publications, Blaise Donnelly displayed a keen interest in this project from the outset, and I would not have signed the contract if it weren't for my genuine respect for and trust in him. He has not let me down throughout this project.

That leaves support and cooperation. In addition to Sage's support, I've enjoyed the support of my wife, Pat, and my daughters, Tammy and Tiffany, who have been willing to forgo a considerable amount of "family time" while I worked on "the book." Fortunately, Tammy and Tiffany are now teenagers, so it was no great sacrifice on their part to do without some parental involvement.

Finally, and most important, I've enjoyed the total cooperation of 16 colleagues who contributed chapters and a foreword to this book. Without their research and their knowledge, the project could not have succeeded. I am deeply indebted to all of them for their efforts to add to our knowledge base and our understanding of this important and changing phenomenon known as "gangs."

I'll leave it to the critics to assess the extent to which this book represents an important contribution to the scholarly literature on gangs. My intent has been to bring together in one book two generations of gang researchers for the purpose of updating and reassessing our knowledge of this subject. To the extent that this goal has been met, my contributing authors deserve the primary credit.

C. Ronald Huff

Introduction:
Two Generations of Gang Research

C. RONALD HUFF

This book was born out of controversy. The controversy involved discussions with other researchers on whether the recent research on gangs was sufficiently important to justify a new book on the subject. Although we never did achieve unanimity on this point, the great majority of persons I consulted told me that they thought such a volume was badly needed and would fill a critical void in the literature on youth gangs in the United States. Those of us who supported the idea of an edited volume cited the following recent developments as compelling reasons to update the knowledge base: (a) the emergence of youth gangs in smaller and medium-sized cities previously reporting none, (b) the increased diversity in the composition of these gangs, (c) the increased sophistication in weaponry and greatly elevated levels of violence associated with some gangs, (d) the controversy surrounding the role of gangs in drug trafficking networks and associated violence in the United States, and (e) the controversy associated with the social context of gangs (loosely defined as the "underclass" perspective versus the "subcultural" perspective).

As a sociologist and professor of public policy and management who teaches a graduate course on juvenile justice, I was acutely aware that there is no book currently available for undergraduate or graduate classroom use that provides a solid overview of what is known about gangs. There are classic books on the subject of gangs, books that present single studies of gangs, scholarly articles, research reports, and miscellaneous other publications, but no book that provides a useful and up-to-date overview of research, as well as theoretical and public policy issues, on the subject of gangs.

In agreeing to edit this volume, I established the goal of producing just such a book. This is, admittedly, an ambitious goal—one that required the assistance of some of this nation's best scholars and most insightful writers on the subject of gangs. Of those invited to contribute chapters for this book, all but one agreed. Perhaps this level of enthusiasm is indicative of the perceived need for this project.

Another of my goals for this book has been to bring together in one volume the best-known senior researchers (Cohen, Klein, Miller, Short, and Spergel) and many of the "new generation" of gang researchers who have been reporting on the increasing diffusion and diversity of gangs in the United States and, just as the generation before them, wrestling with the implications of their data for theory and for public policy. In Cohen's preceding foreword and overview and in the pages that follow this introduction, readers will have an opportunity to update their knowledge of contemporary gangs within an overall context of historical continuity. Readers will have ample opportunity to learn "what's new" and then assess for themselves how new it really is, what its causes and correlates are, and what can be done about it.

This book includes disagreement and controversy. This is both a sign of intellectual vitality and an accurate reflection of the state of gang research in 1990. That is intentional on my part and was, for all intents and purposes, predetermined by the invitations I issued to contributing authors who I knew would disagree on some important points. In my own judgment, we have not yet arrived at a point where we can embrace a general theory of gangs or recommend by consensus the policies that ought to be pursued to prevent and control gangs. There is a place for books that offer a unified theoretical and/or policy perspective, but this is not intended to be such a book. Rather, this is a book that provides an accurate reflection of the diversity that exists among gangs and gang researchers. I do believe, however, that the following chapters offer a great deal of insight into these questions, and I shall return to the matter of public policy choices in the final chapter.

But first, allow me to provide a "sneak preview" of the chapters that follow. The two chapters that compose Part I introduce the reader to both sociological and anthropological perspectives on gangs and their community contexts. In Chapter 1, Horowitz claims that she was wrong about her prediction (Bookin-Weiner & Horowitz, 1983) that the gang research of the late 1980s would focus on social control issues using official data rather than face-to-face methods of inquiry. Many of us would argue that her *mea culpa* is unnecessary, because face-to-face studies of gangs remain all too rare (see Chapter 11 for a vigorous critique of studies relying on official data or "intermediaries"). Horowitz notes that there is little agreement on definitions of and explanations for gangs, gang involvement, gang activities, or the relationship of gangs to the larger social structure, but she argues that agreement on definitions may not be as necessary as is often believed. She asserts that despite much recent research on gangs, we still do not know enough about them to formulate a general theory. Moreover, she believes that confining gang research to some rigid definitional criteria may constrain our creativity in exploring distinct aspects of the gang experience. Horowitz emphasizes the importance of understanding how people experience their lives and impute meaning to their actions. Finally, she contrasts gang research based on a cultural perspective with studies proceeding from an economic model and provides a critique of the cultural model used in early gang studies.

In Chapter 2, Vigil and Long employ an anthropological perspective in analyzing Chicano gang subcultures. They note that emic studies of culture focus on an attempt to understand phenomena from the viewpoint of the participant in that culture, while the etic perspective emphasizes categories and rules derived from the vocabulary of science, which the participants may or may not find meaningful. Vigil and Long argue that both perspectives are necessary for a full appreciation of a culture or subculture and, because both of them grew up in Los Angeles, with many gang members in their schools and communities, they have been able to use both perspectives in their research. They describe their involvement with community participants in their research, analyzing four major aspects of Chicano gang subcultures: adaptation, variability and change, age and gender roles, and role enactment and self-empowerment. Their chapter concludes with an insightful discussion of the factors that have perpetuated and exacerbated barrio gangs in Los Angeles and that continue to fuel the recruitment of the most marginalized youths. Vigil and Long caution that any attempt to address the problems posed by barrio gangs must be grounded soundly in an understanding of the barrio gang subculture.

Part II addresses an issue that has major political and public policy implications, as well as theoretical significance—the definition and measurement of gang violence. Maxson and Klein (Chapter 3) note that with the spread of gangs to many cities across the nation, it is important to ask: (a) How is the "gang problem" socially constructed? (b) How generalizable are the findings of gang research from one city to others? and (c) How valid are our assessments of the seriousness of gang violence, and can these assessments serve as the basis for ranking gangs as a problem on the public policy agenda? They note that the "gang sweeps" in Los Angeles were both massive and costly, and they question whether such draconian measures would have been perceived as necessary if an alternative definition of "gang-related" homicides had been utilized—for example, a more restrictive definition such as that employed in Chicago. They present a detailed analysis of data from Los Angeles and Chicago and discuss the implications of substituting the more restrictive Chicago definition (essentially requiring gang "motive" rather than mere "membership," as in Los Angeles). Although the substitution would result in a significant reduction in the number of cases considered gang-related, some of their other findings are counterintuitive and may surprise readers interested in assessing the prevalence and character of gang violence.

Part III introduces the reader to much of the "new generation" gang research, which documents the increasing diffusion and diversity of gangs and assesses the relationship between gangs and drug use. Like Vigil and Long, Taylor (Chapter 4) grew up with gang members in his neighborhood—in Taylor's case, Detroit. He later undertook a study of Detroit gangs, which, he argues, are spreading in an "imperialistic" manner, fueled by the incentives of the illegal drug economy. Taylor argues that drugs represent a unifying economic force for gangs, just as alcohol did for organized crime during Prohibition. He classifies contemporary gangs as "scavenger," "territorial," and "corporate," with members ("players") who correspond to five distinct types ("corporate," "scavenger," "emulator," "auxiliary," and "adjunct member"). Taylor believes that Yablonsky's near-group theory is useful in understanding contemporary gangs, some of whom he sees as evolving from the scavenger to the territorial and corporate stages. Finally, Taylor argues that drug-related violence in Detroit today is analogous to the gang wars in the Capone era and that for the first time in modern U.S. history Afro-Americans have moved into mainstream organized crime via the "corporate gangs" of Detroit.

In Chapter 5, Vigil returns for a solo performance, analyzing the relationship between *los cholos* and gangs in Los Angeles. After explaining the origin and meaning of the term *cholo,* Vigil provides an analysis of the increasing marginalization of this segment of the Mexican-American population, caught between two cultures. *Cholos* arriving in the United States are clearly at risk of becoming gang members for reasons that become all too clear from Vigil's discussion. Marginalized in Mexico, they suffer from what Vigil terms "multiple marginality" in this country. Vigil describes the processes by which a gang subculture grows out of culture conflict and the "choloization" of the second and subsequent generations of immigrants. A barrio gang subculture has evolved over several decades, and Vigil's analysis suggests that an underclass has formed and is characterized by a lack of education, training, jobs, and other opportunities—an all-too-familiar theme in gang studies.

Chapters 6 and 7 focus on another new variant of gangs in the United States—Asian gangs. Diversity even among the

Asian gangs will become apparent from reading Chin (Chapter 6) on Chinese gangs and the versatile Vigil and his colleague Steve Chong Yun (Chapter 7) on Vietnamese gangs.

Chin analyzes the growth in Chinese criminal activity and Chinese gangs in the United States since 1965, tracing it to 1965 U.S. legislation that greatly affected Chinese immigration and the corresponding age structure of the Chinese population in the United States (many more teenagers). This expanded immigration had an adverse impact upon Chinese communities, especially the families and the district associations, who could not cope with it. As a result, newcomers received little help. Chin notes that although there are fewer than 2,000 Chinese gang members in the United States, they have been involved in some of the worst violence and in heroin trafficking. Utilizing a variety of qualitative methods, Chin describes the individual and group characteristics of New York City Chinese gangs, compares them with other ethnic gangs, and provides an analysis of the functions and social processes of extortion, which he classifies into four subtypes. Finally, Chin explains the persistence of Chinese gangs as rooted in Chinese communities and not dependent on either youth fads or drug use.

Vigil and Yun (Chapter 7) report that while the media popularly portray Asian-American youths as academic "whiz kids," a recent *Los Angeles Times* survey revealed that the Vietnamese residents of Orange County, California, listed "gangs and crime" as their primary concern. Their exploratory study of these emerging Vietnamese gangs is based on interviews with law enforcement officers, social workers, California Youth Authority (CYA) administrators, and 17 Vietnamese youths detained by the CYA for gang-related crimes. Vigil and Yun argue that the concept of "multiple marginality" originally developed by Vigil (1988b) for Chicano gangs is very useful in understanding Vietnamese youth gangs as well. Vietnamese gangs in Southern California appear to offer an alternative route to what the authors term "acquisition without assimilation." Finally, the history and dynamics of Vietnamese gangs suggest that they are not comparable to organized crime groups, Chinese gangs, or other ethnic street gangs, but must be understood within their own cultural context.

In Chapter 8, Campbell explores the world of the female gang and analyzes what she terms "the invisible female peer group" by discussing three myths that help fuel the image of the socially isolated female delinquent. Campbell argues that girls have at least as good peer relations as boys and that their delinquency is as much peer dependent as is that of boys. She then traces the history of female involvement in gangs from the early nineteenth century in New York and discusses some of the distortion that characterized much of the early research on female gangs, carried out from an all-male perspective. Campbell notes that more recent qualitative studies, especially those focusing on Chicanas and Puerto Ricans, have analyzed these female gangs as collectivities in their own right. Finally, she discusses the functions of female gangs by analyzing the problems facing poverty-class girls, looks at the dynamics and symbolism of gang behavior, and analyzes the relations within and between female gangs and between male and female gang members. Campbell concludes with a call for more research on female gangs—especially Black, White, and Asian gangs, which have received very little attention.

The final contribution to Part III is authored by Fagan (Chapter 9), who carefully and methodically explores the relationship between gang membership and drug usage by comparing survey data from gang and nongang high school students and dropouts in Chicago, Los Angeles, and San Diego. Fagan notes that although it is clear that serious juvenile offenders are disproportionately involved in substance abuse, it is less clear what the *causal* dynamics are and to what extent gangs are linked to this problem. Fagan's study attempts to determine whether theories that view gangs as a form of adolescent social network are useful or whether gangs have evolved into criminal organizations, thus requiring different theoretical perspectives. Using an integrated control/learning theory framework, Fagan assesses drug use, delinquency, and violence among gang and nongang youths. The results of his data analyses are in keeping with one of the themes of this book—diversity. Both gang and nongang youths are involved in substance abuse, although there are differences in frequency. Finally, he notes that gangs represent only one type of peer network, and these diverse networks (rather than individual differences) may represent useful explanatory variables.

Part IV consists of two different types of assessments of the changing knowledge base concerning gangs. In Chapter 10, Short notes that gangs are not a new issue, but he sees a new urgency to an old issue. He reviews recent research on communities and crime, which reveals the critical importance of local communities and their conditions. He also notes that communities have their own careers in crime and delinquency. Drawing upon his own work and more recent gang research, Short analyzes the nature of relationships among individual, group, and community careers in delinquency. He presents an engaging discussion of the Vice Lords and the Nobles and their respective Chicago neighborhoods. The contrasts between their neighborhoods, the dynamics of their gangs, and the developmental histories of the two gangs and their members are both striking and informative.

Short notes that contemporary gangs are more sophisticated, more lethal, involve members for longer periods of time, and appear to be more involved in drug abuse and drug trafficking than gangs of the past. He argues, however, that more important than changes in gangs are the persistence and urbanization of poverty, the development of a segmented labor market, and the rise of a ghetto underclass. He concludes by discussing the importance of establishing functional communities and generating social capital, illustrating his points by citing exemplary efforts such as Chicago's Beethoven Project and important research such as Coleman and Hoffer's (1987) study of performance in Catholic, other private, and public high schools.

Hagedorn (Chapter 11) argues that although this book reflects renewed academic interest in gangs, he doubts that we have conducted sufficient research on which to base theory and public policy. He criticizes the "lower-class culture" hypothesis of gangs and contrasts it with the developing "urban underclass" perspective that characterizes his own research. Hagedorn issues a strong plea for more field research in the context of the gangs' urban environments, and he delivers a scathing critique of other types of research on gangs, which he characterizes as "courthouse criminology" (reliance on official records and other secondary data) and "surrogate sociology" (reliance on "intermediaries" for access to data).

Hagedorn provides a very useful discussion of what he regards as the principal objections raised about field research, concluding that at least some of these objections are essentially "cop-outs" and that more good field research on gangs is both desirable and possible. He cites examples of such studies and issues a call for bold and innovative new field studies in the best traditions of the old Chicago school. Finally, Hagedorn argues that typical quantitative approaches, employing secondary (usually official) data, cannot provide answers to the problems posed by the emergence of an urban underclass.

Part V focuses on public policy issues associated with gangs and gang research. In Chapter 12, Miller notes that the youth gangs of the 1980s and 1990s are more numerous, more prevalent, and more violent than was the case in the 1950s. He then asks why the United States—a very rich and powerful nation—has failed to ensure the safety of its citizens in communities feeling the impact of youth gangs. Although crime in general has persisted and it may be naive to believe it could be ameliorated greatly, Miller argues that the youth gang problem could be reduced substantially in both frequency and severity. He analyzes five characteristics of youth gangs that suggest they may have more potential for amelioration than we realize, provided that intervention strategies are well designed.

Miller summarizes the history of gang control programs in the United States, emphasizing that we did not do a good job of basing programs on imaginative approaches and did not pay sufficient attention to carrying out rigorous program evaluations and then paying attention to their results. Miller deplores the lack of an adequate and ongoing federal commitment to addressing the youth gang problem, indicating that we lack a national strategy and a national approach. He reviews historical efforts to address this problem, especially in the 1960s via the President's Commission on Juvenile Delinquency and Youth Crime, which developed a nine-step conceptual strategy that Miller regards as superior to any more recent proposal. Finally, Miller provides a comprehensive analysis of the factors contributing to the failure to provide adequate resources to address this problem or even, in his view, to conceptualize the problem's social context adequately.

Spergel and Curry (Chapter 13) assess the relationships between youth gang suppression and intervention efforts and their programmatic outcomes with respect to the gang problem. In their National Youth Gang Survey for the Office of Juvenile Justice and Delinquency Prevention, they collected data from 254 respondents in 45 cities and six institutional sites. They assessed five different types of program strategies: community organization, social intervention, opportunities provision, suppression, and organizational development and change. They categorized the cities in their study as having either "chronic" or "emerging" gang problems. Their outcome measures included perceived improvement in the youth gang problem, perceived agency effectiveness, and perceived community-level effectiveness. Spergel and Curry argue that their data underscore the importance of community organization and opportunities provision in combination as significant predictors of perceived effectiveness. They believe that the key problem components are economic deprivation, lack of opportunities, social disorganization, and the failure of community institutions.

In Chapter 14, I provide a closing essay that addresses the processes typically followed by cities when initially confronted by a youth gang problem (denial, followed by overreaction and misidentification of gang "members" and the "causes" of gangs). I try to indicate in that chapter some of the dysfunctional outcomes of adopting this approach. Finally, I attempt to distill from existing gang research some conclusions and recommendations that may find common ground among observers adopting diverse theoretical and policy perspectives. I argue that we may find more consensus by shifting our focus to ecological units of analysis and targeting specific neighborhoods that generate the highest rates of crime, delinquency, incarceration, mental illness, and public assistance. Whether one adopts an underclass (economic) perspective or a social disorganization (or other subcultural) perspective, it seems to me that we are inevitably focusing on the same neighborhoods. By undertaking prevention programs targeting such neighbor-hoods, we can address generically the costliest problems in our society. In an era of limited funding for social programs, it makes sense to invest in prevention programs that have a chance to effect improvements in the overall quality of life and social justice.

Sociological and Anthropological Perspectives on the Gang and the Community

1

Sociological Perspectives on Gangs: Conflicting Definitions and Concepts

RUTH HOROWITZ

After almost 15 years of little research, why did gangs again become an important focus of research in the mid-1980s, and why are qualitative studies embedded within largely economic models? Bookin-Weiner and Horowitz (1983) predicted that much of the gang research of the late 1980s would be concerned with issues of social control and would use official statistics because other more face-to-face techniques might be not only unwanted by local communities but considered too dangerous. We were wrong, and a far wider range of gang research has been published (Campbell, 1984; Curry & Spergel, 1988; Fagan, 1989; Hagedorn, 1988; Klein & Maxson, 1989; Spergel, 1984; Vigil, 1988a). Moreover, many of these studies are based on in-depth interview and observational data, unlike much recent research in criminology, which is quantitative, based on official statistics or survey data, and driven largely by government research grants and priorities (Manning, 1989).

In these new research projects, there continues to be significant disagreement among the researchers on the definition of

AUTHOR'S NOTE: I would like to thank David Sciulli, P. K. Manning, and Jane Davidson for their helpful comments on an earlier version of this chapter.

a gang and how to explain membership and activities. One purpose of this chapter is to demonstrate why it is not necessary to agree on the parameters of what constitutes a gang. Agreement likely will never be achieved, and definitions often obscure problematic areas and may not encourage the development of new questions, for example, as some of the most recent studies raise. Most of these new analyses focus on the invariant properties of social life and are abstract and distant from social experience. These models have very different views on the degree to which actors make choices. For example, do young people make rational choices whether to join a gang or are they pushed to join by their social and economic circumstances?

Using data provided in recent studies permits examination of how people experience their social worlds: the multiple meanings of actions, the way events and lives evolve, and the way people make sense out of their lives. People create the realities to which they respond through appraisals and evaluations of people and relationships. Another purpose of this chapter is to show that people experience their lives very differently, such that it is possible for some to experience their lives as constrained by circumstance and for others to make choices.

Renewed Interest in the Gang

Interest in the serious delinquent (the youth frequently involved in serious offenses) rather than the typical delinquent found in the self-report survey (infrequently involved and in less serious offenses) has had a resurgence in recent years, spurred on by studies such as those by Strasburg (1978) and Hamparian, Schuster, Dinitz, and Conrad (1978). These studies showed that some delinquents are involved considerably more in illegal activities than are the typical delinquents sampled in the early self-report studies. These serious delinquents are not distributed evenly among social groups as are typical delinquents. Moreover, there is some evidence that gang members tend to be involved in more illegal activities than other serious delinquents (Tracy, 1979).

Although gangs continued to exist through the 1970s (Bookin-Weiner & Horowitz, 1983; Klein & Maxson, 1989), officials and the media paid little attention. By the late 1970s and early 1980s, however, police and city officials appeared increasingly concerned about gang activity (Hagedorn, 1988; Miller, 1975) and responded by rebuilding their gang units and by accumulating more statistics (Klein & Maxson, 1989), which provide a useful data source.

Relatedly, gangs were unnewsworthy for more than a decade. More recently the media have focused considerable attention on the gang as an important distributor of drugs, especially crack, and as the perpetrator of much violence, especially gun shots that have hit innocent bystanders. News reports have often attributed many violent incidents to gangs (Hagedorn, 1988; Sanchez-Jankowski, n.d.). Researchers knowledgeable about gangs were concerned to address what they viewed as incorrect or exaggerated images in the press and beliefs held by agencies of social control (Hagedorn, 1988). Some research—such as that of Klein, Maxson, and Cunningham (1988)—was undertaken in order to test police and news accounts of heavy gang involvement in crack distribution.

Researchers discovered that many of the media's and officials' views were distorted. For instance, although more gangs have formed in new types of locations—suburban, rural, and new cities (Hagedorn, 1988; Vigil, 1988a), they are not extensions of big-city gangs as police and the news have reported (Hagedorn, 1988). Moreover, only some are involved in the distribution of drugs (Fagan, 1989; Klein et al., 1988). Despite the impression given by news reports, gang members are not necessarily the most likely victims or perpetrators of homicides in all inner-city neighborhoods, though in some they are (Curry & Spergel, 1988; Spergel, 1984). Other reports were substantiated: There are gangs of girls who are involved in both property and violent offenses (Campbell, 1984).

Second, they wanted to wrest the dominant image of the inner city and minorities from the political right, whose image of the poor and poverty dominated public policy debates and blamed the poor and minorities for their own situation. This view justified the government's lack of provision of resources to the poor and minorities. Concerned about the lack of industrial jobs in the inner cities, the new researchers tended to embrace perspectives more sympathetic with economic disadvantage (Wilson, 1987) in their attempts to understand gang behavior, particularly Hagedorn (1988) and Vigil (1988a). Although these explanations differ, they both are embedded in underclass models.

Third, new researchers continued to redirect the focus of research itself. Economic models had replaced almost entirely the cultural approach to understanding gangs and poverty. In the older cultural values approach, the actor pursues some consensual nonrational values; culture, not interests, orients actions. Culture as an explanation for the formation of gangs and gang behavior has been in disrepute among sociologists since the late 1960s. There are several reasons for its demise, including the model of culture that was used, the seeming tautology of its explanation, the shift in methods from fieldwork to survey research, and the conservative political position that the cultural explanations appeared to support. Researchers such as Miller (1958), Lewis (1965), and Wolfgang and Ferracuti (1967) were accused of blaming the victims.

Part of the problem that these cultural explanations had was that they adopted a Parsonian notion of culture. Parsons (1951) views culture as a quasi-objective entity in which values and norms are objects and invariant points of reference to which people orient their actions. Such values and norms give everyday interaction its stable qualities, give moral and affective meaning to social relationships and role performances, and control choices by indicating the relative merit of different courses of action. Culture is the most general factor in a hierarchy of control and also the least variant analytic component of action.[1]

This position came under increasing attack for both political and methodological reasons. Many claimed that cultural analyses were tautological. The culture was found by the sociologist in the behavior of the group, and then the "culture" was used to explain that behavior. This attack was focused particularly on the work of Lewis (1965), who provided a list of many different characteristics and behaviors of the poor that were their culture and were passed on from generation to generation. This perspective was criticized for supporting the notion that nothing can or should be done to help the poor and delinquent because the model implies that they are this way by choice. The position seemed to justify the position of the political right: If people choose to live that way, then there is no reason to try to change their situation. Despite the subcultural perspective's focus on the lack of economic opportunities, it did not focus on the large-scale economic forces that eliminated well-paying blue-collar jobs, particularly from the older industrial cities. This became an important focus of later studies (Hagedorn, 1988; Moore, 1978).

Fourth, some of the new researchers wanted and had the skills to resuscitate an earlier tradition of gang research. Although gang research traditionally has used qualitative methods,[2] from the early gang descriptions of Thrasher (1927) to the biographies of Shaw (1930) and later to Whyte (1943), Miller (1958), Suttles (1968), Klein (1971), Moore (1978), and Horowitz (1983), many during the 1970s and early 1980s argued that fieldwork was too dangerous and difficult, surveys were impossible with this population, the political climate was wrong for outsiders to do gang research in minority communities, and officially generated statistics were of little use.

These potential difficulties have been overcome by several researchers. Some grew up in gang neighborhoods (Vigil, 1988a; Sanchez-Jankowski, n.d.) and taught in or organized neighborhoods with gangs before doing research (Hagedorn, 1988; Vigil, 1988a). Moore (1978), Hagedorn (1988), and Vigil (1988a) have developed research relationships with older former gang members who became part of their research teams. Fagan (1989) used community residents and social service workers to locate gang members and then to read questionnaires to them. Others have used in-depth interviews (Campbell, 1984) or traditional participant observation (Horowitz, 1983).

Additionally, as the police became concerned with gang activity, they began to develop more rigorous data-gathering techniques, thereby providing some sociologists with data (Curry & Spergel, 1988; Klein & Maxson, 1989). Most of the studies, however, have been limited to one ethnic group (Moore, 1978; Vigil, 1988a), one gang (Horowitz, 1983), or a small number of respondents. There is only one long-term qualitative study of 37 gangs in three cities and including Irish, Chicano, Puerto Rican, and Black gangs (Sanchez-Jankowski, n.d.). Although most of these recent studies have some limitations, they provide extensive new data.

Current Models as Partial Truths

Although many of the gang studies are limited by their small samples, this is probably only a minor factor in accounting for the continuing disagreements about the findings (who joins gangs) and explanations (why they join). Some of the differences are more fundamental. They arise in part from an effort to make sociology more scientific by identifying the invariant properties of social life. The models are conceptualized in highly abstract terms, distant from everyday life and experiences of social groups. These studies often develop definitions by which the phenomenon to be explained can be bounded; however, restricting the boundaries of what constitutes a gang may limit the types of questions asked, and looking for invariant properties and generating highly abstract categories to explain social experiences may not be as useful as many sociologists assume.

Some of the apparent contradictions in explanations may be partly reconciled, therefore, by examining how gang members experience their social worlds and construct the meaning of their experiences, and how situations and the experiences within them can carry the action forward. Rather than looking immediately for how experience is made stable by collective representations, it is necessary to explore the social world as a more continuing, evolving, and situationally constructed social experience.

Defining the Gang

Miller (1980) argues that it is critical that social scientists define what a gang is in order to counteract the manipulation of the term by people outside the social science research community. He argues that police broaden or narrow the concept depending upon their own needs and interests. The media tend to broaden the concept to include whatever they want that might make a good (read dramatic, blood-and-guts) story. Additionally, social scientists who want to explain the gang phenomenon need a definition of *gang* in order to specify what they are explaining. There is little consensus, however, about the type or extent of the parameters that should define "the gang" (Klein & Maxson, 1989). Although many sociologists decry this lack of a firm definition, there are at least two reasons a firm definition may not be helpful. First, every group (police, media, a community, or social scientists) has its own interests and taken-for-granted assumptions and will never agree on a definition. Second, definitions tend to focus research in particular ways that may narrow the topics studied and questions asked. New conceptions may encourage refocusing the questions and the development of new understandings.

There are many more reasons for keeping the definition pluralistic. Each study uses its own definition, partially determined by the research technique and the sociological questions asked. Research that employs statistics collected by justice system personnel depends on the definitions of gangs and gang-related incidents used and how the individuals apply those definitions to people and incidents. This varies among police jurisdictions and among individual coders who attribute gang status to an event or an individual (Curry & Spergel, 1988; Klein & Maxson, 1989; Miller, 1975). Although this poses problems for jurisdictional comparisons, it may be useful for understanding the relationship between justice system personnel and the community, the gang, and the individual members. It may affect publicity, the manner in which gangs are treated by the justice system, and the distribution of resources. For example, it does affect the way suspected gang members are identified and treated by the justice system (Zatz, 1985).

Definitions that rely on the community's conception of a gang also may be useful, but they may take for granted differences between the criminal justice system's and the community's relationships to the gang. Fagan (1989) used community workers and gang members themselves to identify gang members meeting the parameters developed by Klein (1971) and modified by Klein and Maxson (1989). According to Klein and Maxson (1989), there are three criteria for defining a street gang: community recognition as a group or collectivity, recognition by the group itself as a distinct group (of adolescents and young adults—added in the 1989 definition, p. 205), and enough (illegal—added in 1989, p. 205) activities to get a consistent negative response from law enforcement and/or neighborhood residents. Although the updated version helps to expand the definition substantially, it reveals some possible problems: We do not know if the situation has really changed or if people failed to raise issues because of the definition. For example, there may have been older youths who were affiliated with gangs, but no one may have noticed because gang members were defined as "juveniles." More recent studies have found many older youths in gangs (Horowitz, 1983; Moore, 1978; Sanchez-Jankowski, n.d.). Klein and Maxson (1989) have changed the definition to reflect this reality. Is there some new experience that promotes the continuation of membership into adulthood, or have older groups always existed?

This definition might also focus researchers' attention away from exploring the community-gang relationship. It implies a generally negative relationship and does not take into account the complexity of, possible variations in, and evolution of the relationship. For example, Sanchez-Jankowski (n.d.) found that gangs often have a positive relationship with their local communities and serve as a local police force. Horowitz (1987) explored the kinship and cultural connections between the gang members and the adults and how in certain situations the fragile ordering of the situation could be dissolved. Moreover, this definition appears to assume that the gang is at least somewhat isolated from the political system and adult institutions. This is still the topic of much debate. On one side are those who see the gang as isolated (Vigil, 1988a), and on the other are those who see a complex and integrated relationship between conventional adults and institutions and the gangs (Sanchez-Jankowski, n.d.).

Miller's (1980) analysis of the different types of collectivities of law-violating youth provides new insights. He argues that there are many different types of law-violating youth groups, but the problem is to decide which ones should be defined as gangs. Miller (1980) used a consensus of opinion among justice system personnel and other professionals who worked with youths to determine which types of groups should be considered gangs. He ended up with the following definition:

> A youth gang is a self-formed association of peers, bound together by mutual interests, with identifiable leadership, well-developed lines of authority, and other organizational features, who act in concert to achieve a specific purpose or purposes which generally include the conduct of illegal activity and control over a particular territory, facility, or type of enterprise. (p. 121)

Not all of these characteristics fit the groups that many sociologists consider gangs, and using the list also may obscure important distinctions among those groups that are included. Although definitions that exclude the element of illegal activities (Morash, 1983) are not particularly useful, it is not clear that all youths in all gangs are involved in illegal activities (Moore, 1978). By relying on definitions, we may fail to see real variations in gangs: Some are more involved in gang homicides, others are less so (Curry & Spergel, 1988); some claim a territory (Moore, 1978), others do not (Hagedorn, 1988); some use and/or sell drugs, others do not (Moore, 1978; Fagan, 1989); some are located in large industrial cities, others exist in smaller cities (Hagedorn, 1988), rural areas, and suburbs (Vigil, 1988a). By defining the gang primarily in terms of illegal activities, we may shift attention away from the complex and problematic relationship between legal and illegal actions (Hagedorn, 1988; Horowitz, 1983; Vigil, 1988a).

Moreover, the inclusion of only certain types of organizational characteristics may be too restrictive and may tend to obscure real variations. Should only groups that have for-malized organizational roles be included? Images of gang or-ganization vary from Yablonsky's (1962) near-group with sociopathic leadership to formal leadership with very specific roles, rules, and sanctions for rule violations. Although no recent data support Yablonsky's position, there is significant support for an organizational image of a friendship-based group with a variety of more or less informal leadership posi-tions and rules (Horowitz, 1983; Moore, 1978; Vigil, 1988a). There is also substantial evidence that there are gangs with several different formal organizational patterns (Hagedorn, 1988; Sanchez-Jankowski, n.d.).

The nature of the organization is important, as it appears to affect the gang's involvement in a variety of activities. For example, Fagan (1989) found that social organization and other processes of gang cohesion were partial explanations for why gangs differ in violence and drug involvement. It is not clear, however, to what extent the differences in organization are a result of the observers' research techniques, theoretical focuses, or real differences. Limited samples may produce lopsided views of organization depending on the choices made by the researcher. This issue has to be debated and studied further. Groups should not be excluded from the analysis because they do not meet some rigid definitional criteria.

Conceptualizing gangs as "street elites" who exhibit a dra-matic style of presentation of self, Katz (1988), an essayist, compares the forms of the collective youthful deviant styles of urban, lower-income minority youth with styles of middle-class suburban youth. He argues that gangs are "committed to the artificial *construction* of segregating geographic boundaries" while middle-class youth tend to use "deviant forms of collec-tive behavior to affect the collective *destruction* of geographic boundaries" (p. 119). He then explores the differences in styles between these two types of collectivities on a number of impor-tant dimensions: aristocrats versus rabble, horizontal versus vertical directions of authority, opposing versus transcending authority, and emphasizing versus obscuring gender differ-ences. Traditional definitions of gangs do not invite these types of comparisons. Nor do they point to explorations such as that of Chambliss (1973), who found that the behavior of middle-class youth was more destructive than that of the more traditionally defined gangs.

The search for parameters of what constitutes a gang is not as important as some argue it is. It may have important implications for policy-making, and these implications should be studied, but it is unlikely that social scientists will ever agree to one definition, let alone be able to persuade practitioners and officials of its merits. New definitions are useful because they uncover phenomena and connections previously unseen and thus unexplored.

Abstract Causes and Assumptions About Human Action

With the variations found in activities and organization, and with methodological issues, it is not surprising that explanations differ substantially regarding why people join gangs and the nature of the relationship of the group to larger social structures. Part of the reason for the continuing differences is the pursuit of invariant properties of social life to explain behavior. These properties are distant from the actual actions of people and the explanations are based on assumptions that people either make rational choices or are determined by circumstances, either cultural or economic. The wooden dicotomy may be made productive by examining the way people experience their lives, viewing the meanings of actions as problematic and exploring the construction of actions by the actors in daily interaction as they make sense out of their social worlds. Both are possible.

For example, Sanchez-Jankowski (n.d.) makes a very convincing argument that joining a gang is part of a rational decision-making process on the part of the individual and the gang. The gang member is a rational actor just like the businessman, and the gang is similar to any business organization: It wants actors who can best support and carry out the collective goals of the organization. Sanchez-Jankowski's view is based on Hechter's (1989) rational choice model, which argues that the collective good produced by the group is better than what rational actors can get on their own. Group solidarity is produced by individuals' dependence on the group and the group's ability to control its members by surveillance and sanctions.

Sanchez-Jankowski argues, in turn, that the gang offers delinquents better criminal opportunities, more girls, or better parties. He argues that poverty produces a particular character type—not necessarily the poorest or those from single-parent or troubled families—that finds the gang especially attractive. The survival of the gang depends on dealing with this type. Gangs that do not offer sufficient incentives to this character type or that do not monitor their members' behavior will collapse because they will be unable to sustain the solidarity necessary. Those gangs that are organized successfully may exist for long periods of time, and members may remain as long as the gang offers them more than they can get on their own or in other organizations. Sanchez-Jankowski explores the organizational structures, their leadership, rules, and sanctions, and the relationship to the individuals and how individuals benefit.

Although Sanchez-Jankowski's actors make rational choices, Vigil's (1988a) actors are pushed into gangs by their condition of poverty and status as minorities. Those who join gangs are the most marginal to the wider society, to their communities, and to their families. Many people who live in the barrio are subject to "stressors" in some of these arenas (economic, ecological, social, cultural, and psychological), but some selected actors are subject to difficulties in all areas. Vigil calls this "multiple marginality," and those who approach this status are the most likely candidates for gang membership. Joining a gang gives these actors a sense of place and importance and provides them with social relationships.

Perhaps these views could be reconciled at the level of how people experience their lives. People bring orientations to events and into relationships, not merely rational calculations. People use these orientations to interpret symbols and to pattern their responses based on readings of situations that may, in turn, reinforce or change the meaning for them. Some people experience their lives as being pushed and buffeted about by factors beyond their control, while others experience their lives more as a series of choices. Campbell's (1984) extensive biographical data, for instance, include one gang member who talked about the threads of her life in terms of a series of choices and another who experienced no control over her life.

Connie is a woman who usually experiences her life as a series of decisions. Although she had a difficult and unstable childhood—moving several times from New York to Puerto Rico and back again, each time with different relatives—she told Campbell (1984), "I told you that when I was six years old I had my own conscious mind and I had to dodge a lot of people in order to survive" (p. 63). When she was pregnant at 15, others admired her independence (p. 67). At 19 she enrolled in the Job Corps and then attended college and held a good job until her involvement with her husband. She explained to Campbell that "she felt released from the 'machine-like' existence of work, school, and childrearing" (p. 69) after leaving school. Her husband's actions and the way she understood that behavior and responded to it created the situation in which she decided to abandon her education and become head of the female group of her husband's gang. She saw her life as a series of decisions, some of which she had to be talked into, but she made the decisions in the end.

Connie's biography can be juxtaposed with Weesa's, the woman who framed her experiences as though she had little control and did not make active decisions. Weesa comes much closer to Vigil's idea of multiple marginality. Like Connie, she too was sent from New York to different relatives in Puerto Rico on several occasions. She too dropped out of school early, had kids as a teenager, and then lived with several men. She talks, however, as though she has made few decisions inspired by either real or perceived choices. At 15 she was living with her boyfriend. "He just wanted me to stay home, home, home. He used to hit me for nothing. And that's when I came out pregnant" (p. 120). It happened to her again at 17: "He liked me, but I didn't like him, you know, but he was alright" (p. 121). She also sees her life as directed by the deeds of others: "Weesa tells what she believes to be a prophetic story about the whore whom her father knifed. In retribution, the women swore that her father's daughter would become a whore" (p. 129). She does not appear to experience control over her life; others control what happens to her.

By accepting a materialist position—as the rational choice model does—immediate material self-interest provides the motivation, whereas the expressive or symbolic aspects of gang involvement are minimized. Acts or aspects of actions that stand for what a person is or who he or she wants to be play little or no role. Although the origins of what drives the youth to membership vary considerably—from family and economic failure with the gang serving as a substitute family (Vigil, 1988a) to a rational decision-making process of the individual and the gang (Sanchez-Jankowski, n.d.)—the gang is joined "in order to." These activities are instrumental. Much of childhood is supposed to be oriented to learning the skills necessary for youths to take their places in the economic realm of work. Instrumental activities are intended to get the actor something else—in the conventional realm, attending school gets one the skills and knowledge to get a job in the legitimate world to make money. One also is supposed to go out with the opposite sex in order to find a spouse. In the same way, one joins a gang in order to improve one's criminal options or social life.

Expressive aspects of peer group activities include those activities youths do with others that do not have practical goals, or those aspects of an activity that are part of expressing to others what kind of person the individual is. Whether that expression is approved by others and how that makes relations pleasurable are communicated by symbols and actions that have moral and aesthetic meanings (Schwartz, 1987). Behavior such as fights, putting down a teacher or police officer in front of others, or breaking into a difficult building might be done as much for communicating to others that the actors are certain kinds of people—that is, persons with particular virtues—as for other reasons. The group may then approve or disapprove of these attempts to construct an identity and by doing so publicly affirm or clarify what is regarded by the group as an approved style. These identities can develop and become important when they are understood and appreciated by others.

Although models of human action tend to be either largely materialistic or symbolic, the actors may construct and interpret their activities and those of others as materialistic or symbolic or both. It is necessary to look at the situation and how it is framed as part of the ongoing interaction. It is possible that the same activity can have very different meanings for the participants and can be framed as an incident that must be done "in order to" or as dramatically expressive of who they are. One such incident, in which she and a gang are going by subway to a party in another gang's territory, is described vividly by Campbell (1984). Gang members often may not pay subway fares, sometimes because they lack money but also because they wish to indicate dramatically that they do not have to go by the rules. On this occasion one of the members jumps a turnstile. The gang leader explains that they are going to a party and must use the subway often, so why cause trouble. He pays for himself and the others with a large wad of bills. The gang splits up so that they do not look too conspicuous on the train (p. 58). On this occasion there is a conflict about paying and what it means, and the leader decides to be pragmatic. Yet he may also be expressing to the group that he is a man with resources.

Analysis of previous research has lead Katz (1988) to argue that although membership is largely expressive—that is, a style and identity—the act itself is seductive. Most important, he examines the experiences of the youths as they participate in "deviant" events. He puts the "fun and thrills" back into delinquency and argues that the attractive properties of the criminal act itself are part of the motivation process. The act itself elicits a sensual moral reaction, a point made many years ago by Bordua (1961) in a critique of delinquency explanations for taking the fun out of delinquency participation. Katz (1988) argues that

> the violence of these groups does not necessarily follow from the nature of the ghetto as an oppressive background; rather, groups must use violence to create an oppressive background if they are to bring into relief their effective presence as an

elite on city streets. For without the violence, would-be street elites would appear to be bound to the social world of childhood. (p. 129)

Katz argues that material benefits play a minor role in the decision-making process. Extreme positions do not allow for the evolution of events and the various ways activities can be structured—choices yield different pictures, and *that* is social reality. An example of how events develop within the immediate situation was described to Vigil (1988a) in an interview. The incident evolved after the young gang member wandered back and forth between home and the park several times. Some friends arrived and they took some "reds":

> At 1:00 A.M. me and my brother and Paul and Mike went to a 7-11 store to steal some more beer. I got a case from the back and set it on the counter as the clerk asks, "Cash or check?" All I could do was laugh, 'cause I knew that I was going to run. When I went back for more beer my brother jumped the counter and hit the clerk over the head with my billy club. Then he handcuffed him and took him to the back of the store and opened and robbed the safe. [They hadn't intended to do this.] As this was happening I hear a cop and can't figure out what is happening. (p. 140)

Although there may have been a materialistic cost-benefit analysis to stealing the beer in the first place, the rest of what happened evolved out of what the participants experienced in the immediate situation.

Conclusions

Gang research has progressed substantially in the last several years, though the results are difficult to compare in part because of the small number of cases included in most of the studies. It may not be possible yet to develop a general theory of gangs. We do not know the parameters of what makes up a "gang" and enough about the nature of the gangs as social/ business organizations or the relationships among gang organizations and ethnicity, the local community and its institutions, the wider society, and the legal and illegal activities of members.

Looking at gangs in different ways allows for the exploration of distinct aspects of the gang experience. Although it may be important for an author to set the parameters of what he or she is researching, there is little reason to confine our research to one particular definition of the gang. Katz's interesting analysis of the importance of the sensual dynamics of illegal actions adds significantly to our thinking, as does Sanchez-Jankowski's organizational analysis. Despite all the research on gangs, there are many questions that have not been asked.

Perhaps we ought to look at how people experience their lives and the conditions or situations in which different experiences are embedded. What permits some people to experience their lives as making a series of rational choices or leads others to experience their lives as more directed and controlled by others? How do those different experiences help to give meaning to individuals' actions? These questions might help further understanding of gang membership and group involvement in illegal activities as a process.

Notes

1. This view of what constitutes "real" culture is held by the proponents of both the strain/subcultural and the cultural perspectives. For the strain perspective, the lack of opportunities or structural inequalities make it impossible to achieve the values constituted by the American dream, so that an alternative subculture, belief system (Gans, 1962), or shadow culture (Liebow, 1967) develops as a substitute to which people are not really committed. That is, they do not have a "real" culture. On the other hand, those who hold that there is cultural relativity in this country and that delinquency arises from an alternative culture believe that it is a "real" culture that causes people to become involved in deviant behavior. They describe a variety of alternative cultures, such as lower-class culture (Miller, 1958), the culture of poverty (Lewis, 1965), the subculture of violence (Wolfgang & Ferracuti, 1967), and the southern culture (Gastil, 1971).

2. The increased use of survey instruments may have helped bring about the demise of cultural explanations and also interest in gangs.

Self-report studies focused on the garden variety of delinquents who were found spread throughout the social structure. Consequently, cultural or subcultural explanations could not account adequately for this finding. Moreover, surveys can best ask general questions about individual attitudes rather than collective definitions.

2

Emic and Etic Perspectives on Gang Culture: The Chicano Case

JAMES DIEGO VIGIL
JOHN M. LONG

U rban immigrant neighborhoods throughout the United States have spawned street gangs for most of the twentieth century. Scholars since the 1920s have reviewed the broadly similar structural circumstances that give rise to these gangs—poverty, substandard housing, poor-paying jobs, low levels of education, estrangement between parents and their more acculturated children, and widespread discrimination (Shaw & McKay, 1942; Short & Strodtbeck, 1965; Thrasher, 1927). Facing these conditions, a significant minority of the youths in ethnic minority neighborhoods founded by immigrants, in defiance of their parents' cultural proscriptions as well as those of the American majority, have coalesced into street gangs with their own syncretic subcultures. Typically, the core of such youth groups is recruited from among those youths with the most marginalized backgrounds. Others join the gang simply for adventure, and still others virtually are coerced into joining.

In addition to the many similarities they share, these street gangs also have differed in many respects. Some of the dissimilarities stem from regional and urban differences, particularly adaptation to environmental circumstances and social forces. Moreover, the unique culture and unique set of acculturation patterns of each ethnic group affected how the youth gangs fashioned a new subculture combining elements from the minority and dominant Anglo-American cultures. As a result, street gang subcultures in various times and places have differed in such aspects as the core values of the groups, the intensity of their disaffection with their parental cultural traditions and the national culture (and its regional variants), the cohesiveness and extent of the gang as a social entity, and, not least, their longevity.

Among the longest-lived youth gangs in America are the Chicano[1] *barrio* (neighborhood) gangs of Southern California. In some Los Angeles barrios, for example, established street gangs have maintained a continuous presence for more than half a century; they have become virtually institutionalized (McWilliams, 1968; Moore & Long, 1987). The continuity of these barrio gangs stems from the same conditions that initially gave rise to the gangs. Throughout the decades, large numbers of poor and poorly trained Mexican immigrants—with and without official permission—have been drawn into Southern California. Each new wave of immigrants has settled in or near existing barrios and created new ones. It is in these barrios where ecologically, economically, and socially marginal links to the larger society are established. Thus each new wave of immigrants provides a new generation of poorly schooled and partially acculturated youths from which the gangs draw their membership. Most of these youths do not, in fact, join gangs. Those who do, however, have significant and lasting effects in their neighborhoods and beyond.

The gang subculture that has evolved in the course of these developments is embedded in and representative of the larger *cholo* (marginalized) subculture to which large numbers of Chicano youths (especially urban youths) subscribe (see Chapter 5). In many regards, the cholo subculture is but a variant of the tendency of teenagers and even preteens in other communities to establish separate behavioral norms and distinct symbols. With new clothing and grooming styles, slang, and so on, this "image" helps distance them from older generations, thus enhancing and facilitating group autonomy and bonding. Additionally, the cholo subculture functions as a source of

identification for Chicano youths with problematic accultura-
tional experiences. Especially important is the break with
Mexican-American traditions, and their tenuous status and
role behavior pattern within the larger Anglo-American culture
(Vigil, 1979). The core membership of the gang—what Vigil
(1988a) has termed the "regular members"—tends to come
from among those cholos with the least attachment to the
behavioral roles available to them in either Mexican-American
or Anglo-American culture.

Methodological Considerations

In describing and analyzing a culture, anthropologists often
find it useful to distinguish between etic and emic[2] understandings of cultural phenomena. In emic studies of a culture,
one attempts to understand phenomena from the viewpoint of
the participants in that culture, that is, to discover the categories and rules one must know in order to think and act as a
native. Etic description, on the other hand, employs "categories
and rules derived from the vocabulary of science" that the
culture's participants might (but might not) find meaningless
(M. Harris, 1988, p. 133). An emic understanding thus affords
a better opportunity for empathic understanding of a way of
life, whereas an etic approach can more efficiently examine the
causes of sociocultural similarities and differences. A full
understanding of a culture or subculture, therefore, would
address both emic and etic aspects. Bernard (1988), for example, suggests that the investigator systematically shift from an
emic to an etic perspective (and vice versa) as a means of
checking the validity of explanations.

A major technique for investigating cultural phenomena
is participant observation, that is, participating in cultural
scenes or behavioral episodes while systematically noting the
behavior of all participants and—when needed and appropriate—seeking explanations of particular behavior (e.g., the
meaning of a word or the rules of a game) from other participants. This is, of course, simply a more systematic application
of one of the two major modes by which we are enculturated

to our cultures: observing others around us, testing the appropriateness of various responses, and asking pertinent questions. We were both engaged informally in participant observation of cholo and gang subcultures while growing up, Vigil in South Central Los Angeles and Long in East Los Angeles. We both attended school with gang members, joined in informal bull sessions with them, played in ball games at the park with them, and—rarely—fought with them. This background has facilitated the sometimes difficult task of establishing sufficient rapport with groups and individuals we subsequently have attempted to study in a more formal fashion. Vigil, in particular, has engaged in systematic participant observation in barrios over several years, throughout Los Angeles and adjacent counties. He has interacted with gang members in parks, in their street hangouts, "cruising" with them in their cars, and in their homes, all the while compiling records of his observations.

There are practical limitations to direct observation of behavior, of course, such as time constraints. Investigations of gang activities impose special restrictions, for individuals engaged in illicit activities often are reluctant to be observed, and an investigator's ethical concerns may preclude his or her participation in any case. In the course of any individual's enculturation, much culture learning that goes unobserved by him or her is inferred from conversation or gained through deliberate instruction. Similarly, many of our findings about cholo and gang subcultures include much information garnered in the course of informal conversation and through instruction by "experts" (i.e., through structured and semistructured interviews). Of special note are the dozens of life histories obtained by Vigil in semistructured interviews with younger gang members and the often less complete but nevertheless detailed life-history materials compiled by Joan Moore and her colleagues at Community Systems Research, Inc. (formerly the Chicano Pinto Research Project), to which we have had ready access.

Moore and her colleagues have developed a very productive methodology for incorporating emic and etic considerations into the aims, design, and execution of research into gang activities and other barrio experiences. Moore (1977) has provided a detailed description of this methodology. It involves a collaborative effort on the part of academic investigators (including, of course, Moore herself and intermittently each of us, among others), members and former members of local barrio gangs, and interested members of the barrio community at large. This wide-ranging collective helps select the gang and/or barrio problem, thereby ensuring that each research project addresses matters of concern to the community itself. (This strategy relates to and has similar origins as the advocacy or collaborative research approaches in applied anthropology; see, e.g., Chambers, 1985.)

The design of the research and the construction of questionnaires to elicit required information are also collaborative affairs. Academic participants construct the instruments after continual consultation with community residents—office staff, gang members, and former gang members employed and trained to use the questionnaires, members of their families, and others whose information would be especially pertinent to the project at hand. These collaborative efforts continue throughout the data collection and (at least initial) interpretation of the data. There are also periodic reviews of findings and tentative interpretations discussed at general staff meetings. More frequently, ideas are honed in smaller discussions between academic investigators and field interviewers. In this fashion, a comparative perspective combining social scientific literature and the perspectives of community participants provides an insider-outsider breadth of knowledge.

We have attempted, in the following paragraphs, to summarize some of the information and insights concerning Chicano gang subcultures that we have acquired by these means. In particular, we have attempted to address the issues of the gang subculture as a mode of adaptation, variability and change in the gang subculture, and the gang subculture as provider of age and gender role protocols and as an arena for role enactment and self-empowerment.

The Subculture as a Mode of Adaptation

In heterogeneous societies, subcultures generate and maintain variant adaptation strategies to match the different backgrounds, different current conditions, and hence different needs and opportunities of the various social categories that constitute the society. The subculture of the gang provides a general strategy for adaptation for the troubled youths who make up the gang. As Cohen (1955) has noted, a gang subculture can persist "only so long as it continues to serve the needs of those who succeed its creators" (p. 65). In the barrios of Southern California, a significant number of youths continue to turn to street gangs to provide for their needs.

The cholo subculture in which the barrio gang subculture is nested incorporates selected and reshaped elements of Mexican-American, Anglo-American, and (to a lesser degree) African-American cultures. It also contains innovative elements not too readily traceable to external influences—like teenage subcultures throughout the United States, it has adopted characteristics that principally serve to render its participants distinct. The cholo subculture of Southern California was born in marginal urban areas where small houses exacerbated the crowded living conditions for large families. Poverty and discrimination in employment generated continual stress within those households. Few parks and playgrounds existed in such areas. The youths who created the cholo subculture and those who have maintained it have been excluded by distance and discrimination from adult-supervised park programs. They have fared poorly in school because of language and cultural differences and limited encouragement from school personnel who expect little of them and parents who often are preoccupied with day-to-day economic crises. It is no wonder that the streets have held such attraction for these youths.

The cholo subculture that has evolved, accordingly, places a high value on friendship—often expressed by employing fictive kinship terms to designate friends—and "partying." Responsibilities beyond one's friends and family are not emphasized. Scholastic achievement is devalued and a job is praiseworthy only if it requires little effort or pays enough to finance one's need to party, or—best of all—both. Alcohol and drug use is valued for enhancing the fun of partying and as a means of demonstrating *machismo* (manliness), for example, by drinking substantially more than others. Machismo has been selectively reforged to emphasize sexual prowess, fighting ability, and a quick readiness to fight. Corresponding attributes of responsibility in the machismo of Mexican culture largely have been shed, except in terms of defending one's honor and family and backing up friends in altercations. Adult authorities—school officials, police, and to a lesser degree even parents—are regarded with suspicion and latent hostility, which in occasional stressful situations erupts into violent encounters over restrictions imposed on the youths' partying.

For barrio youths who despair of succeeding in school and thus can only dream of (rather than plan for) productive adult careers, cholo subculture rejects traditional American and Mexican-American models of success, and in their place offers an arena for status attainment and enhancement in which these youths are capable of functioning. The barrio gang subculture draws its core participants from among the most marginalized of these cholo youths. They join the gang seeking a sense of belonging. Gang membership affords a clearly defined set of peers with whom friendship and familylike relationships (*carnalismo*) are mandated. The egalitarian ethic prevailing within the gang provides a haven from insult to supersensitive pride. Machismo in combination with *locura* (literally, craziness or wildness) as core values of the gang motivate violent conflicts with outsiders, especially rival barrio gangs. These conflicts often focus on protecting the streets of the home barrio from encroachment by other gangs and on violating other gangs' claims to similar control of their own barrios. Such fighting, in turn, provides gang youths with opportunities to release aggressions and hostilities engendered by their marginal upbringing. Fighting and frequent partying together are the most noticeable activities of the barrio gang.

Once established, barrio gangs of course constitute an environmental entity to which other residents must adjust. Adults generally attempt to avoid interaction with gang youths, although indirect contact (e.g., with widespread gang graffiti) is

unavoidable. Youths who have not adopted the cholo subculture do the same. Cholo youths, however, often are both
repelled by the intensity of gang violence and its concomitant
dangers and attracted by the gang's party emphasis and its
defiance of authority. This mixed reaction to the gang and its
subculture leads most cholos to try to establish a live-and-let-
live relationship with local gang members, whose way of life
they partially envy. Such arrangements, however, are brittle,
because the slightest dispute with even one member of the gang
can target an individual for attack by other members. In such
circumstances, not surprisingly, some barrio youths—only
partially reluctant—join the gang to avoid attacks on themselves. Vigil (1988a) cites a 14-year-old who succinctly expressed this mixed motivation: "It was either get your ass
kicked every day or join a gang and get your ass kicked
occasionally by rival gangs. Besides, it was fun" (p. 154).

Variability and Change in the Subculture

Differing in their motivations for joining a street gang, the
gang's members also vary in the intensity of their attachment
to the gang and the extent of their participation in gang
activities. For some individuals, the gang subculture provides
the principal arena for social interaction and the foremost
elements of their social identities. Others who also have strong
identification with the gang participate less frequently in gang
activities because of their interests in other areas. Vigil (1988a)
has categorized such participants in the gang as, respectively,
its "regular" and "peripheral" members. In addition to these,
he distinguishes two types of more marginally committed
members: "temporary" members, who typically join the gang
later and remain a part of it for a shorter length of time; and
"situational" members, who join in gang party activities but
avoid the more violent activities when possible. (It sometimes
is not possible. A leisurely cruising episode may bring one
inadvertently into contact and quick violence with rival gang
members, for example, or may be maneuvered into a drive-by
shooting by a more *loco* member riding in the same car.)

Different barrio gangs and successive cliques in the same barrio often will differ considerably in the relative proportions of members of these varying types. These shifts in clique composition also can affect the nature of a particular barrio's gang activities—for example, the extent and intensity of inter-gang violence, drug and alcohol consumption, and participation in such criminal activities as burglary and robbery by gang members. (The last is rarely a gang activity as such, but the gang norms of bravery and disdain for external authorities tend to condone or even encourage some members to pursue such crimes; see Moore & Vigil, 1987.) Macrostructural factors in the larger social and economic environment, such as the availability of productive employment for barrio residents or the adequacy of funding for social services and recreational programs in the barrio, are of greater influence on the course of barrio events, as discussed by Vigil in Chapter 5 of this volume. In part, of course, such influences affect the proportions of each category of gang members available to each successive clique. Higher unemployment and fewer intervention programs, for example, will exacerbate the stress and strain that shapes those most marginal youths who tend to become the most loco regulars in the gang.

The Subculture as Provider
of Age and Gender Role Protocols

Early adolescence in Western cultures typically is a time in life when rapid biological changes and interaction with a much greater number of individuals from different backgrounds (in junior high school, for example) generate problems in one's sense of identity, especially in regard to appropriate age and gender role behavior. Using Erikson's (1956) label of "psycho-social moratorium" for the adolescent's mind state in this regard, and amplifying a suggestion by Burton and Whiting (1961), Vigil (1988b) indicates that the physical pummeling that is part of the initiation to membership in most barrio gangs serves to help resolve gender identification in youths raised in matricentric households. The initiation also serves, as gang members explain, to test a prospective member's toughness and desire for membership (and thus suitability for membership) and to enhance loyalty to the group (a function of all initiations).

Intergang fighting provides further opportunities for troubled male egos to demonstrate manliness to self and to others. Heavy drinking and experimentation with other drugs often are viewed similarly, because drinking is deemed especially appropriate in adult male gatherings. The gang value of locura encourages both of these activities. Most gang members selectively and periodically act out in loco fashion—to deter potential attacks, for example, or to intimidate others into accommodating their wishes. Many cliques, however, contain one or more individuals whose loco behavior is much less episodic and situationally employed. Although valued for their deterrent and intimidating effects on outsiders, such *vatos locos* (wild guys) sometimes become—by too frequently "starting trouble"—an unwanted liability for the clique.

To enhance egalitarian relations with the clique and provide a readily identifiable image to outsiders, behavioral role models and norms prescribe a "cholo front" for gang members (Vigil, 1988a). This set of role prescriptions includes standardized clothing styles, nicknaming practices (clique members often will not know the formal names of their fellows), tattoo and graffiti techniques, speech practices, and even distinctive patterns for face and hand gestures, body posture, and walking. Members also are expected to employ a particular terminology in addressing one another, with terms such as *carnal* (suggesting blood relationships) and *camarada* (comrade) used to reinforce the bonds of loyalty and friendship prescribed by gang ethics.

The Subculture as an Arena for
Role Enactment and Self-Empowerment

The cholo front provides for a large measure of uniformity in gang members' appearances, and gang norms and values generally are adhered to in gang settings. But gang members, of course, are not uniform; like the rest of us, they differ in physical attributes, temperament, and personality. They will accordingly enact the roles of barrio gang members with varying emphases, seeking different rewards and modes of enhancing personal satisfaction. We have noted above the way in which particularly volatile youths will persist in loco behavior, sometimes to the extent that the clique will oust an overly troublesome youth from membership. Similarly, some members are more attracted than most to heavy drug use; youths who regularly engage in heroin use take on the role of *tecato* (addict) in their late teens and partially segregate themselves into a distinct subclique.

Some gang members (especially, but not exclusively, among the situational members) fear intergang violence or disapprove of it for ethical reasons; they will try to limit their interactions with other members to parties, bull sessions, athletics, and other usually nonviolent activities. Some will admit to such feelings and strategies during interviews, and most will report that other members of their cliques display such behavior; others report that they know (or strongly suspect) some members have "snitched" to the police. Despite the fact that both of these behaviors are serious deviations from the ethical values of loyalty and "backing up the barrio" (gang members use the term *barrio* to refer interchangeably to the gang and the neighborhood in which it is located, implicitly suggesting an identity of interests between the two), such members are not always expelled. Some are so valued as regular suppliers of desired resources (e.g., drugs) or for special abilities (e.g., skill in effecting liaisons with girls) that their breaches of the norms are overlooked. Others are accepted more grudgingly because of their friendship or kinship ties with an especially influential member.

Most gang members feel free to drop their cholo front in situations where it would impair their ability to obtain a particular goal. An individual intent on theft may abandon cholo clothing for something less likely to make people suspicious of him; Vigil (1988a) cites the case of Wizard, who would don an athletic jersey for his shoplifting forays, switching back to khaki pants and a T-shirt later. Similarly, a youth attracted to a girl whose parents strictly supervise whom she can see will dress up in his least cholo outfits and switch to more conventional speech patterns when he calls on her.

Personal approaches to members' behavior often are reflected in nicknames: Names like "Loco," "Crazy," or "Psycho" often are given to the more volatile clique members, for example. A youth who claims authoritative information in discussing current events or who simply wears glasses that make him appear (to clique members) scholarly may be dubbed "Teacher" or "Professor." Telling jokes and playing pranks may earn an individual the sobriquet "*Payaso*" (clown). Although nicknames by no means always suggest personality or behavior traits (they may refer to physical characteristics or idiosyncratic personal experiences, or may simply be variations on given names), this sampling suggests the range of personal approaches that individuals bring to their enactments of gang roles.

Conclusion

There is good reason to believe that the problematic issues that characterize youths growing up in the barrios of Southern California have intensified over the years. Although many of the more overt forms of racial discrimination against Mexican-Americans have lessened dramatically since the 1960s, opportunities for unskilled workers to find permanent productive roles in the local economy also have decreased dramatically. Moreover, the employer penalties introduced by the recent amnesty program have created even more difficulties for large numbers of immigrants. At the same time, spiraling rent increases and inadequate low-income housing construction have resulted in a worsening of already-crowded housing conditions in the barrios. Thus barrio youths are now more apt than ever to be raised in overcrowded family (even multifamily) households. Further, the adult principals of such households often are unemployed, underemployed, or employed in dead-end jobs that pay little and offer no hope of better opportunities in the future.

To compound matters, the gangs themselves have become more pervasive features of the barrio environments to which barrio youths must adapt. The first gang clique (or *klika*, in the syncretic terminology and spelling of the barrio) in any given barrio typically consists of youths between the ages of 12 and 15. By the time the clique has developed fully and is reaching its peak in terms of organized gang activities (at about ages 15 through 18), it has become an influential model for the members of a new younger cohort to pattern themselves after. (A clique also may influence youths in other barrios, as its exploits—often distorted by the media and enhanced by the processes of urban folklore—are heard or read about.) The younger clique, in turn, will provide a similar model for a succeeding generation as it reaches its peak level of activity. Usually, it is at this time that the first clique will be beginning to dissolve, as its members marry, get jobs, or find themselves in recurrent or long-term incarcerations. Each new clique is designated by a specific name, which is appended to the barrio name. Reference to a specific barrio gang, then, usually includes all active cliques or, in some circumstances, all cliques, active or inactive. Two of the oldest barrios in Los Angeles (both located a few miles east of downtown) have experienced, respectively, 14 and 17 such successions of gang cliques (Moore & Long 1987).

Only a small minority of any barrio's youths have joined gangs, and most of those have matured out of the gang by adulthood. Nonetheless, each generation has produced a small number of *veteranos* who retain an active gang identity and affiliation well into their 20s and 30s. Many of these have established what Moore and Vigil (1987) have termed a "cholo family" household. In such households, one or both parents continue to participate more or less overtly in illicit activities while raising their children. Their children are thus virtually preselected to associate and unite with other troubled and disaffected barrio youths in emergent cliques, often at far younger than typical ages. Combined with the increasing availability of illicit drugs and access to firearms since the 1970s, this pattern of in-family socialization to the gang has resulted in a far more violent pattern of gang behavior. In short, the contemporary gang probably is peopled with a larger proportion of highly marginalized and volatile individuals (Vigil, 1987). Accordingly, it is increasingly important that proposals to address the problems that the gangs pose be grounded in an understanding of the barrio gang subculture.

Notes

1. *Chicano, Mexican-American,* and *Mexican* will be used interchangeably in this chapter to mean any person from Mexican background now living in the United States.

2. These terms are derived from linguistics and apparently were coined by Pike (1954). *Phonetic* describes the actual speech sounds employed in a speech community (i.e., among speakers of a common language) and *phonemic* refers to how these sounds are differentiated to convey meaning in an utterance.

PART II

Defining and Measuring Gang Violence

3

Street Gang Violence:
Twice as Great, or Half as Great?

CHERYL L. MAXSON
MALCOLM W. KLEIN

*Let me make the definitions
and I'll win any argument.*
anonymous attorney

Recent increases in street gang violence and the reported spread of major street gang activity to a broad array of American cities (Hagedorn, 1988; Klein & Maxson, 1989) require a careful assessment of our current state of knowledge about street gangs. Further, recent research in such gang-involved cities as Chicago (Spergel, 1985a) and Los Angeles suggests that changes of importance have taken place since the decades of the 1950s and 1960s, when much of our gang knowledge was gathered (Klein, 1971; Klein & Maxson, 1989; Quicker, 1981). For instance, this research suggests higher

AUTHORS' NOTE: We acknowledge with thanks the assistance of Mei-chun Liu Chiang in carrying out the bivariate and discriminant functions analyses. The data used in these analyses were collected as part of an earlier project, funded by the National Institute of Justice, U.S. Department of Justice.

levels of violence, greater numbers and sophistication of weaponry, broader age ranges among gang members, especially on the adult end, and increasing involvement of gang members in drug distribution systems.

Theoretical interests among recent writers have stressed group processes and community contexts of gang activity (Horowitz, 1983; Moore, 1978; Spergel, 1984; Vigil, 1988a). This chapter adds to these the issues of the social construction of the gang problem (see Zatz, 1985)—at least with respect to its seriousness—and the generalizability of the problem. Operationally, we are concerned with whether gang data gathered from one city are immediately comparable to those from another and, by extension, whether gang knowledge must be city specific or can be generalized across cities.

There are obvious policy issues here as well. How validly can we judge the seriousness of gang activity and thus its priority among an array of social problems? How sure can we be that statements of serious or spreading gang violence deserve the allocation of more municipal resources? This latter issue was highlighted in April 1988, when the Los Angeles Police Department sought and received funds from the City Council to mount a series of 1,000-officer sweeps through various gang areas of the city, arresting anyone who looked like, talked like, or acted like a street gang member. The sweeps followed a new annual city high in gang-related homicides in 1987 that appeared to be accelerating even further in early 1988. We will suggest in the pages to follow that this new rate would have been far lower with a different definition of *gang-related* to be found in other cities; would the lower rate have called forth such massive efforts at control and suppression?

Research Purposes

Recent descriptions of Chicago's gang-related homicides struck us as quite remarkable in two regards. First, the Chicago data (Spergel, 1983) closely resembled similar patterns we had noted among gang-related homicides in Los Angeles (Maxson, Gordon, & Klein, 1985). Second, the operational definition of gang-relatedness employed by the Chicago Police Department (the source of Spergel's data) was very substantively different—more restrictive—from the comprehensive definitions used by both the Los Angeles Police and Sheriff's departments, the sources of our data. Do such definitional disparities then yield similar patterns of gang activity and therefore no conceptual problem, or would adjustments to common operational definitions yield very different gang violence descriptions?

Our approach to these issues is to apply the basic Chicago definition of gang-related homicides (Block, 1985; Bobrowski, 1988; Spergel, 1983) to Los Angeles homicide data gathered as part of an earlier project (Maxson et al., 1985). This first analysis will simply "purify" the Los Angeles cases by including only those meeting the Chicago definition. This will indicate how much the gang homicide rate would be reduced by employing this more restrictive definition.

The second analysis will involve bivariate comparisons of gang and nongang homicides in Los Angeles using the Chicago definition, and comparing these to the bivariate analyses reported earlier (Maxson et al., 1985) for gang and nongang cohorts in Los Angeles. These involved both personal characteristics of gang members on victim and suspect sides of homicide incidents (age, ethnicity, and so on) and characteristics of the incidents themselves, such as type of location, numbers of participants, and involvement of autos. One might reasonably expect that the more restrictive definitions would yield "purer" gang cases and thus increase the descriptive differences between gang and nongang incidents. On the other hand, if the definitional disparities are not important, then classifying the eliminated gang cases as part of the nongang pool could reduce these differences (i.e., purifying by the Chicago definition might only mean discarding the less obvious but no less gang-involved incidents).

The third analysis will repeat our earlier application of discriminant analysis to the gang/nongang differences in Los Angeles (Maxson et al., 1985), but this time using the Chicago definition of gang-relatedness. As with the bivariate comparisons, the earlier obtained findings might be exaggerated or reduced, depending on the "real" effect of the purification by using the more restrictive definition. The results, especially in terms of classification success, should have important implications for generalizability of data on gangs across many cities, some of which use restrictive and some of which use comprehensive definitions of gang-relatedness.

Definitions

The situation in the Los Angeles Sheriff's Department is a bit unique, in that the working definition of gang-related events as reflected in the official statistics evolved principally from the concern and activities of one individual. This Sheriff's Department sergeant started collecting gang homicide statistics in 1974 in the most active gang area, East Los Angeles. He expanded the definition well beyond gang-on-gang to include almost all incidents in which any participant was a gang member. In such incidents, he looked for what he described as an "identifiable gang trait." Two examples illustrate the approach:

(1) A gang member gets involved in an isolated incident with his nongang neighbor. The gang member is killed. This would *not* be labeled as gang-related. However, if the neighbor was the victim, then the designation would be questionable and the sergeant would look closely at the circumstance (e.g., "if he was backed up by his homies").

(2) A gang member shoots a clerk in the process of robbing a store. This definitely would be labeled as gang-related because "if he were not a gang member, he probably wouldn't be carrying a weapon."

The specifics are spelled out in the department's official statement, Procedural Memorandum 81-4:

It is the responsibility of the Youth Services Bureau, Street Gang Detail and Safe Streets Detail, to monitor street gang members involved in criminal conduct. This directive establishes criteria for identifying incidents as street gang-related criminality.

The following criteria shall determine if an incident is gang related:

(1) When an incident occurs wherein participants, suspects or victims are identified gang members or associates.

(2) When a reliable informant identifies an incident as gang activity.

(3) When an informant of previously untested reliability identifies an incident as gang activity and it is corroborated by other attendant circumstances or independent information.

(4) When there are strong indications that an incident is gang-related but it does not fit the above criteria, it shall be considered as gang activity.

It is the policy of the Street Gang Unit to identify gang members based on the following criteria:

(1) When an individual admits membership in a gang.

(2) When a reliable informant identifies an individual as a gang member.

(3) When an informant of previously untested reliability identifies an individual as a gang member and it is corroborated by independent information.

(4) When an individual resides in or frequents a particular gang's area and affects its style of dress, use of hand signs, symbols, or tattoos, and associates with known gang members.

(5) When an individual has been arrested several times in the company of identified gang members for offenses which are consistent with usual gang activity.

(6) When there are strong indications that an individual has a close relationship with a gang but does not fit the above criteria, he shall be identified as a "gang associate."

The gang designation process in the Los Angeles Police Department differs somewhat. The official statistics come from the Gang Intelligence Unit, which receives copies of all homicide investigation reports and determines therefrom which will be listed as gang-related. This determination is based upon Special Order No. 21 (8.22.80), which reads as follows:

> *Gang-related Crime*—a) When homicide, attempted murder, assault with a deadly weapon, robbery, rape, kidnapping, shooting at inhabited dwellings, battery on a police officer or arson is reported and the suspect or victim is on file as an active gang or associate gang member. b) When the investigation reveals that the incident involves a gang member, although neither the victim nor the suspect is known to be an active or associate gang member, i.e., "A" shoots "B" and yells the name of a gang during the commission of the crime.

A supplemental description in Central Bureau in October of the same year (1980) provides even broader guidelines:

Gang-relatedness may be established when:

a) Suspects yell a gang name during the crime or when leaving the scene;
b) Suspects yell "where are you from?" before the crime;
c) Witness says the suspects were gang members;
d) Victims are gang members.

Note: Gang affiliations may be determined by the victim's appearance, dress, vehicle, or known gang association.

Thus, in effect, the different LASD and LAPD processes yielded definitional approaches that are very similar. Official statistics for each agency are based upon very broad definitions of gang-relatedness, definitions that could yield a considerable amount of discretion in their application among cases, among investigators, among stations, and over time. Whether or not such discretion has led to systematic differences is of course an empirical question, one that has been discussed elsewhere (Klein, Gordon, & Maxson, 1986). Briefly, both departments appear to use their definitional approaches in a consistent fashion that contributes little variance to the distinctiveness of gang from nongang violence. The basic element is evidence of gang membership on either the suspect or the victim side. We will refer to this as the *gang member* definition.

The Chicago definition, especially with respect to identifying homicide cases as gang-related, is far less ambiguous: "A killing is considered gang-related only if it occurs in the course of an explicitly defined collective encounter between two or more gangs (a 'gang fight')." Further, the department is quite clear on the exclusions. Spergel (1985b) notes, "Criminal and violent activity by gang members, individually or collectively, unrelated to intergang encounters is not considered gang-related."

Spergel (1985b) offers, in addition, two examples that make the contrasts with the earlier LASD examples very explicit:

A gang-related incident, according to the Gang Crime Unit, represents a serious act or alleged acts or threat of violence involving actual, suspected, or putative members of two gangs or even intragang factions. Thus, an attack on an individual mistakenly identified as a member of an opposing gang or intimidations and attempts to recruit individuals currently not gang members, are classified as gang crimes. But an act of robbery of a jewelry store by a recognized gang member, for example, is ordinarily not considered a gang crime in Chicago, as it might be in Los Angeles. (p. 16)

Although Block and, indirectly, Bobrowski dispute Spergel's statements of Chicago's reliance upon the elements of gang affiliations of the participants and the collective nature of the encounter, there is uniform agreement regarding the import of a gang-related motive to the designation of a gang-related incident in Chicago. A recent listing includes nine motives, prominent among these being retaliation, territoriality, recruiting, and "representing" (graffiti, wearing gang colors, shouting gang slogans, and so on). In practice, these overlap very substantially.

The rationale for the Chicago definition has been stated for that police department as follows:

The presence of these indicators alone, however, does not serve to define the event as street gang related. During the review process, the report is carefully studied for information which would lead one to reasonably conclude that the incident grew out of a gang function. The gang membership of either party to the offense does not constitute gang relatedness unless the event contains some element which establishes the nexus between the incident and the animus of the gang.

This definition has been viewed as somewhat restrictive as it tends to limit the volume of reported street gang crime. But it occupies a reasonable middle ground somewhere between those definitions which require that the incident involve group participation, and the other extreme, which requires only that some party to the event be a gang member. The "Chicago definition" admits the misconduct of individuals apart from the presence of the group, and is concerned with providing tactically significant information—not with describing the delinquencies of persons whose misbehavior also happens to include gang membership. If it is restrictive, it is so because it serves the interests of operational personnel concerned with interdicting the illegal activities of street gangs, and avoids the generation of a large body of less useful data. (Bobrowski, 1988, pp. 8-9)

For purposes of our analyses, we can select as Chicago-defined Los Angeles homicide incidents all those with known gang victim and suspect, and all those with clear gang motives for the encounter. Collectivity clearly is subsumed by these. The prior coding of the Los Angeles incidents fortuitously allows us to apply these Chicago criteria with considerable confidence. For purposes of this report, we will refer to this Chicago-style approach as the *gang motive* definition.

We would only add, at this point, that although the contrasting definitions come from Chicago and Los Angeles, they are not used only in those two cities. A recent symposium of police gang unit commanders[1] revealed gang motive definitions used by police departments in Philadelphia, Jackson (Mississippi), and Seattle, and gang member definitions in New York, Detroit, Evanston, Fort Worth, Miami, and Minneapolis. Five California cities that we studied recently revealed variations ranging from narrow gang-on-gang (motive) definitions to broad inclusive (member) definitions approaching those of Los Angeles.

The Data

The data on which the analyses are carried out were gathered in connection with the earlier project (Klein et al., 1986; Maxson et al., 1985). They were taken from the investigation files of the Los Angeles Police Department for the years 1979-81 and the Sheriff's Department for the years 1978-82. Gang-related incidents were the entire populations of homicides in 3 stations of the LAPD and 19 of the LASD, limited to cases with at least one name-identified suspect aged 10 to 30. All gang cases were so designated by the gang units of each department, a surprisingly reliable process as revealed in our earlier project (Klein et al., 1986). Comparable (one name-identified suspect aged 10 to 30) nongang homicide cases were selected by stratified sampling by proportion of gang cases per station to the total sample pool, but limited to 50 cases per year. The resulting numbers are 135 gang and 148 nongang homicides from LAPD, and 226 gang and 200 nongang cases from LASD.

Of additional relevance is the fact that 1980 was, until recently, the peak year of gang-related homicides in Los Angeles County. Thus these cases represent the situation immediately before and after a particularly horrendous period; 351 gang-related homicides were recorded throughout the county in 1980. We are comparing the effects of contrasting definitions during a period of unusual activity.

Analysis 1: Case Numbers

Included in the original Los Angeles data collection were the appearance of gang members on either the suspect side or the victim side of a gang homicide and a categorizing of motives noted in the investigation file. Motives included retaliation, territoriality, previous gang conflict, conflict over graffiti, and a residual "other" category. The basic elements of the Chicago definition are therefore available, yielding the appropriate re-analysis of the Los Angeles cases. Using the gang motive definition—a side is classified as gang if any one person on that side has a gang affiliation or suspected affiliation (via clothing or behavior)—we find that 44.4% of the LAPD cases classified by the gang member definition would still be designated as gang-related, as would 57.1% of the LASD cases. The combined percentage (there were more LASD than LAPD cases) is 52.4%.[2]

Empirically, it seems that gang-on-gang and the presence of a gang motives, as both are recorded in gang incident investigation files, are highly redundant. Excluding cases that have only gang-on-gang *or* gang motive, the figures are reduced by only a few percentage points. It seems fair to conclude that the narrow definition of the Chicago variety would reduce the reported Los Angeles gang homicide rate by about half—more in one jurisdiction, less in the other.

In 1987, a new peak of 387 gang-related homicides was recorded in Los Angeles County. Partly on the basis of this, and the subsequent publicity associated with it and the increase in crack cocaine distribution, the police sweeps referred to earlier were inaugurated. One reasonably could question whether the same reaction would have occurred following a "peak" year of 203 cases; this latter is a figure exceeded in each of the last 10 years using the gang member definition.

Analysis 2: Bivariate Comparisons

In previous analyses, we compared gang and nongang homicides on three categories of variables; those describing the setting of the event, those describing the participants, and those relating to the thoroughness of the police investigations. The third of these is not germane to the current discussion; we compare here the differences revealed by bivariate comparisons of gang and nongang setting and participant variables, using the earlier data and the new data as created by the application of the gang motive definition.

The first step is to ask about the half of the member-defined cases that drop out using the motive definition. Does this "purification" process yield two sets of gang-related cases that are substantially different (i.e., are gang-related cases without gang motives substantively different from their motive-defined counterparts)? We can answer this question by comparing both sets of cases with respect to the incident characteristics and participant characteristics shown in our prior work to distinguish gang from nongang cases. Table 3.1 summarizes this comparison, based on probabilities of .05 or less associated with t tests and chi-squares, as appropriate.

The principal finding to be derived from Table 3.1 is that, for the most part, cases defined by motive and cases defined by gang member involvement do *not* differ substantially. This is true in both jurisdictions. Of 29 variables describing homicide setting and participant characteristics, about one-third in LAPD and one-half in LASD yield differences attaining statistical significance. This is far more than one would expect by chance, but far fewer than might be expected from a serious attempt to alter the meaning of gang-relatedness, especially an attempt involving half (or double) the number of cases.

There are slight patterns discernible in Table 3.1. For instance, the significant differences relate more to participant than to setting variables. Second, a number of the significant differences make more sense with respect to the gang-on-gang than to the motive component of the Chicago-defined incidents—more drive-by shootings, more clear gang affiliations, younger victim ages, fewer robberies, and more murder attempts. Perhaps "motive" really serves as a proxy measure of gang-on-gang. Block's (1985) Chicago analysis indirectly suggests this, as almost every motive-defined case involved a gang assault rather than robbery or other offense setting. Because inferring a motive is considerably more judgmental than checking for gang affiliations in investigative and intelligence files, it may in the future be more expedient simply to look for gang membership on both sides in cities and studies opting for the narrower, motive-defined approach to gang-relatedness.

We move on, now, to the more central comparison in this second approach to the analyses, the question of whether

TABLE 3.1: Setting and Participant Characteristics of Gang "Motive" Versus Gang "Member" Cases in Two Jurisdictions

Characteristics	LAPD (n = 137)	LASD (n = 231)
Location[a]	no difference	no difference
Car[b] involved	"motive" more drive-bys and other car involvement	"motive" more drive-bys and other car involvement
Time of day	no difference	no difference
Total number of weapons	no difference	"motive" more
Gun present	no difference	no difference
Knives present	no difference	no difference
Other weapons present	no difference	no difference
Presence of associated charges	no difference	no difference
Associated charge for		
attempted murder	"motive" more	"motive" more
robbery	"motive" fewer (in fact, none)	"motive" fewer
assault with a deadly weapon	"motive" more	no difference
other	no difference	no difference
Other injuries	no difference	no difference
Unknown suspect	no difference	no difference
Fear of retaliation	no difference	no difference
Prior contact[c]	"motive" more (in minimal category)	"motive" more (in minimal category)
All male victims	no difference	no difference
All male suspects	no difference	no difference
Affiliation of victim[d]	"motive" more	"motive" more
Affiliation of suspect[d]	"motive" more	"motive" more
Number of victim participants	"motive" more	no difference
Number of suspect participants	no difference	"motive" more
Total participants	"motive" more	no difference
Mean age, victims	"motive" younger	"motive" younger
Mean age, suspects	no difference	no difference
Proportion Black victims	no difference	"motive" fewer
Proportion Black suspects	no difference	"motive" fewer
Proportion Hispanic victims	no difference	"motive" more
Proportion Hispanic suspects	no difference	"motive" more

a. Street versus residence versus other.
b. None versus car involved versus "drive-by" shooting.
c. None versus minimal versus clear prior contact.
d. Gang affiliation explicitly noted.

gang/nongang homicide differences are affected by the definition one uses. The data in Table 3.1 might lead one to predict either way, as there were a number of significant, definitionally determined gang case differences, yet not in a majority of the comparisons.

Once again, our procedure is to use selected characteristics of homicide cases. We know from our prior research which of these yielded differences between gang and nongang cases, using the gang member definition. Now we make the same comparisons using the gang motive definition, which, as described earlier, yields only about half as many cases.[3] The question here is, Do the gang/nongang differences take on a different look, either quantitatively (number of distinguishing variables) or qualitatively (pattern of variables)? The detailed data are presented in Tables 3.5 and 3.6 at the end of this chapter. Here we present a summary in Table 3.2.

The proper way to read Table 3.2 is to read down and compare the two LAPD columns, and then the two LASD columns separately. Within the LAPD columns, we see that the character of the gang/nongang comparisons differs between the two definitional approaches for 9 of the 30 characteristics, and none of the 9 constitutes a reversal of direction. There is little pattern to the changes other than those related to associated charges cited in these incidents. When we review the LASD comparisons, we find that there are only 2 out of 30 changes, again with no reversals.

Thus, despite the loss of half the gang cases that accompanies the adoption of the motive definition, there is essentially no change in the described *character* of the homicide incidents. Reference to the levels of association listed in Tables 3.5 and 3.6 does suggest, however, that the motive-defined differences tend to be greater, especially in the case of the LAPD incidents. There is, in the motive approach, some greater "purification" of the gang cases, but this is only within the overall limits of the display in Table 3.2 above. If we were to characterize gang-related homicides in comparison to nongang-related cases, the choice of motive or member definition would make little difference empirically, conceptually, or in policy relevance.

TABLE 3.2: Summary of Two Gang/Nongang Comparisons

Characteristics	LAPD		LASD	
	Member-Defined	Motive-Defined	Member-Defined	Motive-Defined
Location	no difference[a]	no difference	gang more street	gang more street
Car involved	gang more drive-bys	gang more drive-bys	gang more drive-bys	gang more drive-bys
Time of day	no difference	no difference	no difference	no difference
Total number of weapons	no difference	no difference	gang more	gang more
Guns present	gang more	gang more	gang more	gang more
Knives present	no difference	gang less	no difference	no difference
Other weapons present	no difference	no difference	gang more	gang more
Presence of associated charges	no difference	no difference	gang more	gang more
Number of associated charges	gang more	no difference	gang more	no difference
If associated charges, for				
attempted murder	no difference	gang more	gang more	gang more
robbery	no difference	gang fewer	gang fewer	gang fewer
assault with a deadly weapon	no difference	gang more	gang more	gang more
other	no difference	no difference	gang fewer	gang fewer
Other injuries	no difference	gang more	gang more	gang more
Presence of unknown suspects	gang more	gang more	gang more	gang more
Fear of retaliation	gang more	gang more	gang more	gang more

(continued)

TABLE 3.2: Summary of Two Gang/Nongang Comparisons

Characteristics	LAPD		LASD	
	Member-Defined	Motive-Defined	Member-Defined	Motive-Defined
Prior contact	gang more (in no prior and minimal categories)	gang more (in minimal category)	gang more (in no prior and minimal categories)	gang more (in no prior and minimal categories)
All male victims	no difference	gang more	gang more	gang more
All male suspects	gang more	no difference	gang more	no difference
Gang affiliation, victims	gang more	gang more	gang more	gang more
Gang affiliation, suspects	gang more	gang more	gang more	gang more
Number of victim participants	gang more	gang more	gang more	gang more
Number of suspect participants	gang more	gang more	gang more	gang more
Total number of participants	gang more	gang more	gang more	gang more
Mean age, victims	gang younger	gang younger	gang younger	gang younger
Mean age, suspects	gang younger	gang younger	gang younger	gang younger
Proportion Black victims	no difference	no difference	gang fewer	gang fewer
Proportion Black suspects	gang fewer	gang fewer	gang fewer	gang fewer
Proportion Hispanic victims	gang more	no difference	gang more	gang more
Proportion Hispanic suspects	gang more	gang more	gang more	gang more

a. "No difference" here means the difference is not statistically different at the .05 level. The values of location, car involved, prior contact, and gang affiliation are defined in the notes to Table 3.1.

Analysis 3: Discriminant Functions

We come now to what is technically the most complex analysis, and one that can assess for us a bit more clearly what may be gained or lost by adopting one of the competing definitions of gang-relatedness. Discriminant analysis organizes all the variables—the characteristics listed in Tables 3.1 and 3.2—that relate to our homicide cases in such a way as to maximize their capacity to discriminate gang from nongang cases. The result is a *function* (a term referring to the variables plus the weights associated with each of them) that best separates the two kinds of cases. A perfect function will not emerge; some gang cases will look more like the typical nongang case, and some nongang cases will look quite "gangy." Still, we should be able to describe the variables that are the best discriminators between gang and nongang cases and we should be able to discern the relative contribution of each variable (the "weights") to that discrimination.

Finally, this process will permit us to ask how successfully—less than with perfection, but more than by chance—we can classify cases as gang or nongang. In this case, "successful" classification means the degree to which our variables, the setting and participant characteristics, predict the assignment of cases by the LAPD and LASD to the gang and nongang categories. We then can determine if this classification success is higher when these agencies use the member definition or the motive definition of gang-relatedness.

The process is similar to collecting a lot of data on variables thought to be relevant to males and females, where some official agency has separated people into those two sexes. The variables might be such things as height, weight, length of hair, occupation, mechanical skill, preferred sports, and hobbies. There is overlap on most of these items, and some are better discriminators than others. Thus we must find the best discriminators and weigh them accordingly (the discriminant functions). Having that function, we can then ask how well it correctly identifies males and females as determined by the official agency. The difference in our analysis will be that the "official agency" can itself apply two different "gender" definitions (i.e., the member and motive definitions) so that our task is to compare *two* discriminant functions and two classification success rates.

Tables 3.3 and 3.4 list the variables,[4] the weights (*standardized discriminant coefficients* is the technical term), and two important statistics, variance explained (eta squared, technically) and classification success. The signs next to the weights indicate a positive or negative association with the gang category. The magnitude of the weights shows the relative power of that variable to distinguish between gang and nongang cases.

In the LAPD cases, the overall pattern is one of shared variables, although there are several unshared variables in each function. There is considerable shifting in the order of the weights between the two functions. Participant age loses some importance in the motive-defined function and associated charges gain importance.[5] There is a very slight gain in the amount of variance explained by the motive-defined function, as well as a gain in classification success, especially for the nongang cases.

The LASD's functions show the same level of stability as the LAPD's in variables emerging in the functions and the same change in the presence of associated charges; the age difference is less apparent, and the import of the lack of a clear prior relationship increases. Changes in variance explained and classification success are of the same order as in the LAPD data.

It seems reasonable to suggest that associated charges in both cases are variables that relate to the inference of gang motives because violence is more salient in gang than nongang events generally (Maxson et al., 1985; Tracy, 1979). Even more obviously, the greater weight (particularly in LASD) shown by the lack of a prior relationship in the motive-defined function speaks directly to our earlier suggestion of the redundancy between a motive definition and the presence of gang members on both sides of the fray ("gang-on-gang"). Our prior research has shown that gang violence is characterized by participants who don't know each other.

TABLE 3.3: Summary of Discriminant Analyses, LAPD

Characteristics	Member-Defined Weights[a]	Motive-Defined Weights
Mean age, suspects	−.736	−.442
Mean age, victims	−.342	−.324
Proportion Black suspects	−.248	−.243
Guns present	+.238	n.s.
Proportion male suspects	+.218	n.s.
Number of suspect participants	+.196	+.150
Prior contact[b]	+.189	−.219
Car present	+.188	+.371
Number of victim participants	−.063	+.181
Fear of retaliation	n.s.	+.360
Associated charges, attempted murder	n.s.	+.154
Associated charges, assault with a deadly weapon	n.s.	+.152
Variance explained (eta^2)	.42	.45
Classification success (%)		
gang	84.6	88.5
nongang	74.5	84.1
overall	79.2	85.2

a. These weights are taken from Maxson et al. (1990).
b. In the "member-defined" analysis, prior contact is a dichotomous variable for *no* prior contact. In the "motive-defined" analysis, prior contact is positively coded for a *clear* prior relationship between suspects and victims.

The better classification success for the motive-defined functions certainly was to be expected. However, the success of the member-defined functions was quite good to begin with, given the inherent ambiguities of homicide investigations and gang designations combined. Thus there was a limit to how much improvement might be expected for a "purer" definitional approach. A small gain in variance explained and classification success has come at the expense of giving up half the cases otherwise labeled as gang-related.

TABLE 3.4: Summary of Discriminant Analyses, LASD

Characteristics	Member-Defined Weights[a]	Motive-Defined Weights
Mean age, suspects	−.491	−.373
Proportion Hispanic suspects	+.415	+.264
Location on street	+.322	+.150
Number of suspect participants	+.307	+.255
Guns present	+.279	+.146
Mean age, victims	−.237	−.163
Proportion male suspects	+.185	n.s.
Prior contact[b]	+.164	−.539
Number of victim participants	+.156	+.065
Associated charges, any violent	+.152	n.s.
Mean age difference between suspect and victim	+.113	n.s.
Associated charges, attempted murder	n.s.	+.130
Car present	n.s.	+.179
Associated charges, robbery	n.s.	−.322
Fear of retaliation	n.s.	+.240
Variance explained (eta^2)	.49	.58
Classification success (%)		
gang	85	88.7
nongang	80	86
overall	82.6	87

a. These weights are taken from Maxson et al. (1990).
b. In the "member-defined" analysis, prior contact is a dichotomous variable for *no* prior contact. In the "motive-defined" analysis, prior contact is positively coded for a *clear* prior relationship between suspects and victims.

Discussion

This chapter is the latest in a series of papers in which we have used California gang incident data to test propositions about the uniqueness and generalizability of street gang offense patterns. The prior work has established that gang violence is substantively different in character from nongang violence. It has established, at least for jurisdictions with sophisticated gang intelligence units, that the character of reported gang violence is primarily a function of the setting and participant characteristics of the violent events, not the investigative and reporting procedures of the police. It has established that the character of "big-city" gang violence is quite similar to that found in smaller cities with more recent development of street gangs.

In addition, we have noted in our prior work the vast increase in the number of cities facing gang problems, the changes and stability in the character of gang structure over several decades, and an early assessment of the limits of gang involvement in new patterns of drug distribution.

Throughout this work, however, we have been troubled by the realization that much of our work was based on the broad, member-defined designation of violent gang offenses. Other cities, we knew, varied in the definition of gang-relatedness, but the definitions were difficult to elicit and even more difficult to operationalize. Recent work in Chicago both by researchers and by operational personnel in the Chicago police department, in combination with the openness and cooperation of the police and sheriff's departments in Los Angeles, has provided an excellent opportunity to investigate limits to generalizability arising from differences in operational definitions. Importantly, these definitional differences can affect not only the pertinent enforcement operations but also the basic research operations upon which social science understanding of gangs largely is (or should be) based. Knowledge about street gang behavior has very limited value if its generalizability is unknown.

What we have learned from the present analysis includes the following:

(1) A motive-based definition of gang-related homicides yields about half as many gang homicides as does a member-based definition.

(2) The characters of motive-defined and member-defined gang homicides are quite similar. The character of the former may be related more to the gang-on-gang nature of

the incidents than to motive; certainly there is redundancy between the two.

(3) When contrasting gang with nongang homicide incidents, it does not matter much which definitional approach is used for purposes of describing the settings and participants of each.

(4) The motive-defined approach allows one to classify gang and nongang cases a bit more successfully on the basis of setting and participant characteristics, but not at all in proportion to the information at hand. That is, the slightly greater classification success is far less than might have been expected by a 50% "purification" of cases labeled as gang.

It seems clear, then, that estimates of the *prevalence* of gang violence can vary widely among cities using different definitions of gang violence. Within a given city, estimates of prevalence will be comparable over time only if the definitional operations remain constant. Comparisons across cities and across time must be made very cautiously. Studies of the etiology of gangs and gang violence that use such prevalence estimates must also be wary of the definitional problem.

Generalizations across cities with respect to the *character* of gang homicides, however, seem less vulnerable to the definitional problem. Coupled with our earlier finding of similarities in a few smaller California cities (which did not share the same definitional approaches), this suggests that gang homicides—and gang violence more generally—can be viewed in a generic fashion. This is what science hopes to find—general principles, along with situation-specific qualifications. Because gang research almost never is carried out in more than one place at a time, establishing grounds for some confidence in extrapolating findings to other places is certainly helpful.

For federal and local agencies trying to ameliorate a fast-developing national problem, it is also helpful to consider that the character of the problem being addressed has many common features across places and even across time. Current research funded by the federal Office of Juvenile Justice and Delinquency Prevention is attempting to establish intervention

TABLE 3.5: Characteristics of Gang Versus Nongang Homicides (LAPD)

	Member-Defined Gang (n = 135)		Nongang (n = 148)		p^a	Motive-Defined Gang (n = 60)		Nongang (n = 164)		p
	%	No.	%	No.		%	No.	%	No.	
Location					n.s.					n.s.
street	49	66	34	50		50	30	36	58	
other public	22	30	27	39		22	13	26	43	
residence	29	39	39	58		28	17	38	62	
missing		0		1			0		1	
Car involved					.294**					.491**
none	36	49	51	75		17	10	52	84	
car involved	44	59	46	67		47	28	45	73	
shooting out of car	20	27	3	4		37	22	3	5	
missing		0		2			0		2	
Time of day					n.s.					n.s.
daytime	14	19	12	18		10	6	14	22	
afternoon/evening	41	55	39	57		40	24	37	59	
nighttime	45	60	48	70		50	30	49	79	
missing		1		3			0		4	
Weapons										
mean total number of weapons		1.63		1.57	n.s.		1.75		1.54	n.s.
guns present	82	111	67	99	.175**	87	52	69	111	.182**
missing		1		2			0		2	
knives present	23	31	36	53	n.s.	17	10	36	58	-.185**
missing		4		3			1		4	

(continued)

TABLE 3.5. Characteristics of Gang Versus Nongang Homicides (LAPD) (Continued)

	Member-Defined Gang (n = 135)		Nongang (n = 148)			Motive-Defined Gang (n = 60)		Nongang (n = 164)		
	%	No.	%	No.	p^a	%	No.	%	No.	p
other weapons present	12	16	15	22	n.s.	12	7	15	24	n.s.
missing		4		3			1		4	
Associated charges										
cases with associated charges	48	65	38	56	n.s.	47	28	39	64	n.s.
mean number of charges		.71		.48	.136*		.72		.50	n.s.
If associated charges, type	[n = 65]		[n = 56]			[n = 28]		[n = 64]		
other homicide (e.g. attempt, conspiracy)	51	33	41	23	n.s.	75	21	38	24	.345**
robbery	38	25	29	16	n.s.		0	38	24	-.393**
assault with a deadly weapon	28	18	25	14	n.s.	43	12	20	13	.233**
other	23	15	23	13	n.s.	25	7	25	16	n.s.
Other victim injuries present	21	28	14	20	n.s.	28	17	12	20	.192**
Unknown suspects present	23	31	10	15	.174**	30	18	11	18	.229**
Fear of retaliation	33	45	13	99	.304**	40	24	11	18	.329**
Prior contact					.465**					.493**
no prior contact	49	63	27	37		38	22	31	48	
minimal or indirect relationship	31	40	8	11		46	26	8	12	

(continued)

TABLE 3.5. Characteristics of Gang Versus Nongang Homicides (LAPD) (Continued)

	Member-Defined Gang (n = 135)		Nongang (n = 148)			Motive-Defined Gang (n = 60)		Nongang (n = 164)		
	%	No.	%	No.	p^a	%	No.	%	No.	p
clear prior contact	20	26	65	91		16	9	61	94	
missing		6		9			3		10	
Gender										
all homicide victims male	93	126	88	130	n.s.	97	58	88	144	.132*
all homicide suspects male	81	110	71	105	.123*	82	49	72	118	n.s.
Gang affiliation										
homicide victims					.526**					.790**
no mention	51	68	97	142		19	11	96	155	
at least one clearly gang	40	53	2	3		69	41	3	5	
at least one possibly gang	9	12	1	2		12	7	1	2	
missing		2		1			1		2	
Homicide suspects					.746**					.763**
no mention	16	19	90	114		2	1	85	118	
at least one clearly gang	78	91	8	10		94	48	14	19	
at least one possibly gang	5	6	2	2		4	2	1	2	
missing		19		22			9		25	
Participants										
on victim side	2.83		1.83		.225**	3.85		1.82		.381**
missing	9		8			6		9		
on suspect side	3.82		1.92		.254**	4.39		2.07		.277**
missing	9		8			6		9		

(continued)

94

TABLE 3.5. Characteristics of Gang Versus Nongang Homicides (LAPD) (Continued)

	Member-Defined Gang (n = 135) %	No.	Nongang (n = 148) %	No.	p^a	Motive-Defined Gang (n = 60) %	No.	Nongang (n = 164) %	No.	p
total	6.96	8	3.77	6	.281**	8.93	5	3.90	7	.372**
missing										
Mean age										
homicide victims	23.79		30.65		-.301**	20.24		30.06		-.374**
missing		2		2			1		3	
homicide suspects	19.44		23.86		-.483**	19.12		23.40		-.416**
missing		19		22			9		25	
Ethnicity										
homicide victims										
proportion Black	.44		.56		n.s.	.46		.54		n.s.
missing		2		1			1		2	
proportion Hispanic	.52		.39		.132*	.51		.42		n.s.
missing		2		1			1		2	
homicide suspects										
proportion Black	.54		.67		-.131*	.45		.65		-.185*
missing		19		22			9		25	
proportion Hispanic	.46		.32		.139*	.55		.34		.192**
missing		19		22			9		25	

a. Significance levels were determined as appropriate by chi-squares or t tests ($^*p < .05$; $^{**}p < .01$). Levels of association were determined by phi, Cramer's V, or Pearson's r, respectively, for 2 × 2 tables, 2 × N tables, and interval-level data.

TABLE 3.6: Characteristics of Gang Versus Nongang Homicides (LASD)

	Member-Defined Gang (n = 226)		Nongang (n = 200)			Motive-Defined Gang (n = 129)		Nongang (n = 219)		
	%	No.	%	No.	p^a	%	No.	%	No.	p
Location					.392**					.400**
street	48	109	14	27		54	70	16	36	
other public	27	61	34	67		22	28	33	73	
residence	24	55	53	106		24	31	50	110	
missing		1		0			0		0	
Car involved					.264**					.444**
none	34	76	43	85		22	28	45	98	
car involved	44	98	53	104		44	57	52	114	
shooting out of car	22	48	4	7		34	44	3	6	
missing		4		4			0		1	
Time of day					n.s.					n.s.
daytime	11	24	13	25		7	9	13	27	
afternoon/evening	32	73	34	66		34	44	33	71	
nighttime	57	127	53	102		59	75	54	114	
missing		2		7			1		7	
Weapons										
mean total number of weapons		2.23		1.68	.160**		2.47		1.75	.189**
guns present	80	180	60	120	.218**	82	106	63	137	.204**
missing		0		1			0		1	
knives present	31	70	37	73	n.s.	27	35	38	82	n.s
missing		1		2			0		2	

(continued)

TABLE 3.6. Characteristics of Gang Versus Nongang Homicides (LASD) (Continued)

	Member-Defined Gang (n = 226)		Nongang (n = 200)			Motive-Defined Gang (n = 129)		Nongang (n = 219)		
	%	No.	%	No.	p^a	%	No.	%	No.	p
other weapons present	31	70	23	45	.128*	35	45	24	52	.116*
missing		0		3			0		3	
Associated charges										
cases with associated charges	72	164	52	105	.212**	73	94	55	121	.175**
mean number of charges		1.12		.90	.108*		1.14		.94	n.s.
If associated charges, type	[n = 164]		[n = 105]			[n = 94]		[n = 121]		
other homicide (e.g. attempt, conspiracy)	45	73	22	23	.230**	51	48	24	29	.280**
robbery	20	32	34	36	-.166**	7	7	37	45	-.345**
assault with a deadly weapon	57	94	39	41	.178**	64	60	40	48	.240**
other	23	38	50	53	-.282**	23	22	47	57	-.244**
Other victim injuries present	30	67	10	20	.243**	33	42	11	25	.259**
Unknown suspects present	19	43	7	14	.169**	20	26	8	18	.173**
Fear of retaliation present	33	75	10	19	.290**	38	49	10	23	
missing		1		0			1		0	
Prior contact					.494**					.576**

(continued)

TABLE 3.6. Characteristics of Gang Versus Nongang Homicides (LASD) (Continued)

	Member-Defined Gang (n = 226)		Nongang (n = 200)		p^a	Motive-Defined Gang (n = 129)		Nongang (n = 219)		p
	%	No.	%	No.		%	No.	%	No.	
no prior contact	53	114	24	46		56	68	27	56	
minimal or indirect relationship	28	59	8	16		37	45	8	17	
clear prior contact	19	40	68	129		7	9	65	10	
missing		13		9			7		10	
Gender										
all homicide victims male	92	208	82	164	.151**	91	118	83	182	.117*
all homicide suspects male	78	177	70	139	.101*	78	101	69	151	n.s.
Gang affiliation										
homicide victims					.521**					.699**
no mention	46	102	94	188		26	33	93	204	
at least one clearly gang	47	106	4	9		65	82	5	11	
at least one possibly gang	7	16	2	3		9	12	2	4	
missing		2		0			2		0	
Homicide suspects					.762**					.790**
no mention	16	30	91	152		6	7	86	154	
at least one clearly gang	76	143	5	8		88	95	11	19	
at least one possibly gang	8	15	4	6		6	6	3	5	
missing		38		34			21		41	
Participants										
on victim side		4.70		1.79	.262**		5.21		2.11	.269**
missing		6		7			2		9	

(continued)

TABLE 3.6. Characteristics of Gang Versus Nongang Homicides (LASD) (Continued)

	Member-Defined Gang (n = 226)		Nongang (n = 200)			Motive-Defined Gang (n = 129)		Nongang (n = 219)		
	%	No.	%	No.	p^a	%	No.	%	No.	p
on suspect side	4.07		1.79		.386**	4.63		2.06		.408**
missing		7		7			3		9	
total	8.96		3.59		.344**	9.65		4.50		.309**
missing		3		6			1		7	
Mean age										
homicide victims	23.41		29.20		−.215**	20.48		29.57		−.314**
missing		2		0			2		0	
homicide suspects	19.36		24.11		−.428**	18.96		23.77		−.396**
missing		38		34			21		41	
Ethnicity										
homicide victims										
proportion Black	.12		.32		−.231**	.09		.29		−.241**
missing		2		0			2		0	
proportion Hispanic	.83		.39		.448**	.86		.44		.408**
missing		2		0			2		0	
homicide suspects										
proportion Black	.23		.38		−.161**	.12		.38		−.278**
missing		38		34			21		41	
proportion Hispanic	.75		.34		.412**	.84		.36		.469**
missing		38		34			21		41	

a. Significance levels were determined as appropriate by chi-squares or t tests (*$p < .05$; **$p < .01$). Levels of association were determined by phi, Cramer's V, or Pearson's r, respectively, for 2 × 2 tables, 2 × N tables, and interval-level data.

models that can be implemented in differing sites (see Chapter 13 of this volume). Our data should be encouraging for such efforts.

Another way of contrasting the implications of the two definitions is to suggest that the character of gang violence is now less of a social science problem, and that the prevalence of gang violence is now more of a political problem. How much useful information is one willing to sacrifice in order to claim a lower level of violence?

Notes

1. This symposium was held March 1, 1988, under the auspices of the University of Chicago and convened by Irving Spergel as part of a national study funded by the Office of Juvenile Justice and Delinquency Prevention.

2. The validity of the prior designation by the gang units is suggested by the fact that only 0.68% of LAPD nongang cases and 2% of LASD nongang cases fit the Chicago definition.

3. The member-defined data are taken from our prior report. Because *motive*-defined cases omit almost half the member-defined cases, some of the latter now become nongang cases under the motive definitions. These were assigned, by random selection, to the nongang category in proportion to the station contribution to the totals. This amounted to 24% of the member-defined cases in both jurisdictions.

4. The variables entered into the discriminant analysis were limited to those having significant bivariate relationships to the gang/nongang distinctions, those being nonredundant with others on the list, and those not showing heavily skewed distributions.

5. The apparent sign reversal in the prior contact variable is attributable to the different coding approaches adapted in the two analyses.

PART III

Diffusion, Diversity, and Drugs

4

Gang Imperialism

CARL S. TAYLOR

The increase and spread of youth gangs in today's United States constitute a movement that must be recognized and understood. Gangs can no longer be defined in traditional, preconceived terms. Social and economic factors have redefined them, and their imperialistic spread is a multidimensional movement.

Illegal drugs play a significant part in this new imperialism. When the Volstead Act placed alcohol in the illegal realm, an incredible demand was created—and eventually supplied by organized crime. American alcohol consumption financially solidified criminal syndication. Similarly, today's drug appetite has created the economic boom needed to trigger gang imperialism. Using fundamental economics, gangs are the suppliers of a continuing and increasing demand. Drugs, as a commodity, have become the same unifying economic force for gangs today (adult and juvenile) as alcohol was during Prohibition.

Traditional gangs have evolved from early industrial times (Spergel, 1989a; Thrasher, 1927). The public image of gang members, or young thugs, is somewhat fixed in the image of *West Side Story*. This classic tale portrays the old gang type of

AUTHOR'S NOTE: The majority of this article is excerpted from my forthcoming book, *Dangerous Society* (Michigan State University Press, 1990), with the permission of the publisher.

the 1950s. In the 1980s and into the 1990s, the impact of drugs—both economic and social—is changing yesterday's Sharks and Jets into corporate drug businesses intent on expansion.

Recognition of this gang imperialism is still under some debate. Although some researchers caution society to define the term *gang* carefully (Moore, 1989c), others are finding that politics and political concerns are influencing government assessment of the situation (Huff, 1989a). The bottom line is that gangs in 1990 are not the same as gangs in 1950 or 1970—a fact that cannot be ignored.

Background

The origin of serious youth gang development is rooted in the shift from agrarian to industrial society. Gangs of young toughs were plentiful in early urban America. From the early 1900s to the mid-1930s, industrial cities experienced drastic population increases. Immigrants filled the ghettos of New York and other eastern cities in the 1900s with groups of youngsters socializing in their respective neighborhoods. Compared with the industrialized states of the East, southern and midwestern states have had smaller teenage populations and less economic growth; consequently, gang growth has been less rapid.

During the 1930s, researchers in Chicago studied ethnic gangs. Frederick Thrasher, a leading authority on gang behavior and author of the 1927 book *The Gang*, emphasized that gangs often began as play groups within economically poor ethnic neighborhoods. Youngsters who lived together, went to school together, and participated in neighborhood activities together developed a strong sense of identity. They then formed groups within groups that became more cliquish and close-knit. Gangs that had divergent interests were formed, and attitudes of "us" versus "them" developed. When one group posed any type of threat, it became standard to "protect one's turf."

One of the best examples of a protective youth group was the Jewish gang known as the Sugar House Gang, formed in the 1920s by Harry and Louis Fleisher and Irving Milberg to protect Jewish merchants. Greed drove them to join forces with Norman Purple and form the Purple Gang. Prior to 1920—and prior to the formation of Detroit's Purple Gang—the United States had had no national crime syndicate. The bootleg liquor industry of Prohibition propelled the Purples into major crime with notable connections beyond Detroit.

Though numerous urban youth gangs came and went during the 1920s, 1930s, and 1940s, the Purple Gang was the dominant, most highly organized gang of that era in Detroit. Today, a great number of youth gangs have become just as organized and just as deadly.

Gang Types

Gangs may be defined primarily within three different motivational categories: *scavenger, territorial,* and *corporate.* An evolving or maturing gang will embody scavenger and territorial gangs as growth phases of an organized/corporate gang.

Scavenger Gangs

Members of these gangs often have no common bond beyond their impulsive behavior and their need to belong. Leadership changes daily and weekly. They are urban survivors who prey on the weak of the inner city. Their crimes are usually petty, senseless, and spontaneous. Often, acts of violence are perpetrated just for fun. They have no particular goals, no purpose, no substantial camaraderies. Scavenger gang members generally have the characteristics of being low achievers and illiterates with short attention spans who are prone to violent, erratic behavior. The majority come from the lower class and the underclass.

Thrasher (1927) established that gangs, which evolved from neighborhood play groups, were bonded together without any particular purposes or goals. Thrasher's 60-year-old study continues today to describe scavenger-type gangs accurately. Scavengers are generally poor students and misfits with low self-esteem who commit any number of crimes in addition to car theft, breaking and entering, and vandalism. Scavenger behavior is characterized by impulsive, erratic, chaotic acts.

Recently, Vincent Piersante, former head of Michigan's attorney general's Organized Crime Division, observed that most gang members who start out in scavenger gangs later begin professional lives of crime. Thrasher (1927) identified specific factors that shape gang behavior, such as the significant role the community can play. He found that the environment is "permissive, lacks control, and facilitates gang activity. The presence of adult crime within these communities also influences gang behavior because many of the adults who have high status in the community are adult criminals."

Sociologist Robert Merton's (1938) "strain theory" discusses how a desire for certain goals (e.g., car, money, status) pressures individuals into seeking unacceptable means of acquiring those goals. In the case of scavenger gangs, they become isolated from mainstream society. Most of the urban youth gangs that have existed since early America have been scavenger gangs—groups of youngsters drawn together simply by environment and circumstances. In the early 1920s, Detroit gangs were Polish, Jewish, Sicilian, or made up of other ethnic groups. The socioeconomic conditions of Detroit created an atmosphere conducive to scavengers (Thrasher, 1927).

Shaw and McKay's (1942) theory of "cultural transmission" concludes that disadvantaged environments, lack of social controls, and learning passed from one group to another about crime lead youngsters to criminal activities. Piersante (personal communication, 1988) confirmed this theory based on 25 years' experience in the Detroit Police Department: "All of these gangs start out small, bonded together as low achievers, misfits, committing small petty crimes. However, if they become successful they gain money and with money comes power—

power to influence, power to purchase, and power that brings about status."

Territorial Gangs

A territorial gang, crew, group, or individual designates something, someplace, or someone as belonging exclusively to the gang. The traditional designation of territory as it relates to gangs is better known as *turf*.

When scavenger gangs become serious about organizing for a specific purpose, they enter the territorial stage. During this stage, gangs define themselves and someone assumes a leadership role. It is the process of shaping, forming, and organizing with particular objectives and goals.

Once the gang has defined its territory, the next step is to defend that territory from outsiders. In the process of defining and defending territory, gangs become "rulers." They act as controllers. In the streets, territorial law is more respected and feared than legal, traditional law. It is well known and accepted by most that gang law is, in fact, the law in that particular territory.

Gangs defend their territories in order to protect their particular business. The word is out on the street to everyone: "This is gang territory—stay away." Each street corner, dope house, salesperson, distributor, or customer and so on is part of the territory. Anyone who attempts to enter the territory becomes the invader, the intruder, the enemy. Unlike the legitimate business world, gangs use physical violence as their only enforcement tool to stop competition and opposition. All gang types in this study respect territorial law and the necessity that it generates for punishment.

The concept of territory is not new for youth gangs; neither is violence. The gangs in this study reflect contemporary times. Drugs and violence, rooted in the underworld, have propelled them into major crime, creating an outlaw culture employed by the narcotics industry—an industry generating substantial money and, therefore, substantial power. This power allows them to become mobile, and this mobility leads to the expansion of territorial boundaries beyond the few blocks of their respective neighborhoods.

Mobility through financial power is the distinguishing factor between the traditional definition of territory and the nontraditional concept of territory. The classic movie *West Side Story* gave the world a disturbing picture of two urban youth gangs battling over turf: The Sharks defended their neighborhood honor and the Jets defended their territory. But those territory lines were confined to neighborhood ethnic boundaries; the gangs did not have access to large amounts of money or to the mobility and freedom it could purchase.

Similarly, the gangs of the 1950s, 1960s, and 1970s—particularly scavenger gangs as Detroit youth gangs were then— simply did not have cars. Prior to the windfall of illegal drug profits, territory as a concept was limited to the immediate neighborhood. Today, with the power of organized crime, technology, and escalating wages, territory can be intrastate, interstate, or international.

Organized/Corporate Gangs

These well-organized groups have very strong leaders or managers. The main focus of their organization is participation in illegal money-making ventures. Membership is based on the worth of the individual to the organization. Promotion inside the infrastructure is based on merit, not personality. Discipline is comparable to that of the military, and goals resemble those of Fortune 500 corporations. Different divisions handle sales, marketing, distribution, enforcement, and so on. Each member understands his or her role and works as a team member. Criminal actions are motivated by profit. Unlike in scavenger gangs, crimes are committed for a purpose, not for fun. Although these gangs have members from the lower classes and the underclass, middle-class and upper-middle-class youths also find them attractive.

The famous 42 Gang of Chicago was a textbook example of scavenger/territorial to corporate/organized evolution. In 1931, two University of Chicago sociologists did an in-depth study of this gang of 42 tough juveniles who were aggressive, reckless scavengers (Shaw & McKay, 1942). Though they had no set agenda, they murdered robbery victims, stool pigeons, and police. Considered the worst juvenile gang produced in the United States, the 42 Gang was certainly the best "farm team" Chicago's Capone mob ever had. Members were ready to do anything for a quick buck. They stripped cars, robbed cigar stores, marched into nightclubs and staged holdups, and killed horses, hacking off their hind legs to supply certain outlets with horse meat.

Eventually some of the 42ers graduated into the lower ranks of the Capone mob, a well-organized group of adult criminals. Some of the older gangsters viewed them with caution because of their wild, reckless, amoral attitudes. Although they were impressed by the 42's brazen acts, some felt they were "too crazy" for organized work. More than 30 of the 42 eventually were maimed, killed, or sent to prison for murder, armed robbery, or rape—a primary gang pastime.

Their desire to impress the Capone mob eventually paid off. Many times they would pull off big robberies and leave the word on the street that it was the 42s. They would spend their prized loot at Capone's favorite hangouts. Sam Giancana, who eventually became head of Chicago's crime family, was a 42, as were Sam Battaglia, Sam DeSitevano, and Rocco Potenza—all of these juveniles came from west-side Chicago's "Little Italy" (Sifakis, 1987).

Gang Players

The individuals or players involved with today's gangs, like the gangs themselves, have distinct motivations, identities, and roles:

- *Corporate:* A person whose main purpose is pursuit of monetary gain. Criminal activities are used by corporate gangs as a means of achieving goal(s).

- *Scavenger:* A person who lives off the environment; survival by means of criminal activities; loosely organized; no definite leadership.

- *Emulator:* A person who emulates gang behavior; dresses in the style of or pretends to achieve goals of real gangs. Emulators sometimes truly believe that they are members of real gang organizations. They are on the outside of gang organization, pretenders who generally are not accepted by gang members.

- *Auxiliary:* Gang members who hold limited responsibilities in corporate gangs. Auxiliary membership is very common for females. These members usually do not participate in all aspects of gang business. This position is also part of testing or auditioning potential members for added responsibilities or full member privileges.

- *Adjunct member:* A member who is part of an organization but with a limited membership. Adjunct members are permanent part-timers by choice. Sometimes they have relinquished full membership from the organization. Independent business relationships are adjunct for some members. They are protected and regarded as members by outsiders. Some adjuncts have full-time legal jobs and remain adjunct as it relates to criminal commerce.

Near-Groups

Lewis Yablonsky's (1959) definition of gangs differs from that of Thrasher. Yablonsky labels gangs "near-groups," stating that they fall between mobs and cohesive groups. Yablonsky's definition is based on the unstable, changing, and stable permanent characteristics of the near-group. Yablonsky's near-group possesses a "chameleon-like quality." Later, he expanded near-groups to describe "violent gangs," those gangs formed to provide emotional gratification as well as violent gratification.

Yablonsky names two other gang types besides violent gangs: *social* gangs and *delinquent* gangs. Social gangs are historically the tough guys who hang out at soda fountains and participate in athletics, local dances, and rap sessions. Delinquent gangs are organized mainly for illegal activity, with social interaction a secondary function.

Yablonsky's descriptions of gang types laid a very strong foundation for the gang types in this study. Organized/corporate gangs resemble Yablonsky's delinquent gangs. Scavenger gangs are similar to Yablonsky's social and violent gangs. Thrasher's theory of closeness of play groups fits the scavenger's identity better than that of the corporate type. Yablonsky's near-group defines the ever-changing image, leadership, and purpose of the scavenger gangs. The corporate gang of the 1980s has its roots in Yablonsky's delinquent gang. The depth, power, and interrelated gang members' mode of operations, however, make the new corporate gang a different phenomenon.

Gang Evolution

Scavengers are the entry-level applicants in the job markets of the underworld. Drugs changed the lives of inner-city youths who had been trapped victims of depressed socioeconomics in Detroit. Drug business has meant a new life for many individuals who no longer have the Job Corps or special education programs. Scavengers see the drug business as the way out of poverty. One does not need a GED or other certificate of educational achievements; and past brushes with police may be a plus in the gang world, where, best of all, financial rewards are immediate. In an interview, one member of a large scavenger gang answered the leadership and organization question as follows:

Yeah, we're a crew . . . it's about learning the game from the big fellas. All of us are the leaders, the bosses. If one of the big fellas notices our crew, then we all get paid. You never know when you might get chose by the big fellas. Some dudes go with YBI or Pony Down. It don't matter as long as you get chose. Anyway, our crew is getting known. When I first hooked up with Fenkell Boys, I was ten. You just learn how to roll at first. It's like lots of times you don't even get near the real action. But one of our old boys is rolling, so he'll put in the word for one of us. I can remember Jake's brother bought all of us some new Breaker jackets 'cause he used to

be with our crew. We went to a steak restaurant, about
fourteen of us and paid for everything: jackets and big steak
dinners and dessert. It was def!

Scavenger life is full of doubt, misery, and uncertainty. The lure
of corporate life is the carrot that makes scavengers into gang
members.

Territorial and Corporate Gang Transition

In the 1980s, when gangs moved beyond the scavenger stage,
they took on some aspects of power. During the territorial
stage, gangs must physically take power and designate persons, items, something as theirs. One police official called the
territorial process the "dog and fire hydrant" period for the
gang. The gangs that become successful must have staying
power. In order to have staying power, the gang must become
serious and organized. "No collective category, no class, no
group of any kind in and of itself wields power or can use
it. Another factor must be present: that of organization"
(Galbraith, 1983).

The use of physical and psychological intimidation by corporate gangs is unacceptable to most people of the traditional
culture. One only need look closely to see the correlation. Two
corporate gangs in Detroit used their organizations to sell
narcotics and keep competition out of their business zones.
Protecting a sales area or feudal fiefdom is nothing new or
radical in the United States. "Consistent with long established
policies, the various gangs attempted to create and maintain a
monopoly over a particular territory. Invasion by a competing
organization resulted in gang warfare. Murders were commonplace" (Sifakis, 1987). Drug-related violence in Detroit in the
1980s is no different from the gang warfare of the Capone era.
Both scavengers and corporates accept violence as a part of
doing business in Detroit.

The no-drug-use rule of corporate gangs is a serious, mature,
business-based rule. Scavengers are just having fun and are
not ready to sacrifice their drug habits for themselves or for a
corporate cause. Corporate members pursue their goals and

will achieve them regardless of what sacrifices they may have to make or what they may have to do. All of the corporate gangs in this study indicated that they would use violence against anyone. The scavengers reported that they too would use force. However, it was apparent from the group interviews that corporate members had been schooled to believe that violence is a powerful tool to be used to get what they desired; the scavengers, on the other hand, displayed an attitude that violence was sporadic and perversely fun at times. The scavengers are in the first stage of learning gang behavior. Territorial gangs demand seriousness, power, and responsibility. The commercialization of the corporate stage demands a code of ethics. Although all three stages share different views, the perception gained from this study is that, for the very first time in modern U.S. history, African-Americans have moved into the mainstream of major crime. Corporate gangs in Detroit are part of organized crime in America.

Drugs and Drug Business

Although the debate continues as to whether gangs and gang imperialism exist, one need only focus on the devastation of the inner city for evidence. With no jobs and too little education, inner-city youths have found the scourge of drugs to be a two-edged sword of destruction. Individuals, groups of friends, crews, and gang members all are consuming hard drugs daily. Drug usage by scavengers is normal. If youngsters are not using drugs, then they are trying to sell them. In the midst of the war on illiteracy, the battles go on and on.

According to the 1982 television program *Kids and Heroin*, Detroit had 50,000 heroin junkies. As one drug counselor commented:

> We couldn't treat all the drug addicts if we wanted to today even if they all would come in. Crack has made this city a living hell. Crack addicts are growing [in number] daily and you would be surprised at who's on crack. If you included the [suburbs], you would really be knocked out. Let me tell you, drugs are everywhere, my friend.

The drug infusion has created a city full of fiefdoms. Drugs have caused the study of gangs to move beyond the problem of juvenile delinquency. One retired police official assessed the problem from the perspective of law enforcement:

> It's like feudal China, there are pockets of entrenched drug operations all over the city. War on drugs? We've lost that war, because we didn't have a battle plan. The young punks think they've won and they're flaunting it in our faces. You have warlords over little areas that control their little fiefdoms. There are young people acting as contractors for these warlords. They're out there bidding and competing for jobs to sell dope, deliver narcotics, or worse, to murder for money. Hell, the public is scared to death. I can understand it. I don't like it, but we as law enforcement officials can't protect the public always. The damn drug business is bigger than we like to admit. Kids and adults see the warlords spreading money and fame. They want some of that money. Soon as we put away one bunch, another one takes its place. Then you got professional people, like lawyers, giving these punks their service. It's making me want to cry. Dope has made these characters think they're rich and powerful!

Conclusion

Gang imperialism is based not only on the economic realities of the United States, but also on the social aspects of class. Within the social strata, the emerging underclass provides potential and willing applicants for fledgling narcotic operations. The individuals involved in illicit drug sales more than likely will be "minority," which includes females for the first time in modern times. Females have been cited in recent studies of gangs (see Campbell, 1987; and Chapter 8 of this volume). The intermixing of juveniles, adults, males, females, and others, however, signals that the business element of gang imperialism is a very potent foe. The fact is that drugs have taken street gangs and given them the capability and power to become social institutions.

As in everyday life, the impact and economics of any commerce in a free enterprise zone divide the successful traders and the unsuccessful traders. When young Detroiters invade the state of Ohio, they are in pursuit of the American dream. That dream may appear distorted to middle-class or working-class America, yet it is truly business, the spirit of American entrepreneurship. Cocaine rocks in Detroit sell for $5.00, while in Cleveland, Toledo, or Cincinnati the same rocks will bring $20.00—supply and demand.

Gang imperialism is American capitalism. Those who want to find employment will gravitate toward the gang, or toward individuals who can give them employment. Those who are consumers will welcome anyone who can bring the highly desired commodity—cocaine, heroin, or whatever. The failure of social institutions during the 1960s gave way to urban centers experiencing civil riots. The social fallout of the 1970s and 1980s already has manifested the new wave of gangs and criminal thinking in the 1990s.

5

Cholos and Gangs: Culture Change and Street Youth in Los Angeles

JAMES DIEGO VIGIL

In a 1905 photograph of a Mexican immigrant settlement near downtown Los Angeles, the subtitle prominently displayed is "Cholo Court." The arrangement of a clump of small shanties and haphazard lean-tos set off by a mound of rubbish in the foreground is not the inspiration for the name of this "apartment" complex. Instead, the name is derived from the people. *Cholo* is what the American and established Mexican-American residents called these poorest of the poor, marginalized immigrants. The term itself is several hundred years old and used in various (and mostly Indian) areas of Latin America to describe an indigenous person who is halfway acculturated to the Spanish ways; in short, a person marginal to both the original and the more recent European culture.

Culture change includes modernization, urbanization, and acculturation, and the latter process broadly describes what takes place when two cultures meet (especially when there is an imbalance of power between them), with change taking place in one or both cultures. *Cholo* is a term that, from early times to the present, has been associated with culture change, symbolizing a people caught between two cultures (Vigil, 1988a).

During the Spanish colonial period, *cholo* also meant a "marginalized" person's ethnic background and social status (Vigil, 1984). This chapter will show how the cholo process has continued and persisted in the United States; indeed, Chicano street populations who have undergone intense culture change embrace and use this label with pride to denote their speech, dress, and other customs and habits, as well as themselves. Because of these culture contacts, conflicts, and changes, the "choloization" (i.e., marginalization) of the Mexican population has made some youth more at risk to become gang members. This chapter will outline the macrohistorical and macrostructural events that shaped the cholo subset of the Mexican population, clarify distinctions between the concepts of cholos and gangs, and examine how U.S. choloization affects gang formation. In previous work on gangs (Vigil, 1988a), I have utilized a "multiple marginality" conceptual framework that integrates several interrelated variables, but here I would like to devote attention to the macrohistorical, culture change, and subcultural themes.

Immigration

Continual Mexican immigration in this century has added new elements to the cholo historical phenomenon. Many immigrants, already considered cholos in their native country, underwent further—if different—marginal experiences in the United States to add a binational dimension to the word and process of cholo (Chavez, 1988). Others who were less marginally adapted in Mexico became cholos in the United States, through a secondary process of choloization and in response to conditions in the United States. What this means is that a steady stream of cholos arrive and/or are produced in each generation, and because of their backgrounds they are at risk of becoming gang members. In earlier decades, cholos struggled to keep afloat on the environmental fringes and economic margins, and as the American social and economic system underwent transformations, so did they.

Los Angeles, for example, underwent a major industrialization and urbanization boom in the early twentieth century that required tens of thousands of workers. Mexicans constituted a primary source of labor for such enterprises, and immigrated by the hundreds of thousands in the 1920s (Gamio, 1969). After the late 1920s, economic restructuring with the Depression, the repatriation and deportation of Mexicans to Mexico, and World War II combined to forge something radically new out of the Mexican, and especially the cholo, population. In that period, what Bogardus (1926), a sociologist at the University of Southern California, once referred to as a "boy gang" was now transformed into a gang. The gang membership came from the ranks of cholos; the earlier boy gang was actually a barely changed manifestation of the Mexican *palomilla* (literally, covey of doves) male cohorting tradition.

What factors led to this transformation and acceleration of boy gang to gang? Combined with earlier racist practices in schools, public facilities, and the like, the events of the repatriation added insult to injury; the Mexican people learned anew that they were not welcome. Repatriation involved returning Mexican workers and families, now unwanted, to Mexico (Hoffman, 1974). When the Depression created hardships for the U.S. population in general—especially sharp competition for jobs—it affected the low-income, and especially cholo, Mexican population even more adversely. One can imagine the thoughts that ran through the minds of these people as they lost jobs, household and family stability, and their already tenuous hold on America, and simultaneously learned that they had lost their purpose here and were to be sent home.

One reaction to such racist treatment involved an increase by some Mexicans in challenging and somewhat antisocial behavior, especially among the second-generation youth, who liked to consider themselves American but (as historical events dictated) realized they were being rejected. Indeed, families with what previously had appeared to be successful cultural adaptation strategies were being thwarted. The response of such individuals often was aimed at proving that they were American, by frequenting restricted movie theaters, swimming pools, and restaurants, with the understanding and expectation that they might be turned away. Approximating a mild form of antisocial behavior, such incidents became even more inflamed during World War II, when the Zoot Suit Riots erupted. Preceded by a steady increase in Anglo-Mexican friction, these 1943 riots culminated with servicemen and Anglo citizens hunting down and beating up Mexican youth dressed in "zoot suits" (Mazon, 1985; McWilliams, 1968).

The Zoot Suit Riots, and especially the increase in anti-Mexican sentiment among the Anglo-American population, have been underscored as the turning point in the development of a serious gang problem. Previously, the public and police attitude toward the street youth had produced many forms of harassment, but with the hysteria of the war and the surge of Mexican civil rights strivings, there was a sharp increase in media and police activities that focused on the youth population, cholos and noncholos alike. Newspapers especially took aim at the dress of the *pachucos*, the label for Mexican-Americans who wore zoot suits and affected a "hip" street style. This, however, was a veiled disguise for a more generalized anti-Mexican media campaign. Police, announcing that street "punks" were breaking laws and threatening the fabric of society, launched roadblocks and roundups to drive the youths into jail or into orderly behavior (McWilliams, 1968). According to Alfredo Gonzales (1981), the events of this period mark the beginning of the "labeling" of the youth as gang members; the labeling in turn led to an intensification of gang participation rather than diminishing the phenomena.

As these events unfolded, World War II took many positive Mexican male role models away from the *barrios* (neighborhoods) to fight the war; ironically, this occurred soon after segments of the population had been repatriated. The males that were left in the community for the younger cohort to look up to were those rejected from service, with criminal records, and usually the poorest of the poor cholos. Thus "model absence" was a major turning point in transforming the boy gang into a gang.

In a longitudinal study of two barrios in East Los Angeles, Joan Moore (1978) and her colleagues at the Chicano Pinto Research Project (CPRP) have documented how the war and its aftermath changed the nature and trajectory of youth groups, and in concert with choloization generated negative gang and drug activities, with the latter, in time, acting as a force of change. During the first decades in the barrios of El Hoyo Maravilla and White Fence, the youth groups followed more a palomilla cohorting pattern of mischief rather than mayhem, gradually coalescing into the "boy gangs" that Bogardus noted. In the CPRP investigations, it is remarkable that one of the barrios used the group name of the local parish they attended, Purisima, and only after the war did the name White Fence become common; the name change marks the shift from pal-omilla/boy gang to gang.

With the Depression over, repatriation complete, and World War II under way, there were other changes, especially more immigration. The war made the United States short of labor, and the government was prodded by agribusiness interests—now in need of field and other laborers—to enact laws to bring "guest workers" to work sites. Thus the *bracero* (field hand; from *brazos*, arms) program was initiated; when the war ended, this program continued. With the boom in the American econ-omy in the aftermath of World War II, there was need for even more such laborers; even though there were repetitions of repatriation efforts (such as Operation Wetback in 1954) to complicate and exacerbate choloization further. Mexican immi-gration burgeoned with both documented and undocumented workers entering the United States, a pattern that ebbed and flowed into subsequent decades (Moore & Pachon, 1985).

Meanwhile, many of the original barrios found another type of migration taking place. Improvements in the work and earning powers of many families resulted in social mobility. Moving up also included moving out of the barrio. Barrios became for Mexicans a stepping-stone to the American dream of a better home and neighborhood. Returning GIs were a part of this process. The nation, appreciative of their war record, created many federal programs to aid their readjustment, and Mexican-American GIs—like others—took advantage of these opportunities. Housing loans made it easier to move out of the barrio. A side effect of this process was that the barrio would have even fewer positive role models, thus robbing barrio youths of such influences at both ends of the war.

Acculturational and Generational Change

Through all these transformations there were some families who were unable to become socially mobile, instead suffering one setback after another and thus experiencing long-term poverty. Although most immigrant families were subjected to economic shifts and culture change, some of the families were burdened even more. When generational and status change is throttled, choloization is intensified. In time this tended to change the conditions in the barrios, with the less successful families left behind and with less hope and inspiration shaping the future of the new generations of youth. A budding, incipient underclass began to form.

With the passage of time choloization began to take new twists and turns. Specific time and place revisions affected how the immigrant population would recreate a new culture in the United States. None contributed more to the creation of a cholo subculture than the dynamic events listed above. A general cultural orientation began to evolve in all barrios that became a part of this experience.

At first, immigrants arrived just to work and survive, but soon after, some of the families began to adapt to U.S. culture. With the first generation, it was relatively simple to retain their native lifeways as workplace, home, and social and recreational activities kept most of the population together. Throughout the 1920s and 1930s this connection with their primary ethnicity remained; this is when the palomilla pattern prevailed (Bogardus, 1934). With the second generation, there was a sharp departure from the past. These "Americans" earnestly sought to capture the "dream." Practicing a type of secondary ethnicity, they learned the English language and Anglo-American ways while, in varying degrees and intensities, retaining their association and familiarity with Mexican customs. Assimilation was the answer to some, those who wished to forget their past and look only to the future, especially if rapid social and residential mobility was desired. Acculturation, however, was the more common route for most of those from the second generation. In the Mexican case, as in most immigrant communities, it was more often unidirectional acculturation because of the asymmetrical power relationships dictated by the dominant Anglo-American group.

For a significant group of Mexicans, both immigrant and native cholos, the environmental and socioeconomic obstacles (as well as the historical dynamics noted above) operated to strain cultural adaptation strategies, whether of assimilation or acculturation. As a result, a large segment of the community experienced personal and group alienation from both cultures—the depth and degree, of course, mediated by other circumstances. To reiterate, this is a throttling of generational and status change, and thus an intensification of choloization; it can result in "erring acculturation," where movement to an established conventional life-style is stymied and thus a propensity arises to create a new subculture and/or accept the cholo one.

It is this cultural transitional process that creates the confusion and ambiguity that affect youths' sense of cultural identity and loyalty. When ethnic boundaries are weakened by culture change, as happens in the cultural transition process between the first and second generations, there is a change in the ethnic group's ability to command and retain the involvement, attention, and identity of its members. In such circumstances, a subculture based on new boundaries evolves and becomes a cohesive cultural system. The subculture of cholos can be defined broadly in this manner, but with the understanding that even this subculture can be divided further into smaller subcultures. In short, subcultures and smaller subcultures evolve over several generations (Molohon, Paton, & Lambert, 1979).

The U.S. experiences of Mexicans over several generations have given rise to various subcultural strata within that group. The subcultural strata have been shaped by the dynamics and variations of change reflected in each generation. One must think of partially nested levels of subcultures to appreciate the complexity and diversity of the Mexican-American community. The first generation is the broadest subculture, for it represents the initial phase of adaptation to living and working conditions, racial disparagement, and institutional neglect and is a commonly shared phenomenon. With the second generation as cultural transitionals, another subculture evolves—namely, that of the cholo—and it involves more extensive culture conflict. Most individuals work their way through this phase without knowing they are cholos, as I have defined the term broadly, and opt for assimilation or a mixed acculturation strategy that incorporates elements of Mexican and Anglo-American culture, including in some cases bilingual fluency (Buriel, 1984).

A considerable number of individuals of this group, however, are unable to devise a smooth, consistent strategy of adaptation. For them, often, the effects of racism, the persistent cycle of poverty with little chance of social mobility, and the general malaise engendered by problems with school and employment have dominated their lives and impeded acculturation, as well as overall cultural adaptation. These are the individuals who are the end product of the choloization process, for they become identified with the label *cholo*. Cholo identification is reflective of their plight—no way out, locked in—or what has been referred to as the underclass (Moore, 1985; Wilson, 1987), members of which suffer from "persistent and concentrated poverty"; in short, a cholo is a type of institutionalization of marginalization. This cholo life-style is an American experience set in the strains and stresses of prolonged immobility, of missed opportunities and social setbacks, that affects how Mexican culture is relinquished and American culture acquired, an adjustment process that spawns a mixed culture. An individual's status as a cholo may be of relatively short duration or it may be lifelong in nature. Similarly, gang members drawn from the ranks of cholos may remain in the gang briefly or for prolonged careers; the latter tend to be the individuals who reflect the most intense multiple pressures and conflicts of choloization.

The Syncretization of
a Street Subculture

The rise and formation of the gang subculture revolves around the broader backdrop of culture conflict and choloization of the second-generation Mexican-American population. The process becomes more intensified in the third generation, within which a subculture of the streets has become institutionalized. This gang subculture is nested within and part of the broader cholo and Mexican-American subcultures.

Participants in the gang subculture are drawn largely from youths who, in middle childhood, have relied increasingly on street peers for socialization. Youths with particularly problematic, traumatic family and personal experiences—mostly unsupervised and lacking adult guidance, coming from the most choloized segments of the population—are forced to the streets because it is a convenient open space for play and socializing and a relief from their drab backgrounds. In doing so, these youths—as young as 8 years old—must learn how to survive fear-inspiring situations, particularly encounters with strangers (mostly other youths like themselves) who approach them as fair game. Street peers, some slightly older and a few in their early teens, become the major agents of socialization to help in their adjustment. The friends one makes on the streets and the activities that are learned there often carry over into the school setting, where friendship bonds and street lessons are reinforced as indifference or hostility to school and authority grows.

During adolescence, problems with age and sex role identification exacerbate structural and environmental stresses. Street youths at this point typically become school dropouts, thus providing themselves with more time for street affairs. Lacking training of any sort, too young to fill most jobs, and facing the paucity of employment opportunities for low-income minority youth populations generally, such youths are clearly at risk for joining in and following gang patterns.

Most of the time spent with gang street peers is devoted to having a good time—drinking beer or wine, smoking marijuana, or participating in recreational events such as parties and sports. At times, however, gang activities take on a more deviant character, as members strive to live up to street-induced notions of "manly" behavior or to demonstrate their loyalty to the gang: gang fights, for example, and sometimes criminal activity directed outside the gang arena. It is the latter, less widely accepted activities that have gained the public's attention. Part of this gang pattern derives from tradition (i.e., gang lore and mythology, intergenerational influences) and part stems from technology (i.e., movie and television images of violence, availability of guns, and mind-altering chemical substances). Such socially destructive habits lend a pervasive aura of death to drug use and abuse and barrio gang rivalries. Although participation in such habits enhances one's status and recognition—for doing these "gang" things shows courage and *huevos* ("balls")—it is clear that conditions conducive to street socialization and its processes have altered adolescent "storm and stress" dynamics (Vigil, 1988b).

As Moore (1978) has argued convincingly, the introduction of heroin use, and especially heroin and other drug dealing, in the late 1940s and early 1950s was a major factor in changing the gang into a more formalized unit and furthering its evolutionary path of palomilla to boy gang to gang subculture. It was also in the 1940s in some barrios, and greatly intensified by the 1960s, when third-generation, street-socialized gangs become more extensive, with each new generation of barrio youth growing up in the presence of the institutionalized street gangs. Within each generation are youths with problematic backgrounds who increasingly are pushed into the streets and drawn into the gangs.

This gang subculture has changed realities such that new immigrant children have to adapt and contend with it; one Latino youth even told me that gang-banging (fighting) is like "showing you are American," or assimilated. As Plant (1937) remarked, commenting on "white ethnic" youth in the 1930s, "If it is true that the triumphs and tragedies of the street flow into and become a part of the child, then all programs of personality change must manage somehow to change the street." There is a clear interplay between street socialization and the evolution of a gang subculture. Macrohistorical forces and structural conditions have altered social control institutions in such a way that children are forced to deal with the streets as a social arena.

Conclusion

Immigration, choloization, and the conservation/regeneration of a street gang subculture continue today. Historical events still affect the tone and direction of the gang subculture. The Vietnam War, the War on Poverty, and the Chicano civil rights movement of the 1960s and 1970s, for instance, altered the form, activities, and direction of gang cohorts in new ways.

In brief, the war robbed the barrios of yet another generation of positive role models (Vigil 1988a). This void was tempered somewhat by the government's efforts to combat poverty and choloization with many social programs. Although these efforts were short-lived, there was a noted improvement in the lives of cholos and gang members, especially the curbing of interbarrio youth violence. Concomitant with these events was the Chicano movement, which brought attention to the overall plight of the Mexican-American people, particularly the long-suffering barrio populations. Many cholos and gang members joined such efforts and rechanneled their frustration and rage with some success toward the body politic (Acuna, 1981; Vigil, 1984)—namely, schools and law enforcement, two institutions of social control.

It is no coincidence that gang violence mushroomed in the aftermath of these events, for choloization did return to replace the War on Poverty, and street models began to reclaim their turf from activists and lead new generations of barrio youth. Gangs and gang membership have expanded since then.

Since the late 1960s Mexican immigration has increased, and other Latino groups have been immigrating in large numbers since the late 1970s, causing major demographic shifts throughout the greater Los Angeles area. These first-generation residents have replaced heretofore Black and third-generation Latino ghettos and barrios, respectively; established new barrios in multistoried downtown apartments while making over the downtown shopping district; and generally transformed the spatial and social fabric of greater Los Angeles. Coping with the usual adjustments and difficulties that immigrants confront, they must also deal with added new developments. Many of the immigrant families and their children derive from cholo backgrounds, that is, *primary* choloization from the native country. The *secondary* choloization life-style fashioned in the United States over several decades has been diffused through the media and cultural exchanges to Mexican youth populations across the border, especially in border towns (Cuellar, 1987). Thus some immigrants already have internalized the U.S. cholo style before they begin adaptation to American life; they are precholoized, so to speak. Finally, for all of the immigrants there is the new American experience, where a portion of the people will be subjected to further *secondary* choloization. Thus three forms of cholo influence the adaptation paths of these immigrant groups: native-based primary, diffusion of American secondary, and the American secondary experience.

To compound matters, and irrespective of cholo forms, these immigrants arrive and settle in locales steeped in a long-standing, well-established barrio gang subculture. It is a subculture, as noted, that evolved over several decades of a syncretization process that generated a set of subcultural norms, values, rules, and rituals. Adjustment and adaptation to American realities now includes dealing with this gang subculture. As a result of all these various cholo and gang subculture exposures, first-generation Latino youth are now more likely to skip developmental and choloization stages, as previously outlined, and react quickly to the cultural standards and practices of the gang, either to avoid or to absorb it. For more practical and pragmatic purposes, these newcomers especially have learned youth street attributes as if they were learning about America—becoming "assimilated," as one informant stated. More important yet, they have learned to "gang" together to protect and defend themselves from the aggression and threats posed by established gangs. In recent years there has been a proliferation of such new Latino gangs throughout the area, some of which have even replaced older gangs.

In sum, the process of choloization in the context of immigration history—the ebbs and flows of the economy and social restrictions and major upheavals—has contributed to the rise of a gang subculture. Once rooted, the gang subculture has developed a life of its own to recruit new members by normal street enculturation and socialization, as well as by threats and intimidation. The syncretized nature of the subculture provides choloized, troubled youth with the opportunity to reconcile conflicts and ambiguities by adopting a set of norms and procedures that, at least to them, lessen confusion. It helps reduce personal tensions and allows them to cope with the pressures and strains of the streets. Their past Mexican/Latino realities and traditions must be combined with those of the present American reality, and it is no accident that something new is forged out of this conflicting experience.

As in past decades, most of the new immigrant population will acculturate to the United States and manage a bilingual/ bicultural orientation, and eventually they too will construct strategies for social mobility (Buriel, 1984). Some, perhaps in larger numbers today, will undergo choloization in the face of persisting structural and cultural difficulties and barriers, and will join the ranks of those who are at risk of becoming gang members.

6

Chinese Gangs and Extortion

KO-LIN CHIN

Before 1965, with the exception of group conflicts among the tongs[1] in the late nineteenth and early twentieth centuries (Dillon, 1962; Gong & Grant, 1930), crime rates within the Chinese communities in North America were very low (Beach, 1932; MacGill, 1938). Chinese immigrants were generally law-abiding, hardworking, and peaceful. Official statistics show that the most common offenses were victimless crimes such as prostitution, opium smoking, drunkenness, and disorderly conduct (Tracy, 1980). Offenders were primarily adults who indulged in these culturally sanctioned recreational activities as a respite from work. Among Chinese adolescents, delinquency was also uncommon (Sung, 1977).

In considering the tranquility of Chinese communities in the past, however, it is important to note that before 1965 there were few Chinese teenagers in the United States, a result of the Chinese Exclusion Act passed in 1882 and the National Origins Act of 1924 (Fessler, 1983; Sung, 1979). The Immigration and

AUTHOR'S NOTE: I am grateful to Colleen Cosgrove for her comments. This chapter is excerpted from *Chinese Subculture and Criminality: Non-Traditional Crime Groups in America* (Contributions in Criminology and Penology, No. 29, Greenwood Press, an imprint of Greenwood Publishing Group, Inc., Westport, CT, 1990). Copyright \cpr 1990 by Ko-lin Chin. Reprinted with permission of the publisher.

Naturalization Act of 1965 was a turning point in the history of Chinese immigration because it not only made China a "preferred" nation but also established priorities for admission based largely on family relationships; those already living in the United States could initiate the immigration process for their families overseas (Kwong, 1987; Takagi & Platt, 1978).

Since 1965, the increasing number of Chinese immigrating to the United States has affected the stability of the Chinese communities in unprecedented ways. Traditional groups such as the family and district associations were ill prepared to cope with the influx. Because there were few social service agencies to help the newcomers, they were left mostly on their own to resolve housing, employment, education, and health problems (R. Chin, 1977; Huang & Pilisuk, 1977).

This breakdown in support, coupled with the growth of the Chinese population in isolated and fragmented communities, brought a corresponding increase in criminal activities among the Chinese (Bresler, 1981; Posner, 1988; President's Commission on Organized Crime, 1984; Robertson, 1977). Chinese gangs sprang up in San Francisco (Emch, 1973; Loo, 1976), Los Angeles (Los Angeles County Sheriff's Department, 1984), Boston (Roache, 1988), Toronto (Allen & Thomas, 1987), Vancouver (Robinson & Joe, 1980), and New York City (Chang, 1972; K. Chin, 1986). Although the number of active Chinese gang members is relatively small (there are no more than 2,000 Chinese gang members in the whole country), their involvement in some of the nation's worst gang-related violence (e.g., Daly, 1983) and heroin trafficking (U.S. Senate, 1986) has drawn the attention of law enforcement authorities. Recently, local and federal authorities have predicted that Chinese criminal organizations will emerge as the number one organized crime problem in the 1990s, when they become a dominant force in heroin trafficking, alien smuggling, money laundering, and other racketeering activities (U.S. Department of Justice, 1985, 1988, 1989; U.S. Department of State, 1988).

Although Chinese gangs have been active in the United States for more than 20 years, most of our knowledge about them has come from police and journalists. Other than a few scholarly studies carried out 10 or 15 years ago (Loo, 1976; Miller, 1975; Robinson & Joe, 1980), there has been no recent research on Chinese gangs. Thus it is imperative to improve our understanding of a social problem that law enforcement authorities have suggested is of paramount importance. This chapter describes the individual and group characteristics of New York City's Chinese gangs and compares them with street gangs of other ethnic groups. Additionally, the social processes and functions of extortion—the type of illegal activity routinely and systematically committed by the Chinese gangs—also are considered.

This study was based on four types of data: ethnographic interviews, field notes, official reports and documents, and newspapers and magazines. People who were familiar with Chinese gangs or who had been victimized by gang members were interviewed, including members of the tongs and street gangs, social service providers, officials of civic associations, reporters, police officers, prosecutors, federal law enforcement officials, and victims.

To supplement interview data, I spent some time in the field. Most of my observations were made in gambling dens or bars where gang members hang out. I also reviewed and analyzed official reports and documents, and examined indictment materials and sentencing memoranda related to Chinese gangs. Finally, hundreds of English- and Chinese-language newspaper and magazine articles on Chinese gangs were collected and categorized by type of criminal organization, geographical area, and type of crime.

Demographic Characteristics

Sex

Like other ethnic gangs, Chinese gangs are composed predominantly of males. Although young females do hang around with members or live in the gangs' apartments, they are not initiated into the gangs. Except for carrying guns for their boyfriends, the girls are not involved in either property or violent crime.

Age

According to a police report, members' ages range from 13 to 37 (New York City Police Department, 1983). The mean age for the 192 registered gang members is 22.7. Most members are in their late teens or early 20s. Because the report included active, inactive, suspected, and imprisoned members, the sample may overrepresent seasoned members. Those who are new members may not yet be known to the police.

Country of Origin

In the 1960s and 1970s, most gang members were young immigrants from Hong Kong. A few were American- or Taiwan-born. Of the 25 Ghost Shadows indicted in 1985, for example, 24 were born in Hong Kong. Since the late 1970s, some Chinese gangs have recruited many Vietnam-born Chinese (President's Commission on Organized Crime, 1984). In the 1980s, many young immigrants from China were being recruited. Recently, some Korean youths also were inducted into the newly established Chinese gangs. So far, Chinese gangs have not recruited anyone who is of non-Asian origin. Most gang members, with the exception of a Taiwanese gang, speak the Cantonese dialect.

Structural Characteristics

Size

Each gang has on average about 20 to 50 hard-core members, a few inactive members, and some peripheral members. When conflicts among gangs are intense, they may seek reinforcements from other cities. Law enforcement authorities estimate a total of 200 to 400 active Chinese gang members in New York City, belonging to about nine gangs.

Organization

The structures of the gangs vary. The Ghost Shadows, for example, have four or five leaders at the top, the so-called *tai lou* (big brothers). Most other gangs have either one or two leaders. Under the leaders are a few "lieutenants," or associate leaders, in command of the street soldiers. At the bottom of the hierarchy are the street soldiers, who guard the streets and commit most of the extortion, robbery, and street violence. They are known as the *ma jai* (little horses).

Leaders maintain direct contact with certain tong elders and receive payment from them or from the gambling houses in the community. The leaders are the only liaisons between the tongs and the gangs. Leaders rarely are involved in street violence, although they give the orders. Whenever a leader wants somebody harassed or assaulted, he instructs the street leaders or members to carry out the assignment. The leader may provide the hit man with guns and pay him as a reward after he fulfills the "contract." Usually, the leader monitors the action from a nearby restaurant or gang apartment.

Although the associate leaders do not have much power in the administration of the gang, they control the ordinary members. Therefore, it is not surprising that street soldiers are more loyal to their immediate bosses than to the top leaders. Street leaders usually recruit the ordinary members. Although street leaders sometimes are involved in carrying out assignments, their usual role is that of "steerer"—they bring the street soldiers to their target and identify it for them. Street leaders do not initiate plans to attack specific people.

Among ordinary members, a few tough ones are known as "shooters"; they carry out most of the gang's assaults. The primary function of the soldiers is to watch the streets, guard the gambling places, and collect protection fees.

Most gangs have their own apartments, which are occupied mainly by street soldiers and are used as headquarters and for ammunition storage. The leaders do not live in them, although they drop by occasionally.

Except for the Ghost Shadows and the Flying Dragons, the gangs do not have splinter groups in other cities. The Ghost

Shadows have chapters in Boston, Chicago, Baltimore, Houston, and Toronto, and police in New York City believe that the groups are nationally—or even internationally—linked.

Recruitment and Membership

Some youths join the gangs voluntarily, while others are coerced. Before the mid-1970s, most youths were volunteers. Members treated one another as brothers, and it appeared that there was much camaraderie among them. From the mid-1970s through the early 1980s, however, many youths joined the gangs out of fear. Gangs have employed both subtle and crude methods to recruit new members. Gang members may treat a potential member to a good meal, show him their expensive cars, and provide him with the companionship of teenage girls. Impressionable adolescents may decide to join the gang to enjoy the putative benefits of membership. If potential recruits are unimpressed by what the gang offers, gang members send street soldiers to beat them up, a crude way of convincing them that their lives are more secure if they are gang members than if they are alone.

Usually, gang members recruit youths who are vulnerable—those who are not doing well in school or who have already dropped out. Young newcomers who have little or no command of English, poor academic records, and few job prospects are the most likely to find gang life attractive and exciting. Gang youths also approach adolescents who hang around video arcades, basketball courts, bars, and street corners, and those who talk and act arrogantly. Recruitment activities are carried out by both seasoned members and those who have been in the gang for only a short time.

Once a youth decides to join the gang, he goes through an initiation ceremony that is a simplified version of the Chinese secret societies' recruiting rituals. The youth takes his oaths, burns yellow paper, and drinks wine mixed with blood in front of the gang leaders and the altar of General Kwan, a heroic figure of the secret societies. The oaths taken by new recruits are, in essence, similar to the 36 oaths of the secret societies (see Bresler, 1981; K. Chin, 1990).

Dynamic Characteristics

Conformity to peer pressure is a strong characteristic of Chinese gang members. For instance, after six Ghost Shadows abducted and raped a White woman, two of the offenders initially opposed killing the victim. When the other four argued that she had to be killed, however, the two immediately consented. Nevertheless, group cohesion appears to be weak. Intragang conflicts erupt frequently, and members sometimes transfer from one gang to another. Within a Chinese gang there are usually two or more cliques, each consisting of a leader, one or more associate leaders, and several soldiers. These cliques usually distrust and dislike one another, and the tensions among them are exacerbated easily whenever illegal gains are not distributed properly. A review of the history of Chinese gangs in New York City indicates that leaders constantly are plotting to have one another killed (K. Chin, 1990). A Chinese gang leader is more likely to be killed by his associates than by a rival.

Some intragang conflicts are instigated by tong elders who are associated with a particular clique. These mentors prefer to have a divided rather than a united gang; therefore, they intervene to ensure that no particular clique gains enough power to challenge the supremacy of the tong.

Attachment to the gang is not absolute. To date, no gang member has been attacked by his peers simply because he decided to leave the gang. If a member joins a rival gang, however, he can provoke retaliation from his former associates. On the other hand, if the leaders of the two groups involved can reach agreement about the transfer of members, changing membership and allegiance can be arranged satisfactorily.

Comparison of Chinese Gangs with Other Ethnic Gangs

How different are Chinese gangs from other ethnic gangs? Some researchers report that Chinese gangs are similar to other ethnic gangs in several ways. For instance, Robinson and

Joe (1980) found that the characteristics of the Chinese gangs in Vancouver were identical to those of American gangs. The gangs Robinson and Joe studied, however, were atypical in the sense that they were not related to community organizations as Chinese immigrant gangs in San Francisco and New York City are. They resembled American street-corner gangs or athletic clubs, and were similar to the American-born Chinese gangs that were active in the early 1960s, a period when Chinese gangs were not yet institutionalized by community associations.

Like Robinson and Joe, Takagi and Platt (1978) suggest that Chinese gangs—like other ethnic gangs—are involved only in petty crimes. In their view, the tongs and other adult associations, rather than the gangs, are responsible for the organized racketeering activities and violence within the Chinese communities. Takagi and Platt's findings are not supported by other data. Violence in Chinatown is, in most instances, instigated by Chinese gangs (K. Chin, 1990).

In contrast to scholars of gang delinquency, law enforcement authorities argue that Chinese gangs are unlike other ethnic street gangs. A former captain of the New York City Police Department suggests that Chinese gangs should not even be considered as "youth" gangs because of the way they are controlled and the age of the leaders:

> [Chinese gangs] are well-controlled and held accountable to the various associations in the Chinatown area. They are the soldiers of Oriental organized crime, with strong ties to cities throughout the United States. The associations have international ties in banking, real estate, and import/export businesses and are suspected of being involved in narcotics and alien smuggling. Members of the street gangs range in age from the mid-teens to early twenties. The street leaders are in their early twenties and thirties, with the highest leader being a mature middle-age or senior adult generally in charge of one of the associations. (New York City Police Department, 1983, p. 3)

The data collected for this study revealed that Chinese gangs have the following unique characteristics that set them apart from other ethnic gangs. First, they are closely associated with and are controlled by powerful community organizations. Second, gang leaders invest their money in legitimate businesses and spend a large amount of time doing business. Third, Chinese gangs form national or international networks. Fourth, the gangs are influenced to a great extent by Chinese secret societies and the norms and values of the Triad[2] subculture. Fifth, gang members normally do not go through various stages in which they graduate from delinquent behavior to serious crime. New members often are assigned to carry out the most serious assaults. Sixth, Chinese gangs control large amounts of money, and making money is their main motive. Finally, Chinese gangs systematically victimize the businesses in their communities in ways no ordinary street gangs possibly could. In sum, their strong affiliation with powerful adult organizations, their high level of mobility, and their businesslike methods of wiping out rivals suggest that they more closely resemble adult criminal organizations than typical youth gangs that are concerned mainly with dress codes, turf, and involvement in nonutilitarian, negativistic activities (Cohen, 1955).

According to data collected for this study, Chinese gangs resemble Cloward and Ohlin's (1960) "criminal gangs." Chinese gangs develop in ethnic communities in which adult criminal groups exist and in which the adult criminals serve as mentors and role models for the gang members. They not only provide the youths with jobs but also offer them an opportunity structure in illegitimate activities. The youths can start working as street soldiers and then go on to become lieutenants, gang leaders, and (eventually) core members of the tong. Thus a street youth can work his way up to become a respected, wealthy community leader through the structure of illegal activities provided by adult organizations, if he can survive his years as a gang member.

Nevertheless, gangs such as the Ghost Shadows and the Flying Dragons do not strictly follow the subculture pattern in Cloward and Ohlin's classification. Their long history of street violence shows that, besides securing income, the gangs fought constantly with rival gangs to establish their power to shake down the community. This use of violence to win status is consistent with Cloward and Ohlin's definition of "conflict gangs." It is hard to imagine, in any case, how criminal gangs could protect their illegal sources of income without violently subduing rival gangs to prevent them from encroaching on their territory. Although gang involvement in street violence is not condoned by the adult organizations and is not in the best interests of the gangs themselves, apparently the gangs believe that they must instill fear in rival groups as well as in the community as a whole.

What is the evidence for Cloward and Ohlin's third delinquent subculture, the retreatist? In a study of gangs in three cities, Fagan (1989) found drug use widespread among Black, Hispanic, and White gangs, regardless of the city. Moore's (1978) Los Angeles gangs and Hagedorn's (1988) Milwaukee gangs were involved heavily in drug use and dealing. Drug use among Chinese gang members, however, is rare. Moreover, although gang leaders are involved in drug trafficking, they themselves are not drug users. Tong members do not tolerate drug use in the gangs, and the gangs themselves are reluctant to recruit anyone who uses drugs. If a member begins using drugs, he is expelled from the gang.

Thus Chinese gangs have the characteristics of two of the subcultures described by Cloward and Ohlin: the criminal and the conflict subcultures. Because gang leaders are concerned primarily with the lucrative heroin trade and investment in legitimate businesses and are closely associated with certain tong leaders, they adhere more to norms and values of the criminal subculture as depicted by Cloward and Ohlin. Young members are concerned mostly with their macho image and therefore are more prone to commit violent acts and predatory crimes. These young members seem to be most congruent with Cloward and Ohlin's conflict gangs. Consequently, instead of labeling Chinese gangs as either criminal or conflict gangs, it is perhaps more important to consider the ages and ranks of the gang members and their criminal propensities.

Unlike Chinese gangs that are closely associated with the well-established adult groups, gangs formed by young Chinese immigrants from Vietnam and Taiwan have no adult group to emulate. As a result, these gangs are not as well organized as the Chinatown gangs. Without the stable income from protection and extortion operations that Chinatown gangs enjoy, and without a lucrative commercial district to claim as a territory, Vietnamese and Taiwanese gangs are forced to become involved primarily in extortion, robbery, and burglary. These gangs resemble Cloward and Ohlin's conflict gangs because they are prone to excessive use of violence, they lack supervision by adult criminal elements, and they are outside the illegitimate opportunity structure.

Protection and Extortion

The booming economy and the gambling industry in the Chinese community have provided Chinese gangs with ample criminal opportunities. Of the businesses in the community, gambling clubs are the most in need of the gangs' protection. In order to operate smoothly, the clubs must rely on gang members to protect them and their customers from the police, intruders, and the gangs themselves. To perform these jobs, a few members are dispersed in the street where the gambling club is located. Three or four members guard the entrance, while some stay inside. Members carry beepers to communicate with one another. Street leaders in the gang's nearby apartments oversee the entire operation. Nightclubs and massage parlors owned by Chinese and catering to Chinese patrons also require protection. These businesses need gang members to protect them from members of other gangs.

Gangs supplement their primary activity of guarding gambling dens and adjacent streets with another criminal activity: systematic extortion of Chinese businesses. Police estimate that at least 80% to 90% of Chinese businesses have to pay one or more gangs regularly or occasionally. Only those merchants who are close to the hierarchy of the tongs are said to be able to avoid paying the gangs.

Techniques of Extortion

According to police officers, prosecutors, and victims interviewed, the gangs primarily use two forms of extortion. One explicit technique is for gang members to demand money. Usually, gang members approach a new business during its opening ceremony and ask for *li shi* (lucky money). After the owner pays, they show up again later and identify themselves as gang members, explain how the racket works, and indicate that it is better to pay than to refuse. Occasionally, gang members tell the owners that they need money for food, or to help their "brothers" who have been arrested. There are also times when gang members will ask businessmen to "invest" in their business or give them a "loan."

In the second extortion technique, the demand for money is implicit. For example, the gang members will try to sell festival-related goods such as firecrackers or plants to business establishments for an inflated price. Sometimes, gang members may simply tell store owners that protection from the gang is provided to their businesses.

Gangs employ several common practices. First, a group of youths may enter a restaurant during the lunch or dinner hour, and each of them occupies a table. They tell the manager that they are waiting for friends. They sit for hours, and they act in rowdy fashion to intimidate customers. They may fight with each other, smash the dishes, or insist on remaining in the restaurant after closing hours. An experienced manager knows what the disruptive youths want.

Second, young men may go into a restaurant and order the finest dishes on the menu. When they leave, they write "Shadows" or "Dragons" on the back of the bill and do not pay. Third, some gang members may dine in a restaurant but refuse to pay the bill. While they argue with the manager about it, two or three fellow members walk in and pretend to be customers. They appear to be sympathetic to the manager and chastise the youths who refuse to pay. When the "show" is over, a gang member calls up the manager, demands protection money, and tells the manager that if similar incidents happen in the future, his gang will protect the restaurant. This technique is known as *hei bai lian* (black and white faces), meaning that while members play the role of the "bad guys," leaders will act as the "good guys" who ask money from the frightened victim.

The fourth method is called *tai jiau tsi* (carrying a sedan chair). Gang members will try to flatter a potential victim by calling him "Big Brother" and acting as though they are his loyal followers. If the businessman is unaware of the gang's tactic and associates himself with the gang, he may find out that it is too late for him to get rid of the label "Big Brother." As a "Big Brother," the victim has no other real benefits except to provide financial support to the gang.

The fifth approach is known as *wo di* (literally, undercover). A gang member infiltrates a business by seeking a job there. During his tenure he collects information about the owner, where he lives, when the business will accumulate the maximum amount of cash, and other matters. The gang member provides the information to his associates to draw up an extortion or robbery plan.

Most of the time, the owners negotiate about the amount of payment, but they do not bicker about whether they are going to pay. When the gang gets a victim paying, a schedule is arranged: several hundreds dollars monthly for large stores; less than a hundred dollars per week for modest businesses. The gang usually has designated collectors and keeps records of its income from extortion.

If a retail business refuses to pay, then the gang may vandalize, burglarize, rob, or set fire to the shop. The owner then usually relents and cooperates. In some instances gangs have beaten, shot at, or killed business and retail store owners. For those who do pay, the amount demanded by crime groups escalates rapidly, or another gang will show up soon with the same demand. When businesses are no longer able to meet the gangs' demands, they close down, move to another area, or report the crime to the police. Usually, most business owners try to satisfy the gangs by paying them the first few times. Only when they find out that they have to pay more than one gang or that their payments increase rapidly will they turn to law enforcement for help.

Types of Extortion

Extortion in Chinese communities may be classified into four types. The primary objective of the first and most prevalent type of extortion is monetary gain. The offenders and victim may not know each other prior to the incident, and the extortionate act may be perpetrated without the knowledge of the tong associated with the gang. Regardless of how the victim reacts to the offender's demand, he or she is unlikely to be assaulted physically by the offender in this type of extortion.

The second type is symbolic extortion, which is used as a display of power to indicate control over a territory. Monetary gain is not the major goal; gang members usually demand only free food or other small items such as cigarettes. They also may ask for heavy discounts from restaurant owners. This type of extortion occurs almost on a daily basis, and the victims are usually small store owners or peddlers who do businesses within a tightly controlled gang territory.

The third type is extortion for revenge. Offenders extort victims because of something the victims did to the gang previously, or the gang is hired by a victim's adversary to extort the victim as a form of revenge. Because monetary gain is not the motivating factor, victims are likely to be robbed, beaten up, or killed even if they do not resist the perpetrators. Extortion is used simply as a cover for vengeance.

The fourth type is instrumental extortion, which is used to intimidate the victim into backing down in certain business or personal conflicts. In this type of extortion, the victims are also vulnerable to assault and harassment. The extortionate act is, more than anything else, a message sent to the victim by his rival through the gang members. Gang members also may rob or extort money from the victims for their own sakes. Conflicts pertaining to business territories and business or gambling debts usually result in instrumental extortion activity.

Extortion and Territory

Through extortion, the gangs assert their firm control over certain territories in New York City's Chinese communities. When two or more gangs claim control of a specific area, or when the area is occupied by a weaker gang, store owners within that territory have to pay more than one gang. Currently, Canal Street and East Broadway, the rapidly expanding streets of Chinatown, have no single powerful gang that can claim exclusive sovereignty. Consequently, some of the store owners in those areas have to pay as many as five gangs simultaneously.

The same is true for the Chinese communities in Queens and Brooklyn. Although the White Tigers, the Green Dragons, and a Taiwanese gang are the three most active gangs in these newly established communities, more powerful gangs from Manhattan's Chinatown occasionally invade the area to commit extortion. When two or more gangs are active in a particular area and attempt to extort from the same victim simultaneously, street violence erupts as a result of the power struggle.

Before 1980, most extortionate activities were confined to Manhattan's Chinatown. Only occasionally would gang members venture outside Chinatown to extort money. Beginning in 1980, however, the gangs rapidly spread their extortionate activities to other parts of Manhattan, Queens, Brooklyn, Long Island, New Jersey, and Connecticut. Unlike extortionate activities within Manhattan's Chinatown, which are mostly spontaneous and cost the victims fairly small amounts of money, out-of-state extortion is well planned, and gang members tend to demand rather large amounts.

Since 1984, businessmen in Queens and Brooklyn have been extorted frequently. Unlike in Manhattan's Chinatown, gangs in these areas have no gambling establishments from which to collect protection money. As a result, the only likely source of funds is extortion or robbery of stores in the community. The lack of knowledge about the gangs by local precincts has also contributed to the rapid increase in extortion. In addition, business owners in Queens and Brooklyn are not protected by tongs or other traditional organizations as are business owners in Manhattan's Chinatown.

Conclusion

In order to understand Asian crime groups, the research and law enforcement communities need to broaden their perspectives. Concepts that are adequate for explaining Italian, Black, and Hispanic crime groups may not be adequate for examining criminal organizations of Asian origin. Because Asian people have diverse cultural heritages, we also need to identify the unique features of each Asian ethnic group.

We can isolate three unique characteristics that cause Chinese gangs to persist. First, unlike Black and Hispanic gangs (Hagedorn, 1988; Moore, 1978), Chinese gangs are not based on youth fads or illicit drug use. Instead, they are closely related to their communities' social and economic life. This relationship enables Chinese gangs to become deeply enmeshed in the legitimate and illegitimate enterprises in their communities. Opportunities for money, power, and prestige through various ventures are bestowed on Chinese gang members. No such distinctive opportunity exists for other minority gangs.

Second, unlike other ethnic gangs—which operate primarily in deteriorated, poor neighborhoods—Chinese gangs flourish in rapidly developing and economically robust Chinese communities that are tied closely to Chinese societies in Southeast Asia. Chinese gangs thus can become engaged in economically rewarding domestic and international ventures. Other ethnic gangs are hampered by both the lack of lucrative criminal opportunities in their own neighborhoods and the absence of contacts outside those neighborhoods.

Third, Chinese gang members are embedded in the legendary Triad subculture, a subculture established and maintained by members of the Chinese secret societies. By emulating Triad initiation rites and internalizing Triad norms and values, they can claim a certain legitimacy within their communities. This legitimacy enables them to instill a level of fear that no other ethnic gangs can match, because the community does not view them merely as street thugs.

Nevertheless, the nature, values, and norms of Chinese gangs could change in the future. Chinese gangs with no ties to the tongs or Triad subculture are emerging in newly established Chinese communities. We are now observing the rise of Vietnamese-Chinese and Fujianese gangs (Badey, 1988; Meskil, 1989). Both groups are not only unfamiliar with Triad norms and values, but their criminal patterns—such as street mugging and household robbery—are markedly different from those of the traditional Triad-inspired gangs.

Notes

1. *Tong* means "hall" or "gathering place." Tongs were first established in the United States during the mid-nineteenth century by the first wave of Chinese goldfield and railroad workers as self-help groups. Bloody conflicts among the tongs are known as "tong wars." The most powerful tongs in New York City are the Chih Kung, the On Leong, and the Hip Sing. Since the 1960s, in order to improve their image, the tongs have been renamed as associations. The heads of these associations are normally influential and well-respected community leaders.

2. *Triad* means a "triangle of heaven, earth, and man." Triad societies are secret societies formed by patriotic Chinese three centuries ago to fight against the oppressive and corrupt Ch'ing dynasty. When the Ch'ing government collapsed and the Republic of China was established in 1912, some of the societies began to be involved in criminal activities.

7

Vietnamese Youth Gangs in Southern California

JAMES DIEGO VIGIL
STEVE CHONG YUN

Historically, Asian-Americans have suffered from overt and covert racial discrimination, including explicit legal barriers. More recently, however, the "model minority" myth has masked the problems of Asian-American communities (see Takaki, 1989; Yu, 1988). Asian-American youths, for example, typically have been portrayed as academic whiz kids. Yet in a recent *Los Angeles Times* survey, Orange County's Vietnamese residents listed "gangs and crime" as their primary concern (Emmons & Reyes, 1989). William Cassidy has estimated that in Orange County—home of approximately 140,000 Vietnamese—only 1,000 youths have become part of the gang subculture (Hornblower, 1987). Increasingly, Vietnamese youth gangs are exacting a more visible toll on the community. However, the

AUTHORS' NOTE: The research presented here was funded by the Social Science Research Council: Undergraduate Research Assistantships and by the University of Wisconsin—Madison, Graduate School. Kira Edmunds, Peter and Hyun Hee Kim, Burkhard Karr, and Andrea Libby provided valuable support and comments. We especially thank Karen Heimer and John M. Long for their insightful criticisms.

scarcity of scientific research obscures the Vietnamese youth gang phenomenon.

Using data obtained from interviews with law enforcement officials, social workers, California Youth Authority (CYA) administrators, and, most important, 17 Vietnamese youths detained for gang-related crimes, we have begun an exploratory investigation of the problem. The youths who were our informants included all but one of the Vietnamese incarcerated in a regional CYA center for boys during the summer of 1989. Each initially participated in a questionnaire-guided interview and subsequently was questioned in several brief, informal meetings. All but two were convicted of armed robbery. All were born in South Vietnam and, according to official records, ranged from 15 to 18 years of age. The youths, however, readily confessed that they had underreported their ages upon arrival in the United States; thus the unofficial ages range from 17 to 21 years. (In this chapter, we shall refer to the youths' unofficial ages.) All the youths were from Southern California, particularly the San Gabriel Valley and Orange County. Individuals also were selected for more in-depth life-history interviews, which focused especially on family backgrounds, schooling, and street life experiences. The experiences related by these youths suggest that the concept of "multiple marginality" (Vigil, 1988a), developed as a conceptual framework for understanding Chicano gangs, offers the most fruitful means of understanding Vietnamese youth gangs. The effects of the Vietnam War, low socioeconomic status, governmental neglect, culture conflict, and racism have manifested themselves in multiple interrelated stresses and pressures. This marginality complex, in turn, prevents many youths from attaining their versions of the American dream via the traditional pathways of education and hard work. Unable to adapt to the dominant culture, they turn to gangs as a means of acquisition without assimilation.

A Historical Overview

The Vietnamese community of Southern California, as well as the youth gangs that have arisen within it, are products of the immigration that followed in the wake of the Vietnam War. When seen in this historical context, the Vietnamese youth gang phenomenon can be understood more easily.

The First Vietnamese Refugees

During the fall of Saigon in 1975, the first wave of refugees escaped from Vietnam and were brought to four refugee camps in the United States, including Camp Pendleton, located near San Diego. They were relatively well educated, highly urbanized, of high socioeconomic status, and young. A high proportion came to America with their families intact (Bach & Bach, 1980; Kelly, 1977; Liu, 1979; Marsh, 1980; Nguyen & Henkin, 1982; Stein, 1979).

Many Americans, however, refused to accept the Vietnamese influx. In a 1975 Gallup poll, 54% of the American public opposed resettlement of the Vietnamese in the United States ("A Cool and Weary Reception," 1975). To appease the xenophobism, President Ford promised that the refugees would be dispersed throughout the nation to minimize their supposed threat (Kelly, 1977; Liu, 1979). Under strict time constraints, the government resettled all 130,000 refugees by the end of 1975.

Almost immediately, however, the Vietnamese relocated themselves to form ethnic communities. People as diverse as the gold-rush 49ers and the Joad family in John Steinbeck's *The Grapes of Wrath* have been attracted to California, and the Vietnamese were no different. The attraction of the embryonic Vietnamese communities that grew from Camp Pendleton, rumors of an abundance of jobs, and the favorable climate were the primary factors behind the "second migration" of the Vietnamese to Southern California (Kelly, 1977). By 1979, nearly one-third of all Vietnamese in the United States claimed residence in the "Golden State" (Bach & Bach, 1980). The policy of dispersal had backfired.

Arrival of the "Boat People"

While Vietnamese immigrants in the United States were moving to California, many in Vietnam were planning their own migration. After 1977, a second wave of refugees, the "boat people," formed slipshod armadas and escaped from Vietnam by the tens of thousands. By the middle of 1979, more than 290,000 Vietnamese had escaped (Grant, 1979).

Unable to escape during the fall of Saigon, individuals and families in South Vietnam were forced to adapt to the harsh reality of communist rule. Many were relocated forcibly to "reeducation camps" or "new economic zones." Soldiers routinely searched "suspicious" households; when pressed for money they robbed these homes as well. Children played with abandoned grenades, bombs, and bullets. Citizens were killed openly, in broad daylight.

Although the "push" factors to leave Vietnam were intense, the lure of America was also powerful (Grant, 1979). Unlike the first wave of refugees, the boat people made explicitly clear their desire to come to the United States, the "freedom land." Leaving their homes and all their possessions, they boarded boats that were only minimally equipped for extensive sea travel. Starvation, engine failure, pirates, murder, and sea storms typified life in the boats. During this ordeal, thousands died. From the sea, the survivors made their way into the refugee camps, where living conditions were only slightly improved. After months of camp life, they came to America.

Our Vietnamese informants and their families came to the United States in the second wave of immigration. Each can recount experiences filled with the suffering and horrors noted above. Several had to leave parents behind, because their parents were too poor to pay for their own passage. The youths (and, in most cases, their parents) all sought to reach America. Their motives can perhaps be summarized by the response of one of our informants, a 19-year-old from El Monte, California:

> The communist way is messed up. And my dad dreamed of coming over here to America to make all our family go to school and do good. . . . They said it was rich and you could be free. You didn't have to do it the communist way.

Alienation and Frustration:
The Formation of a Subculture

Southern California, which now had several established Vietnamese communities, was again the primary destination. Today, nearly 40% of all Vietnamese in the United States live in Los Angeles and Orange counties alone. The presence of other Vietnamese helped to buffer the culture shock for the later arrivals, but the boat people were even less prepared for life in the United States. They were generally poorer, less educated, less urbanized, and had fewer salable skills than their counterparts who had arrived in 1975 (Bach & Bach, 1980; Grant, 1979; Marsh, 1980; Nguyen & Henkin, 1982; Skinner, 1980).

The racism that had subsided somewhat after the resettlement of the first wave of refugees was regenerated with the arrival of the boat people. A series of Gallup polls in 1979 indicated that more than 60% of the American public opposed admission of the new refugees (Stern, 1981). Opposition was particularly intense in Orange County and the San Gabriel Valley of Southern California (Arax, 1987a; Date & Foley, 1984). Thus it is not surprising that more than two-thirds of the Vietnamese in Orange County easily recognized anti-Vietnamese sentiment (Emmons & Reyes, 1989).

The federal government, which had failed to address the needs of the first wave of refugees adequately (Kelly, 1977; Liu, 1979; Stein, 1979), enhanced the alienation of the boat people. Although many Vietnamese immigrants have achieved prosperity, the repeated cuts in government aid programs—combined with California's high cost of living—have sent many Vietnamese families into the underground economy, particularly in the garment industry. Unfamiliar with their legal rights, many work for wages as low as a dollar per hour in illegal sweatshops. California state officials estimate that half of the Vietnamese families on welfare may be obtaining illegal income (Arax, 1987b). Current government emphasis on spending reductions seems likely to preclude adequate emphasis on the benefits of vocational training and English classes for the Vietnamese.

Thus, although the average Asian-American household income of $22,075 per year (in 1980) is above the national median, a recent United Way study reveals that the average Vietnamese household income in Los Angeles County is only slightly above $9,000 (Larson, 1988). In effect, a highly prosperous Asian-American upper class inadvertently has masked the plight of those below (Takaki, 1989; Yu, 1988). The alienation from America's financial mainstream is compounded by the monetary habits of many Vietnamese. As a result of cultural and linguistic differences, many Vietnamese forgo the use of banks and instead opt to keep substantial amounts of cash and gold bars within their homes (Berkman, 1984). This practice, as we shall explain later, is exploited by the youth gangs.

Alienation from law enforcement institutions is particularly relevant and acute in the Vietnamese community. Justice officials bemoan Vietnamese reticence in reporting crimes, while business owners victimized by extortion cite the lack of adequate police protection from criminals free on bail. Meanwhile, police officers struggle to adjust to cultural and language differences (Morganthau, Contrepas, Lam, & Sandza, 1982; "Report," 1987); police departments only recently have begun to recruit Vietnamese-speaking police officers. Indeed, as one police officer noted, "the cultural gap is like the Grand Canyon" (Morganthau et al., 1982).

For the youths, alienation from the educational system is especially frustrating. The pressure to succeed in school is extremely intense. Parents transfer their personal aspirations to their children, and school is seen as the key to success (Skinner, 1979). Indeed, the Vietnamese traditionally have made heavy sacrifices for their children's education (Hagerty, 1980; Skinner, 1980). It is no surprise, then, that so many Vietnamese adolescents became an annual part of their high school honor rolls (Brand, 1987).

Many Vietnamese youths, however, first arrive with exaggerated images of America's educational system. Disillusionment and reality quickly set in. The traditional age structure of schools becomes meaningless; initially, many of our informants who came to America as young teenagers found themselves with 8- and 9-year-olds as classmates. This age discrepancy was compounded by the common Vietnamese practice of underreporting a youth's age by several years. By underreporting their children's ages, Vietnamese parents enabled them to enter school at lower levels, to compensate for their poor English proficiency. Unfortunately, the age discrepancy caused embarrassment and conspicuousness for the youths, which led to confusion as they were "promoted" rapidly in an attempt to integrate them with classmates their own ages.

Many of our informants failed to adapt to the rapid pace of instruction; besides fights with other students, the youths cited their inability to understand what was going on as their primary problem in school. Their proficiency in English has improved slowly; only two informants classified their English as "very good," although all had been in the United States for more than five years. Comments such as "I was too scared to talk to the teacher" are common when talking to these youths. Even the simple act of asking permission to go to the bathroom became a degrading ritual.

Although the task of learning English is a major barrier, racism is easily understood. Despite their smaller size, these youths will respond to racist taunts with their fists. One 20-year-old informant from Santa Ana explained, "The Mexican gang over there [in my school] pretty big. . . . A lot of Vietnamese there got pushed around and I can't understand it. I like to stand up for what we are. Feel I'm big, too." Racial harassment often leads to bonds with other Vietnamese youths, as a means of protection and camaraderie. This "extracurricular activity," however, exacts a heavy price: Weapons were brought to school and concentration shifted from schoolwork to the schoolyard. Consequently, all our informants had been disciplined by their schools for fighting, and several had been expelled.

For those unable to meet the challenge, Asians who are academically successful are a source of resentment. A 17-year-old Vietnamese youth from Santa Ana made his feelings clear:

> I just don't look at them or nothing. . . . I don't like those people. Man, they're too smart. They get A's, and you can't

get no A's like that. I get mad. I get jealous. You're in your world, I'm in my world.

Yet this was the same youth who would avoid his "bad friends" and wear his "schoolboy" clothes (nondescript, churchlike clothing) during school, so that his teachers would not think that he was "bad." (After being detained repeatedly for grand theft auto, he finally gave up and began skipping school and wearing his "bad" clothes—stylish, "GQ" clothes that were black in color.) Mental and physical tensions build to the point that skipping school becomes a tempting alternative. Overall, the majority of our informants consistently had received failing grades and dropped out during middle school.

The indisputable academic successes of other Asian youths make this failure seem an isolated phenomenon, but a closer look at the data reveals a growing problem: Asians are three times as likely as Whites to not complete elementary school, and Asian adolescents accounted for a disproportionate 14% of the worst SAT scores in 1985 (Yu, 1988). The Alhambra School District in Los Angeles County, which has the nation's highest proportion of Asian students, reports that over half of its foreign-born Asian student population cannot speak proficient English (Arax, 1987a).

Traditionally, problems at school would be mediated by the family, but the stability of the Vietnamese family in America is marred by myriad cultural and socioeconomic conflicts. At one level, there is a conflict between two value systems. On the one hand, American television, advertisements, and ubiquitous displays of wealth (especially in cities such as Los Angeles) encourage the youths to obtain material wealth and provide constant stimulation to gain the American dream as soon as possible. Simultaneously, their families are preaching the traditional Vietnamese values of hard work, self-sacrifice, and patience. It is a cultural tug-of-war that all too often pulls the youths toward immediate gratification.

Not only do the youths reject their parents' values, they learn to reject the traditional role of parenthood itself. American and Vietnamese concepts of parenthood often differ, and the conflicting images lead to tensions and feelings of inadequacy. One youth, a 20-year-old from Long Beach, lamented the situation: "Most Asian family that I notice, they don't usually show their affection—hugging or nothing. They [are] just like that."

It is not surprising that all of our informants reported that Vietnamese is the primary language within their homes. Thus another problem is the language barrier within the family itself: Parents who can speak only Vietnamese must cope with the fact that their children can speak at least some English. This communication barrier, in addition to an unfamiliar educational system, prevents many parents from taking an active role in overseeing their children's education. As a result, Vietnamese youths—often afraid of blatantly defying authority—are able to circumvent parental control subtly by stealing report cards and scheduling spontaneous "holiday vacations" from school. One youth, acting as the translator, was even able to convince his parents at a school conference that the principal was giving him a "special vacation for his good behavior." (In actuality, he was being expelled for fighting.)

Even if able to speak English, however, many Vietnamese parents work very long hours, leaving them little time to supervise their children. The 1980 census indicates that Asian-American husband-wife teams work an average of six hours more per week than the national median. For one youth, the absence of family unity was particularly bothersome:

> Because when they [his parents] start opening the shop we never had time for each other. . . . Only time we see each other is when we eat. . . . My parents were never there for me.

Rather than reflecting increased wealth, the extra hours reflect a struggle to maintain a basic standard of living while trapped in low-paying jobs. This not only increases strain between the generations, but also places strain on marital stability. Fathers feel guilty and inadequate as they find their wives working longer hours and with better pay (Arax, 1987b). Divorce and separation often result.

Because most of our informants consider their families to be poor, they are hostile to the idea of accepting money from their parents. This youth illustrates the intense desire for financial independence:

> That's why I think my family poor. They don't take care of me enough. I just want to go my own. They take care whatever I need, but I don't want that money from them. I just want my own money. I want to make my own money.

The multiple complex of academic failure, community alienation, racism, cultural conflicts, status incongruity, and personal aspirations leaves the youths with few legitimate alternatives. Unable to conform to the dominant society, the youths gravitate to the gangs.

Before analyzing Vietnamese youth gangs, we must define the term *Asian gangs*. The concept of gangs in the Asian-American context has become especially confusing. The media, law enforcement officials, and government bureaucrats continually use the term *Asian gangs* to refer to both highly organized criminal groups and loosely structured youth gangs. Such use of the term is dangerous, as it furthers the impression that all Asian delinquents are involved in organized crime; it is reminiscent of the "yellow peril" mentality.

A noteworthy example of this phenomenon is California Attorney General John Van de Kamp's 1986 "Report to the Legislature on Organized Crime in California." The report, which was widely criticized by the Asian community, cited an increase in gang activity among the Hong Kong Triads, the Yakuza of Japan, and Vietnamese youth gangs (see Harrison, 1987). Whereas some Vietnamese youths have ties to some individuals involved in organized crime, these relationships tend to be sporadic and distant. Moreover, the Yakuza and Triads are highly organized crime groups, while Vietnamese youth gangs are anything but highly organized. Similarly, Vietnamese youth gangs do not fit the pattern of street gangs as typified by African-American and Chicano youths. Vietnamese youth gangs do not claim turf, adopt particular modes of clothing, or, sometimes, even have gang names. Several informants emphasized that they were not members of a gang, but rather of a "group."

Thus these Vietnamese delinquents do not fit neatly into the traditional pattern of either organized crime groups or street gangs. We use the term *youth gangs* to denote these groups, but acknowledge the unique quality of their structure and values.

Characteristics of Vietnamese Youth Gangs

As Thrasher (1927) notes, "No two gangs are just alike" (p. 45). Describing Vietnamese youth gangs in general terms is a particularly difficult task. In spite of this inherent difficulty, we believe that youth gangs provide their members with what they are unable to obtain from legitimate sources: money, recreation, autonomy, and a sense of family. In addition, youth gangs are characterized by the following traits: a fixation on acquiring money, pragmatism, and fluidity. Although these traits are complementary, we shall examine them separately.

Money

All of our informants agreed that money was the primary focal point within their gangs. Virtually all criminal activities are oriented toward this end. Stealing cars, for example, is not committed for the sake of joyriding, but for money. It is within the gangs that the youths find the means to sustain a free-spending life-style. Often a more sophisticated peer will teach them ingenious, yet simple, methods to steal cars. This informant's remarks illustrate the nature of this interaction:

> At first we just play pool and kick back. But I go out and fuck around and I need money. . . . So I see other Vietnamese they make money a lot of ways. They rob or they steal car. So some of them told me how to get money to fuck around. So I try to

steal a car 'cause I got a man and you give him [a car] he give
you eight hundred [dollars] . . . and he don't ask question.

Automobile theft, however, soon becomes insufficient in
maintaining the life-style, and so they turn to armed robbery.
The victims are without exception other Vietnamese, and the
crime usually occurs within the victim's home. As mentioned
previously, many Vietnamese-Americans tend to keep large
amounts of cash and gold within their homes. Knowing this,
the youth gangs will survey a residence and in small groups
(usually four or five persons) will enter the home armed with
handguns. Victims are beaten and coerced into revealing the
location of their valuables. Sometimes extremely cruel measures are used: One informant had threatened to drown the
victim's infant son in the toilet. As victims themselves of
communist soldiers who robbed their homes in Vietnam, these
youths have few compunctions in using violence. Their methods are efficient and effective. Almost without exception, they
are able to extract $15,000 to $20,000 per residence. On those
rare occasions when they were able to find only a few thousand,
our informants expressed their disgust and frustration.

Although (or because) they have been academic failures,
these youths soon find themselves living a grossly exaggerated
version of the American dream. The extensive Vietnamese
community provides an abundant supply of victims. The stolen
money is then spent in Vietnamese restaurants, nightclubs,
and car dealerships. The cornucopia and camaraderie is such
that intragang conflicts over money are rare. As one 19-year-
old informant explained, "We share money with everybody. . . .
We don't have to tell each other who get what, we use it all
together."

The fixation on wealth leads youths to emulate their older
counterparts who are involved in organized crime. According
to our informants, there is an implicit understanding that
one progresses from grand theft auto to armed robbery and
finally to extortion. Extortion is considered to be the riskiest,
yet the most efficient, means of procuring money because it
requires a great deal of stability and "reputation." Thus it is the

organized crime gangs that tend to be involved in extortion, for, as one informant said, "Extortion is the last thing we [youth gangs] would do."

Nevertheless, many of our informants confessed that prior to their arrests, they had aspired to the level of organized Vietnamese crime gangs such as the Frogmen, the Paratroopers, and the Black Eels. Despite these aspirations, however, the traditional Vietnamese age hierarchy and the secretive nature of the organized crime gangs prevent most youths from immediately entering this stage of criminality. Thus the youths subsist on residential robberies as they bide their time. As one informant stated, "They [the Frogmen] don't kick with us because we just boys." (Interestingly, many Vietnamese youth gangs identify themselves as "boys"; e.g., the Vietnamese Boys, or the Oriental Boys.)

Pragmatism

Given their intense ethnic pride, it is perhaps odd that these youths would victimize their own people. Yet a closer analysis of the Vietnamese-American community reveals the pragmatism in choosing only Vietnamese victims. As one 20-year-old informant explained: "We scared of Whites, [of] any other race, 'cause they know a lot of law and they don't keep cash [within their homes]." Vietnamese, on the other hand, do keep cash at home and also tend to be leery of the police and courts. Indeed, some law enforcement officials estimate that as many as 50% of the residential robberies go unreported, as victims may be intimidated by the legal system, fearful of retribution, or even unwilling to expose their own crimes, such as welfare fraud (Barber, 1987). In addition, the simple fact that both the criminal and the victim often do not speak fluent English is another factor behind the intraethnic nature of this phenomenon.

In fact, virtually all forms of behavior are calculated for their benefit and potential utilization. Rarely do these youth gangs engage in the persistent fighting that characterizes African-American and Chicano gangs. The common rationale is typified by one informant who described such behavior as "stupid": "Black and Ese [jail slang for Chicano] gang they . . . fight for neighborhood. They shoot each other for nothing. For us, [the] most [important thing is] we try to make money. We don't fight for a little neighborhood 'cause that's stupid." This is not to say that gang fights do not occur, for they do. But our informants indicate that physical conflicts are relatively infrequent and usually the last alternative utilized in resolving a dispute (which commonly centers on money).

Drug dealing is shunned for pragmatic reasons also. With the wealth obtained from residential robberies, the youths simply have no need for other sources of income. The "start-up costs" of drug dealing are cited as another factor. Further reflecting their business pragmatism, these youths argue that drug dealing is too risky and that there is "too much competition." Drug use is by no means eschewed, however. Cocaine is used heavily, but heroin is shunned because it makes one "unreliable and crazy."

Conspicuous gang symbols, such as tattoos and hand signs, tend to be avoided because they draw attention. This pragmatism may even result in the refusal to adopt a gang name, for fear that it would invite police recognition. When markers are utilized, they are discreet. For example, one common tattoo is that of a small V, composed of five dots, that is placed on relatively inconspicuous parts of the body such as the webbing between the thumb and first finger. Other markers, although conspicuous, are altered easily. One of our informants, a member of a youth gang that is characterized by 6- to 12-inch Mohawk hairstyles, proudly pointed out that his hair was held vertical by a mix of hair gel and egg white. Apparently, experimentation found that this formula was the easiest to wash out. In an emergency, the Mohawk quickly becomes a ponytail. Likewise, other "tattoos" often are drawn with pens, and are thus removed easily. Similarly, other markers such as gang colors and graffiti generally are avoided. Reflecting the impact of the media, our informants noted that they tended to wear clothes that emulate the fashion styles of new-wave musicians and models in *GQ* magazine. These clothes tend to be baggy, stylish, and expensive, but are not an absolute characteristic of youth gangs, as these clothes are popular among many youths in Southern California. Thus extreme care is taken to protect their criminal life-style, which is their only access to the American dream.

Fluidity

In describing Vietnamese youth gangs, we use the term *fluid* to indicate that the gangs are structured and organized loosely. There is little or no role differentiation and no declared turf, and membership changes constantly. Unlike African-American and Chicano gangs, which have structured initiation rites (commonly referred to as "jumping in"), membership within a Vietnamese youth gang (provided that the initiate is Vietnamese, or, in some cases, Cambodian) is established through previous relationships. One 19-year-old informant explained: "Somebody like your good friend, they look like they cool, they not stab you behind your back and you know them well, so just kick it together." Another informant merely stated, "It's really open."

In addition, membership in the gang does not preclude individual independence. Our informants indicated that one is free to drift in and out of the gang, and even into other gangs. Many of them seized the opportunity to travel (typically in cars) extensively across the United States, forming new and reestablishing old relationships. As a group, our informants have been to 17 different states (as far as Massachusetts), as well as Canada and Mexico. As they travel from city to city, they report, they commit armed robberies to fund their journeys. Thus it is not uncommon for a youth gang to commit a residential robbery in Los Angeles, meet friends the next day in Seattle, and by the next morning be well into Canada. Nights are spent in motels, and commonly 15 to 20 persons of both sexes will inhabit a single room (as renting multiple rooms attracts suspicion). To many observers, the mobility of the youth gangs suggests that a nationwide network exists, but our informants and other sources indicate that it is a loosely organized network, established by mere word of mouth. The geographical fluidity of the youth gangs appears to be a continuation of their rootlessness: As young children, they drifted from city to city to escape the war; as adolescents, they drifted across the open sea and traveled thousands of miles to reach America. In some ways, the youths appear to drift from state to state in search of a stable home they never had.

Despite the mobility and independence offered by the youth gangs, intense personal bonds are formed and maintained. One 20-year-old informant said, "We have a lot of respect and love for each other. We really with together [sic]. We live with each other. We're real close to each other." Another informant emphatically declared, "They were family to me. . . . I love 'em. Something come down, I'll be there for them. . . . I'd die for my homeboys." Affection is declared by calling their homeboys *ahn* (the Vietnamese word for brother) or by using personal nicknames (e.g., one informant was referred to as "*Co*," which means flamingo).

Thus the structural and geographical fluidity of the youth gangs further hinders the attempts of law enforcement agencies to combat the problem. This fluidity, however, does not diminish the intensity of the personal bonds formed within the gang, which becomes their adopted "family."

Conclusion

Past historical experiences are a crucial factor in the creation and establishment of Vietnamese gangs, as personal and family disruptions stem from such background issues. Even the American context of adaptation is colored by these macro-historical forces, especially in light of how the later waves of immigrants were treated shoddily and dispersed throughout the United States. Eventually finding their ways to California, where a sizable Asian-American population was entrenched, these immigrant families and their children began their Americanization journey. Alienation from government social services, law enforcement, and the financial mainstream (which led many into underground economic routes) was central to this process.

To reiterate, the formation of the youth gang subculture stemmed from both external (e.g., racism, schooling problems, economic burdens) and internal (e.g., war trauma, family stress, failure to achieve the "model minority" standard) factors. As noted, most of the youth sought support and social associations during particularly stressful times in their lives. This was especially true in junior and senior high school, where threats and intimidations increased and thus *ahns* (brothers) were needed for protection and friendly comrades to "kick back." The uprooted, dislocated nature of their lives led them to fashion their own type of subculture. The trade-off, unfortunately, included becoming a part of an incipient delinquent pattern headed toward—it appears—an organized crime career. Their tenuous adjustment contributes to a fluid, mobile method of acquiring quick, ready cash. Juxtaposed to African-American and Chicano gangs, in these Vietnamese youth gangs there is little interest in territorial considerations, and the signs and rituals of graffiti and initiation are played down, if not absent. Their residential movement, spatial dispersion, and pragmatic fear of detection preclude such localized and ritualized habits. Survival, for them, includes the acquisition of the American dream despite their multiple marginality and without losing their ethnic pride and culture. It is a quick fix to a fragmented, disjointed history.

8

Female Participation in Gangs

ANNE CAMPBELL

The Invisible Female Peer Group

The peer group has long been identified as one of the most powerful variables in explanations of male delinquency. By contrast, the female delinquent has been depicted as isolated and inept; a pitiful figure trying to assuage her loneliness through brief, promiscuous liaisons with boys (see Campbell, 1980; Giordano, Cernkovich, & Pugh, 1986). I begin this chapter by reviewing three myths that gave rise to this erroneous picture of social isolation (see Campbell, in press, for a fuller discussion).

Myth 1: Female delinquency is equivalent to with sexual promiscuity, and symptomatic of maladjustment and social isolation. In 1968, Cowie, Cowie, and Slater wrote: "The nature of delinquent offenses among girls is completely different to the delinquent offenses committed by boys. A large part of the delinquencies of girls consist in sexually ill-regulated behavior of a type not to demand social sanctions in the case of an adult" (p. 43). The translation of female delinquency into sexual promiscuity led to a characterization of such girls as rejecting female peers in favor of brief, unsatisfactory affairs with exploitative older men (Cowie et al., 1968; Konopka, 1966; Richardson,

1969; Thomas, 1923; Vedder & Sommerville, 1975). Chesney-Lind (1974) challenged this view when she suggested that the prevalence of female status offenders was exaggerated by an overreliance on official juvenile court data. Although boys also engaged in precocious sex, it was girls who were processed systematically and stigmatized for it. Self-report studies óf delinquency have confirmed this (Campbell, 1981; Canter, 1982b; Cernkovich & Giordano, 1979; Gold & Reimer, 1975; Hindelang, 1971; Weis, 1976). Self-report data provide no evidence that girls specialize in the solitary status offenses that previously were thought to characterize female delinquency. Indeed, Emler, Reicher, and Ross (1987) found "that girls are if anything even more likely than boys to commit any offenses in the company of others" (p. 99).

Myth 2: Family factors exert a more powerful influence on female than on male delinquents. Common sense suggests that girls are subject to much stricter control and supervision by the family than are boys, and this observation has been borne out by studies showing that daughters are perceived by their parents to be more vulnerable and to require more protection than boys (Block, 1978; Lynn, 1974; Maccoby & Jacklin, 1974). There are two fundamental issues here. First, are girls in fact subject to stricter parental control than boys? The answer is a resounding affirmative (Canter, 1982a; Cernkovich & Giordano, 1987; Hagan, Simpson, & Gillis, 1979; Singer & Levine, 1988). The second question is of greater concern: Do family variables explain more variance in female delinquency than in male delinquency? If the answer is yes, then we have found strong justification for the relative paucity of attention to the peer group as a factor in female delinquency. Loeber and Stouthamer-Loeber (1986) conducted a comprehensive meta-analysis of the impact of family factors on delinquency; they conclude: "In general, parental behavior was related to child conduct problems to the same degree for each sex" (p. 126). Subsequent studies, although finding gender differences in the nature of the family's impact on delinquency, report no significant differences in the size of the effect (Cernkovich & Giordano, 1987; Hill & Atkinson, 1988).

Myth 3: Girls do not form strong same-sex friendships. Early studies of female delinquency explicitly focused upon "relational strivings" and success in marriage as being the arena of self-expression, status, and competition among girls (Konopka, 1966; Morris, 1964; Rittenhouse, 1963; Sandhu & Allen, 1969). It is hardly surprising, then, that teenage girls were viewed as barely capable of warm same-sex friendships, because adolescence was seen as a marketplace competition for a mate. The data, however, tell a different story. Giordano et al. (1986) interviewed 942 teenagers about their friendships, using 13 dimensions of the quality of these relationships. Of these dimensions, 11 showed significant sex differences favoring girls. Girls were, among other things, more self-disclosing, more caring, and more trusting of and loyal to their friends. Giordano (1978) and Bowker and Klein (1983) found that female delinquency increased as a function of membership of a regular group, the amount of time spent in the group, and the frequency of peer contact. Figueira-McDonough, Barton, and Sarri (1981) reported striking similarity in the models of peer impact on delinquency for the two sexes. A high degree of involvement with peers and normative approval of deviant behavior explained similar amounts of variance in delinquency for boys and girls. Morash (1983) reported that the delinquent behavior of peers outweighed any other single factor in explaining individual delinquency for both sexes (.58 for boys, .44 for girls).

In sum, girls have equally good (arguably better) peer relations as boys and their delinquency depends as much on close association with delinquent others as it does for boys. In spite of this, it traditionally has been assumed that it is girls' relationships with boys, rather than with other girls, that produce delinquent behavior. When the delinquent girl is allowed a peer group, the only meaningful characters in it are male.

Early Accounts of
Female Gang Participation

Notwithstanding the ubiquitous problem of definition (Klein & Maxson, 1989; Miller, 1980), the gang has provided a natural forum for those interested in the interpersonal dynamics of group delinquency. Girls have been a part of gangs since the earliest accounts from New York in the early 1800s (Asbury, 1927). Their presence is not in dispute. The problematic issue revolves around the *form* of their participation.

In early writings girls were defined solely in terms of their interpersonal and structural relations to male gang members. They also were described through three layers of potential distortion: Their roles were described by male gang members to male researchers and interpreted by male academics. This does not in itself guarantee bias, but it introduces some troubling issues. Perhaps an example from the literature can illustrate. In 1965 a street worker reported:

> They just pull the girl off to the side and start rapping to her. . . . Jake will lay a broad right on the bench but most of them will take the girl off somewhere to one of these junked cars and lay her there. . . . They'll discuss who's fucking and who's not, how much time it takes for this one and how much time it takes for that one. (Short & Strodtbeck, 1965, p. 36)

At the first level, male members have much to gain by casting females in secondary roles as cheerleaders or camp followers. To the male gang worker, this reported secondary status may be accepted unproblematically because his avowed focus is upon male members and consequently his direct access to the world of the female gang member may be limited. Theorists who base their work on such information may be led to draw conclusions that fit coherently with theory but not necessarily with the facts. A. K. Cohen (1955), for example, argued that a girl is most likely to express the strain between long-term goals and the realistic likelihood of achieving them through an appropriately female channel—sexuality. Just as the "college boy" must relinquish short-term enjoyment for later benefits, so must the "good girl" learn to maintain her sexual attractiveness without becoming sexually accessible. In this way, she increases her market value in marriage, with its concomitant promise of upward social mobility. The "bad girl," who rejects this ethic, expresses her disdain by allowing free sexual access to males. From such a position, one might expect the girl to wear her promiscuity proudly, as a badge of rebellion. Those who have spoken with the girls themselves rather than accepting male gang members' accounts concur that this is not the case. Young women do not gain positive status from peers if they develop reputations for visible promiscuity (Brake, 1980; Horowitz, 1983; McRobbie, 1978; Smart & Smart, 1978).

The reliance on male gang informants began to change around 1970, and at the same time a rather different image of female participation also emerged. But it would be a mistake to conclude that male gang members had willfully given a distorted picture. It may be the case that the roles of girls did in fact alter gangs or, to put it another way, that the older material was true *at the time it was given.*

With such caveats in mind, it would be fair to say that gang girls, according to early writings, had the unenviable choice of two roles. Rice (1963) describes the problem in a nutshell:

> If a girl fights as well as a boy—and Youth Board workers know girls who do—boys don't like her, and in no walk of life is a girl who boys don't like an object of admiration or envy to other girls. By the same token, the one kind of status that carousing can confer is manly status, and to the extent that gang girls carouse they merely lessen the possibility that they will achieve the womanly status of being considered desirable mates. (p. 153)

Gang girls were either tomboys or sex objects. In terms of the literature, the latter seems to have proved more popular. In using the term *sex object,* I include those behaviors or roles that are distinguished by the fact that they conventionally require a sexually attractive female to perform them. This encompasses being a girlfriend to a male member, providing sexual services to gang boys, luring rival male members to preassigned locations (usually for the alleged purpose of sex or parties), acting as a spy by establishing a romantic relationship with a boy from an enemy gang, and carrying drugs or weapons for the boys (because girls are less likely to be searched by male police officers).

Thrasher's (1927) account of Chicago gangs found them to be overwhelmingly male. Those gangs that did include girls, however, he described as immoral rather than conflict gangs. Their chief activities included petting, necking, illicit sex, and mugging. They had names like the Tulips, the Lone Star Club, the Under the L gang and the Night Riders. They had clandestine signals that were used in the classroom to arrange secret meetings in vacant lots or deserted barns between a boy and a girl.

Bernard (1949) reported the growth of female gang membership in New York. Virtually all the female gangs were affiliated with male gangs, although they took on their own names, such as the Robinettes, the Chandeliers, and the Shangri-la Debs. Probation reports described initiation rituals that required prospective members to have intercourse with male gang members. Older girls were reported to have procured younger girls for the boys, with the express intention of rape. During the war years, groups of gang girls would pick up soldiers and lure them into side streets, where their male accomplices, too young to be drafted, would "roll" them. A girl might be dispatched to seduce rival gang leaders while her own gang notified the police of her whereabouts and claimed she was being raped. Characteristically, the girls' functions were to carry weapons (being immune to search by male officers), provide alibis, act as spies and lures, and provide sex for the male members. The overwhelming impression is of gang girls as sexual property.

The 1950s was the era of the street worker. Social workers attempted to reach and reform (or at least control) the behavior of teenage gangs. In 1950, the Welfare Council of New York City published a report on their attempt to work with Harlem gangs and their girls' affiliates. The girls were either sisters or friends of those in the male group. The majority were described as sexually promiscuous, and illegitimate births were "common." The girls incited and supported the boys' lawbreaking, while playing little part in it themselves. Occasionally, some of the girls drank or used narcotics and a few truanted from school. They are described by the street workers as passive, exploited people of low self-concept and ability. As one male member told a street worker:

> You take what you want from them. When they get off the beam and don't act right, slap them around so they'll know who's who. (Welfare Council of New York City, 1950, p. 16)

Girls were seen as sexual objects to be cajoled, tricked, or forced into sexual relations. No mention is made of the rapes, gang bangs, or homosexual prostitution of the boys—let alone their involvement in normal, if precocious, sex. The street workers' aim seems to have been not to encourage girls' independence from boys, but to inculcate "feminine" middle-class values about their sexuality and its worth by conducting classes in cosmetics and etiquette, organizing sewing parties, and getting together charity boxes to send to foreign countries.

In 1963, Rice reported on the Persian Queens in Brownsville, Brooklyn. The gang numbered only seven girls, whom Rice describes as "dim" and "exceptionally unattractive." The role that Rice concentrated upon most heavily was that of sexual consort for the boys: The girls were "delighted to drink with the Mohawks, sleep with the Mohawks and, if the occasion demanded, carry weapons and furnish alibis for the Mohawks." Hanson's (1964) account of another New York female gang, the Dagger Debs, was based upon accounts drawn from New York City Youth Board's files. The Dagger Debs numbered 12 members, and their structure included a president, a prime minister, and a war counselor. They had a "clubhouse" (an abandoned apartment) that was used for meetings and making out with members of their brother gang, the Daggers. Although Hanson makes passing reference to the girls' involvement in mugging and shoplifting, the major stress is on their sexuality. Hanson documents the girls' early initiation into sexual activities, their universal lack of genuine sexual enjoyment, and their ignorance of reproduction and birth control.

They will oblige on rooftops or in cellars, on park benches or in the grass. They stand in halls and doorways or disappear briefly into dark corners. They behave like prostitutes, but most of them are not. They have such a low opinion of themselves, they don't even charge. (p. 70)

The street worker aimed to turn them into "ladies" by starting a charm clinic and teaching them how to eat in restaurants and shop in department stores.

Fishman (1988) has reanalyzed qualitative data also collected in the 1960s on the Vice Queens, a Black female affiliate of the Vice Kings of Chicago. Their principal roles were traditional—sexual objects, drinking partners, weapons carriers, and lookouts. They fought other female gangs, but took particular pride in exploiting their femininity to instigate inter- and intragang fights among the boys. By reporting "passes" made by members of rival gangs, they manipulated the Vice Kings into fighting for their honor. Their raison d'être was the male group, and they had "little function outside the mating-dating complex." They competed, often violently, for the attention of the male gang members, and status within the group was largely dependent on relationships with particular boys. Going steady with or having a baby by a high-status boy was prestigious, but there was no anticipation by either sex of long-term commitment or marriage.

The gang girl faced a no-win situation. If she had sex, she was rejected by the very boys she sought to attract. If instead she emulated male behavior, she ran the risk of being rejected as a tomboy. Nevertheless, early reports make it clear that some girls opted for this latter role. Asbury (1927) describes young women like Hell-Cat Maggie and Battle Annie, who, in 1850s New York, had reputations for their fighting ability. Thrasher (1927) notes that at the youngest age before adolescence, girls who took part in ganging engaged in the same kinds of misbehavior as the boys and were eager to outdo them. They excluded "feminine" girls from their gang exploits. With the awakening of interest in romantic relationships, however, the girls became self-conscious and left the gang. Miller's (1973) tomboys were the Molls, an all-White, Catholic gang of 11 girls aged between 13 and 16. The Molls played hooky, stole, drank, vandalized, and fought. They attempted to gain favor with their male companion group (the Hoods) by emulating and abetting the boys' criminal activities, but *not* by freely dispensing sexual favors to them. The girls made no effort to deny their dependence upon the Hoods, however, and in fact seemed quite proud to acknowledge their reliance upon them.

This historical emphasis upon the "rogue male" as the Svengali of gang girls has been challenged by more recent quantitative results. Giordano (1978) conducted interviews with teenage girls in which a self-report delinquency scale was used in addition to a number of questions about friendship patterns. Gang girls reported more delinquent acts than nongang girls and, when asked about the degree of approval they would receive for delinquent acts from different members of their peer groups, the highest approval rating came from *other girls* rather than from boys. Bowker and Klein (1983) reported similar results with another female sample. They used six measures of the quality and intensity of female friendships, all of which showed a relationship with number of delinquent offenses, gang membership, or both. They conclude that "relations with *girlfriends are quite a bit more important* than relations with boyfriends in determining gang membership and the seriousness of delinquency among the girls in our study" (p. 745).

Contemporary Accounts: Gang Rhetoric

More contemporary qualitative work on female gangs (in which I include work from 1970 to 1989) has come from direct contact with the girls themselves, rather than once removed, from male members. These works, based upon intensive interviews or participant observation, have taken female gangs as collectives to be explained in their own right. Hispanic girls have been the principal objects of study, both Chicanas in Los Angeles (M. G. Harris, 1988; Quicker, 1983) and Chicago (Horowitz, 1983) and Puerto Ricans in New York (Campbell, 1984). There has been much less attention to Black, Asian, or

White girls (but see Brown, 1977; Campbell, 1984; Hagedorn, 1987; Miller, 1973).

If we are to account for female gang membership in its own terms rather than as an interesting comparative footnote to the male gang, it is important to incorporate the community and class context in which these girls live and to identify what it means to be a woman growing up in and adapting to these conditions. This involves the examination of gang youth in relation to both the parent culture (the ethnic working-class or poverty-class community from which they spring) and the mainstream culture of which their class forms a marginal part. Gangs can be seen as representing a means by which some youths seek to resolve the problems presented by their structural position in relation to both these groups.

The words and actions of gang members seek to resolve the intractable problems of class by simultaneously rejecting and opposing some aspects of community and mainstream values while incorporating and internalizing others (Cohen, 1972; Hall & Jefferson, 1976). Their resulting identity is often apparently contradictory or incoherent (Campbell, 1987). They commit crimes while opposing criminals. They want independence while also wanting strong, dependable mates. They oppose hard drug use while simultaneously counting drug users among their members and dealing drugs on street corners. As Goodman (1960) puts it, "We cannot expect average kids to deviate with genius."

What are the problems that face poverty-class girls, the problems for which they seek answers in the gang?

(1) *A future of meaningless domestic labor with little possibility of educational or occupational escape.* For potential gang members, the possibility of a career is effectively non-existent, and the possibility of a low-paying job is remote. Many come from mothers who have survived largely on welfare, supplemented by the marginal economy (Campbell, 1984; Moore, 1988). They are school dropouts with poor literacy skills (Moore 1989a). When asked about jobs, their standard responses are in terms of hopelessly unattainable goals, such as being a rock star or professional model. They do not aspire to the kind of minimum-wage

opportunities that are realistically available to them. Thus the future that awaits them is within the home.

(2) *Subordination to the man in the house.* In Hispanic culture the right of the male to dictate, control, and discipline his wife is accepted widely (Acosta-Belen & Christenson, 1979). As the breadwinner (and even when he is not a breadwinner), he will make decisions that circumscribe the possibilities that are open to her.

(3) *Responsibility for children.* As a mother, the Hispanic woman achieves considerable status within the household, but the practical constraints of raising children necessarily restrict her options, as does the required demeanor of motherhood (Fitzpatrick, 1971).

(4) *The social isolation of the housewife.* As her children grow up and pursue their lives, she will find herself trapped at home. At best she will have a circle of female kin and near-kin around the neighborhood; at worst she will be isolated in a project apartment.

(5) *The powerlessness of underclass membership.* Much has been written on the structural and cultural roots of powerlessness in poverty-level life (Wilson, 1987). The marginality of these women in relation to the male economic and social world produces a triple remoteness from effective initiative. Handicapped by class, race, and gender, these women are victims of the system at an economic and social level. But they are also, more concretely, victims of crime and violence within their communities and their homes.

For these girls, the period of adolescence (which, defined as the cessation of childhood, may begin as early as age 8) is a brief interlude before they are incorporated into adult Hispanic identity and the economic, practical, and social constraints outlined above. The gang represents for its members an idealized collective solution to the bleak future that awaits. The members construct for themselves, at a rhetorical level, an image of the gang that counterpoints the suffocating futures they face. In short, the members tacitly conspire to portray the gang to themselves—as well as to others—in a particularly romantic light. Irwin (1970) describes a similar process among adult criminals:

This mutual support of each others' delusions among criminals is not simply dissembling. It is more a process of subtle distortion of reality by which they themselves are fooled. It is a process of selecting the most prestigious occurrences, amounts and acts for retelling and forgetting the less prestigious.

Miller (1974) has also noted the tendency for gangs to develop "standardized answers" to outsiders' questions and has expressed surprise at the extent to which their statements are given credence by researchers. Indeed, some writers do seem to have accepted the more romantic presentations given by girl gang members uncritically. The position I adopt is that such gang rhetoric is not designed solely to fool researchers, but also to fool the gang members using it.

Much is made of the "rebel" or "outlaw" nature of the gang. The gang is cast in direct opposition to the straight, anemic world of conformity. Unlike the rest of us, gang members are free from the mundane demands of Mertonian ritualism. Their dress, their swagger, their craziness are all brandished as evidence of their proud independence of the straight world.

> They can't feel the things we feel or the way our life-style is. The [mainstream] Man says, "How can you all be doing this or doing that?" He tries to analyze our life-style. "How do you do this?" and all this kind of shit. We don't want them to get inside us, we don't want them to. (Campbell, 1984)

Boyfriend-girlfriend relationships are elaborated similarly. The boy's possessiveness and his jealousy of potential rivals are seen as clear evidence of his passionate attachment to his partner. For this period of her life at least the girl is young and desirable, inciting passion and stormy emotions. Consequently, the beatings that she may receive at his hands when he believes that she has been unfaithful are interpreted as a direct index of his love for her. The problem lies not in his violent and often insecure disposition, but in the peculiarly extreme nature of their romance. This belief is adhered to even in the face of evidence that would tend to undermine it. For example, his infidelity is blamed upon his desirability to other women, rather than seen as evidence of his less-than-total commitment to her. In this way, the tyranny of males over females is translated into the problem of his passion for her, and the institutionalized female goal of attracting a man is not merely met but exceeded. She lives out the idealized female role that has been fed to her through magazines, soap operas, and romance novels (Brake, 1980; McRobbie, 1978).

> You have to be playing games with your old man. Sometimes you might have to be the sister, sometimes you have to be the lover. I don't want him to be with me because he married me and I'm his wife and he comes home every night to his wife. No, I want him to come home to his WIFE. "Wow, my wife." Sometimes I feel my love for him is too strong. It must be that love is always being jealous. Love does hurt. Love is always saying "I'm sorry." I hate him for loving him and I love him for hating him. (Campbell, 1984)

Gang members refer to one another as "sisters" or "home-girls" and to the gang as "family" (Brown, 1977; Campbell, 1984; Harris, 1988; Quicker, 1983). These terms conjure the sense of belonging and identification that are frequent themes in their conversation. The exaggerated sense of "we-ness" is best exemplified when the group is under threat from beyond, by rival gangs' incursions into the neighborhood or by police arrests. This intense in-group loyalty is particularly important to gang members. The home lives of gang girls are marked frequently by breakdown and dysfunction, at worst resulting in physical and sexual abuse (Campbell, 1984; Moore, 1988). The fragility of family relationships often is compounded by frequent changes of residence and early school truancy and dropout. The girls often speak of themselves as "loners" before joining the gang, barely connected to their schoolmates or to neighborhood peer groups.

> I don't trust anybody else, that's why. They're the only ones I can depend on, 'cause I know if I get into hassles, they'll help me. Like one time we went to B____. We used to go to hang around there, and some girls there were going to jump me, and all the girls I was with took off and they left me there

alone. That's when I said I was only going to hang around with my homegirls. (Quicker, 1983)

The sisterhood of the gang is reinforced conversationally to compensate for the internal divisions that are not uncommon. Quarrels between the girls over boyfriends occur with regularity (Campbell, 1984; M. G. Harris, 1988; Horowitz, 1983; Quicker, 1983). If a girl is challenged on foreign turf, there is a normative prescription for her to state proudly her gang allegiance, even if this leads to an outnumbered attack and serious beating (M. G. Harris, 1988). Much is made of the bravery of girls who adhere to this norm to compensate for the times that discretion triumphs over valor. Even informing on fellow gang members to the police is not unknown. None of this, however, would be evident if one took at face value the idealized collective representation of loyalty in their social talk.

Street talk also highlights the glory days: the spontaneous parties, the pranks, the drink and drugs. More than anything else gang membership is seen as fun. Stories are told and retold of astonishing chemical intakes, of "crazy" behavior and "wild" parties. These events stand as a bulwark against the loneliness and drudgery of their future lives. They also belie the day-to-day reality of gang life. The lack of recreational opportunities, the long days unfilled by work or school, and the absence of money mean that hours and days are whiled away on street corners (Corrigan, 1976; Klein, 1971). "Doing nothing" means hanging out on the stoop; the hours of "bullshit" punctuated by trips to the store to buy one can of beer at a time. When an unexpected windfall arrives, marijuana and rum are purchased in bulk and the partying begins. The next day, life returns to normal.

Toughness and craziness are inextricably linked in the construction of a street reputation. Toughness denotes an unwillingness to back down in the face of threat (real or imagined); craziness indicates the labile, unpredictable nature of their response. The combination wards off the specter of people "fucking with us." As others have noted in connection with male gang members (Miller, 1966a) and British soccer fans (Marsh,

Rosser, & Harre, 1978), much of the violence of these youths occurs in the world of talk rather than of action. The bellicose reputation in which they take pride is given considerably more weight in conversation than is the fear that lurks beneath it. They fear being a "dud"—a victim at the mercy of others. In their neighborhoods, where violence and even death are not uncommon, having a "rep" is preferable to walking scared, to being powerless. But the rep they work so hard to achieve sets them up as targets for others who are seeking to expand their own reps. There is the abiding fear that "there's always someone tougher than you."

> I always get nervous, even when I'm just arguing with somebody. I get nervous. There's times, yeah, I see a real big girl, then I get scared. I think, "Damn, I'm going to hurt her or she's going to hurt me." But once you're in a fight, you just think—you've got to fuck that girl up before she does it to you. You've got to really blow off on her. You just play it crazy. That's when they get scared of you. It's true—you feel proud when you see a girl that you fucked up. (Campbell, 1984)

Contemporary Accounts: Gang Life

Miller (1975) identified three possible relations between female gang members and male gangs: as independently functioning units, as regular members in "coed" gangs, and as female auxiliaries of male groups. Researchers overwhelmingly have found the last of these to be most common. Only Brown (1977) in Philadelphia has documented a wholly autonomous gang of girls. Although such groups may exist, they are far from typical. The female group usually comes into existence after the male gang has been established and often takes a feminized version of the male name. In Los Angeles, as with the male gangs, the girls may be subdivided further into age cohorts or klikas (M. G. Harris, 1988). The older girls may share with the boys the name of chicas, the younger girls locas (Quicker, 1983). Leadership is usually more diffuse than in the boys' groups. Typically the members insist there is no leader and that decisions are made democratically. Observation suggests that some girls clearly have more clout than others, but that this usually is not formalized as a leadership role. Some gangs have "*veteranas*" or "godmothers," older women (often in their 20s or 30s) with considerable gang experience who often counsel on gang-related and personal problems.

Girls from the neighborhood (and beyond) are not pressured or coerced into joining. Potential members come not only through friendship networks but through family ties (M. G. Harris, 1988; Moore, 1988). Prospects or "wanna-bes" spend time with the gang and are screened informally as to their acceptability. Where a formal initiation ceremony exists, it usually takes the form of a prearranged fistfight between the prospect and an established member. The function of this "jumping in" is to prove publicly the new girl's ability to fight. She need not win the encounter; she must, however, demonstrate her "heart" or courage. This initiation also deters girls who might join for the wrong reasons—to "use" the gang as backup in some private dispute, to gain access to the boys, or to act as spies for a rival group.

The girls regulate their own affairs. They may collect dues, hold meetings, and initiate, discipline, or expel members. They are hostile to attempts by the male gang leader to intervene in these matters. Occasionally a male gang member may try to influence the girls to accept a boy's girlfriend into their ranks. The girls insist on putting her through the usual period of supervision and making their own decision. They are usually suspicious of such prospects, believing that the girl's motivation is weighted more heavily toward romance than toward sisterhood. They are possessive of their men and consequently resentful of outsiders who want the kudos of romance with a gang boy without the long-term commitment and dangers of gang loyalty. This hostility usually is couched, however, in terms of a security issue (the outsiders may be spies from other gangs) rather than as a matter of possessiveness (Campbell, 1984).

Disciplinary issues are usually informal. At a group meeting, the misbehavior is described and the group expresses its approbation, warning the offender to mend her ways or risk expulsion. Misbehaviors may include failing to support another homegirl in a fight, failing to identify oneself as a gang member when "hit up" by another gang, theft from other members, informing on group crimes, and association with male members of rival groups. The most frequent source of conflict is stealing another girl's boyfriend (Campbell, 1984; M. G. Harris, 1988).

Gang girls exert strong normative control over one another's sexuality, as do working-class girls generally (Smart & Smart, 1978). They are acutely sensitive to the community's view of them as sexually "cheap" and—for Hispanic girls particularly— this is one of the most painful costs of gang membership (Horowitz, 1983). Serial monogamy is expected. The more cohesive the gang, the more likely it is that the girls will be expected to select their partners from the ranks of the male gang. Association with nonaligned community boys or even with members of other gangs (if they are at peace with them) may also be tolerated (M. G. Harris, 1988). Once a girl becomes involved with a boy she is expected to remain faithful until the relationship ends. Suspicion and jealousy are probably the most disruptive forces in the gang, and the strong enforcement of norms of fidelity helps to minimize the destructive potential.

Fights usually are directed at members of rival female gangs. (It is rare, but not unheard of, for the girls to take on male gang members. To do so confers particular kudos.) Enemies are disparaged as "hos" (whores) and "glue-sniffers." They frequently are characterized as the mere sex objects of their men, lacking the courage to fight for or defend them. Although often insisting that they do not look for trouble (trouble just finds them), they will enter rival territory to provoke a confrontation or to paint their *plaka* or gang symbol (M. G. Harris, 1988). This constitutes a very direct challenge to their enemies. Territory or turf remains a focal issue not only as a symbolic matter of gang integrity but as an economic base where the gang reserves the right to deal drugs. The girls view turf more in the former terms. Although the boys may use guns, the girls most often are involved in fist or knife fights (Campbell, 1984; M. G. Harris, 1988).

The tough image to which the girls aspire is a source of ambivalence for both sexes. For their part the girls take pride in their independent forays against (and triumphs over) other gangs. At the same time, they are gratified both by the boys' determination to protect them from more lethal encounters and their intervention when they see a homegirl being beaten in a fight (Horowitz, 1983; Quicker, 1983). The boys are equally proud of the girls' "heart," although there is often a somewhat patronizing tone to their accolades. They frequently insist that the gang is not the place for girls and may encourage their own girlfriends to stay out of gang affairs (Quicker, 1983).

Because the boys' approval is central to the girl gang's existence, the girls often publicly defer to the males. In Los Angeles, the girls' uniform includes Pendleton jackets, T-shirts, drapes, and flat shoes. In New York, denim sleeveless jackets with combat boots and handkerchiefs were popular. If the boys object to the outfits as too "butch," however, the girls will reserve the full outfit only for encounters with rival gang members (Campbell, 1984). When both sexes are present, the girls tend to remain quiet, allowing the boys to do most of the talking.

This deference is in marked contrast to the way the girls talk when the boys are not present. Then their attitude is transformed into indulgence. Men are infantilized in talk; they are cast as willful, hot-blooded children prone to outbursts of anger and passion. They do not always know what is good for them and it is women's place to steer the men invisibly in the direction that they wish them to go. Nowhere is this more evident than in the discussion of male infidelity. Men are, by nature, unable to refuse an offer of sex. Consequently, it is not the boy's fault when he strays but rather the other woman's. The confrontation is recast as between the girlfriend and her rival, rather than between the girl and the boy. Consequently, sexual betrayal is terminated by an attack on the rival, not on the boyfriend, who simply was following his nature. This view of men seems to be widespread in Hispanic culture, but it is realized in a more public and violent way through the encouragement of other gang members.

For most girls, leaving the gang occurs at the end of adolescence. For many it coincides with the birth of a child and the unwelcome realization of the constraints that this entails. Some have mothers who are willing to raise their children for them, but others, by choice or necessity, take on the full-time care of their children. Some find themselves in juvenile institutions, prisons, or drug treatment centers. An unfortunate few graduate to heroin use, and their dependence on the drug overtakes their loyalty to the gang. Others set up stable relationships with men and slip away from the life on the streets. Some researchers have described more ritualized exits, in which members are "jumped out" (M. G. Harris, 1988; Quicker, 1983). These involve severe beatings by a number of homegirls, sometimes resulting in hospitalization. Whether or not "jumping out" occurs seems to be a function of the extent of the girl's previous involvement, her motives for leaving, and the formality with which she announces her intended departure. Most girls are wise enough to diminish their involvement over time rather than precipitate group sanction by framing their leave-taking as an act of betrayal.

Conclusion

The picture constructed here of female gang membership is incomplete and provisional. Lack of research data makes the task of synthesis similar to trying to construct a jigsaw puzzle with most of the pieces missing. We barely have the pieces to begin a similar picture for Black and White female gangs, and even the above sketch may be distorted by the summing of data from Chicana and Puerto Rican girls (Moore, 1988). The economic and social plight of male gang members has encouraged considerable research; our concern should be no less for women than for men. Recent data suggest that the future awaiting gang girls is bleak indeed: 94% will go on to have children, and 84% will raise them without spouses (Hagedorn, 1987; Moore, 1988). One-third of them will be arrested, and the vast majority will be dependent on welfare. The attraction of the gang is no mystery in the context of the isolation and poverty that is awaiting them.

9

Social Processes of Delinquency and Drug Use Among Urban Gangs

JEFFREY FAGAN

S ince the early work of Thrasher (1927), the terms *gang* and *violence* often have appeared together in the popular and social science literatures. In recent years, drug use and drug dealing have been added to the stereotype of urban youth gang activities. Despite the historically uneven relationship between gangs and drug use or selling (Klein & Maxson, 1989; Moore, 1989a; Spergel, 1989a), attention to youth gangs in this decade has focused on their growing involvement in drug use and distribution and, in turn, the violence that is intrinsic to street-level drug trafficking. In the public eye, the involvement of youth gangs in volatile drug markets (such as crack) has signaled a transformation of youth gangs from transitory adolescent social networks to nascent criminal organizations (e.g., Reuter, 1989).

These concerns reflect recent trends in the drug-crime relationship among adolescents. First, several studies have

AUTHOR'S NOTE: Support for this research was provided by Grant 87-JN-AX-0012 from the Office of Juvenile Justice and Delinquency Prevention. The opinions are those of the author and do not reflect the policies or views of the Department of Justice. James Deslonde (1943-1987) was co-principal investigator for this research, and made it all possible.

183

reaffirmed the strong association between substance use and delinquency (Elliott, Huizinga, & Ageton, 1985; Fagan, Weis, & Cheng, 1990; White, 1990). Each study carefully points out that the relationship may be spurious rather than causal, however, and that "third factors" may explain either behavior separately or their joint occurrence. In fact, White, Pandina, and LaGrange (1987) warn that the putative predictors of either serious drug use or serious delinquency will lead to unacceptable rates of overprediction. Regardless of whether the relationship is causal, spurious, or reciprocal, serious juvenile offenders are involved disproportionately in substance use.[1] And the association seems to be facilitated by the strength of involvement in peer social networks where drug use and delinquency are normative. Nevertheless, adolescent drug use has become a focus of media attention and public policy despite its steady decline in this decade (Johnston, O'Malley, & Bachman, 1988).

Second, the sudden proliferation of youth gang involvement in crack use and sales in Los Angeles and a small number of other cities has led to the confounding of the two social problems (Maxson & Klein, 1986). Coming in the midst of declining tolerance of drug use and outrage against drug-related violence, these reports have fueled the public perception that gangs have transformed into emerging organized criminal networks conspiring to distribute drugs nationally through nationwide networks of affiliates and franchises ("Kids and Cocaine," 1986). Young crack sellers have been portrayed as ruthless entrepreneurs, highly disciplined and coldly efficient in their business activities, often using violence selectively and instrumentally in the service of profits.[2]

Yet, drug selling has always been a part of gang life, with diverse meanings and variable participation by gang members. Fagan (1989) found diverse patterns of drug selling and other criminal involvement among gang members in three cities with extensive, intergenerational gang traditions. For some gangs, drug distribution is an incidental and instrumental part of gang life, serving only to finance gang activities or provide income or drugs for gang members (Dolan & Finney, 1984). For others, drug selling is a form of social "glue" that binds gang members (Feldman, Mandel, & Fields, 1985; Moore, 1978).

But other studies contend that the lucrative and decentralized crack market has led to a new generation of youth gangs (Skolnick, Correl, Navarro, & Rabb, 1988; Taylor, 1990). In the "new gangs," there are more older members (in their 20s) and more members with prison records or ties to prison inmates. Participation in these new gangs may be motivated by instrumental goals of profit rather than the cultural or territorial affinities that unified gangs in earlier decades. These events have coincided with basic social and economic transformations in inner cities (Tienda, 1989; Wacquant & Wilson, 1989) that have weakened the formal and informal social controls that in the past have mediated gang behaviors and adolescent violence (Curry & Spergel, 1988; Sampson, 1987).

Drug use among gang members also is a diverse phenomenon. Stumphauzer, Veloz, and Aiken (1981) have noted varying patterns of drug use within and among Chicano youth gangs in East Los Angeles. Others describe a variety of drugs used, meanings, and functions of drug use within gangs, and the commonplace role of drug use in gang life (Campbell, 1984; Dolan & Finney, 1984; Vigil, 1988a). Feldman et al. (1985) describe distinct styles and functional values of drug and alcohol use among gangs in three Latino neighborhoods in San Francisco. Yet other gangs eschew or prohibit drug use among their members who are involved in drug selling (Chin, 1990, and Chapter 6 of this volume; Taylor, 1990, and Chapter 4 of this volume).

Accordingly, the extent and meaning of gang participation in drug and alcohol use, drug selling, and their involvement in the violence that often accompanies selling, still appears to be quite variable. Because gangs are primarily adolescent groups that are also are involved extensively in illicit activities, the drug-crime association among adolescents should also be evident among gang members. In turn, the factors that explain the drug-delinquency association should be similar for gang and nongang youths. If gangs have transformed in this decade and become a distinct organizational form of criminal activity, however, the putative predictors of drug-crime involvement among gang members may vary from other adolescents.

Research Problem

Comparisons of gang and nongang youths from homogeneous social areas have been rare, and have suffered from definitional problems (see Chapter 3 of this volume).[3] Few studies have examined the validity of theories of crime and delinquency to explain either gang participation or differences in illicit behaviors between gang and nongang youths. Moreover, the few studies comparing gang and nongang youths have not examined drug-crime relationships in this decade of changing cities and changing patterns of drug use and selling.

Delinquency research more typically has examined the role of group or subcultural processes in the complex etiology of criminal behavior, as well as the group properties of crime events (e.g., Farrington, Berkowitz, & West, 1981). Although gang members commit more crimes and more violent crimes than nongang youths (Tracy, 1979; Tracy & Piper, 1984), it is uncertain whether the differences reflect the positive correlation between group crime and violence, features of the gang itself, or the state of social controls in the inner cities where gangs are most evident. Gangs may represent marginalized youths within inner-city neighborhoods that already are isolated socially and economically from conventional norms and opportunities (Curry & Spergel, 1988; Fagan, 1989; Vigil, 1988a), and where social controls have been weakened.

Nevertheless, the explanatory power of "group norms" has been a critical concept bridging delinquency theory and gang research (Erickson & Jensen, 1977; Gibbs, 1981; Zimring, 1981). If youth gangs represent an extreme form of group delinquency, then understanding the microsocial processes of their social networks may be critical to explanations of gang behaviors.

Because gangs also are adolescent social networks, explanations of illicit behaviors by adolescents should apply comparably to gang and nongang youths. If gangs in cities such as Chicago and Los Angeles have evolved into distinct criminal organizations, however, explanations of deviant behaviors among nongang youths may be irrelevant for gang participation or behaviors. These questions are examined in this chapter.

Theoretical Framework

Historically, youth gangs have played an important role in theories of crime and delinquency. Both Eckland-Olsen (1982) and Jackson (1989) cite the important contributions of differential association processes and control theories to the study of youth gangs. The disruption of social controls in inner-city neighborhoods, the result of macrosocial processes launched by social structural factors (Sampson, 1987), provides fertile ground for gang formation and processes leading to violence (Curry & Spergel, 1988). Short (1989) notes that the collective nature of gang delinquency calls for theoretical integrations that include the study of microsocial interactions between individual behaviors and the ecological context of behavioral events: social controls, situational factors, and group processes.

Recent theoretical integrations have been applied to delinquency (Conger, 1980; Elliott, Ageton, & Canter, 1979; Johnson, 1979; Weis & Hawkins, 1981), substance use (Kandel et al., 1986; Johnson, Marcos, & Bahr, 1987), and the joint behaviors (Elliott et al., 1985; Fagan et al., 1990; White et al., 1987). These studies disagree on the primacy of constructs from one theory or the other in understanding behavior, but do agree that an integration of learning and control perspectives is superior to either in isolation (Johnson et al., 1987). Few studies, however, have tested this integration of theories to explain gang participation, differences in deviance between gang and nongang youths, or differences in individual characteristics of gang and nongang youths.

Integrations of control and social learning theories attempt to explicate fully the role of deviant peers in facilitating the learning of criminal values and behaviors (Johnson et al., 1987), and also the development or attenuation of social bonds. Conger (1980) suggests that these learning processes provide instrumental value or meaning to behavior (acquisition of behavior definitions), opportunities for practice (imitation) and reinforcement, and exposure to definitions. Learning processes leading to deviance may occur in associations with deviant peers, through aversive negative experiences in conventional activities, or in the context of social disorganization that disrupts conventional social groups and activities (Sutherland & Cressey, 1978). Short (1989) suggests that both internal group processes and pressures from the external environment influence not only learning processes within gangs but also precisely what is learned.

The theoretical framework in this study proposes that social bonds develop through socialization experiences in the domains of family, school, peer groups, and neighborhood (Weis & Hawkins, 1981). Johnson et al. (1987) add religious influence as an early influence in social development. Fagan and Jones (1984) suggest that both positive and negative bonds can develop through socialization experiences in each domain. The model also specifies neighborhood influences on delinquency and substance use, a departure from earlier theoretical integrations that overlook the influence of youths' perceptions of neighborhood norms on illegal behavior and the influence of contextual factors.

Recent theoretical integrations also specify the temporal sequence of their influence. The causal paths hypothesized in the model may include nonrecursive reciprocal effects—that is, delinquency may disrupt social bonds (Thornberry & Christenson, 1984) and lead to problems in the family or at school. Therefore, bonding may be alternately a predictor and an outcome of deviance, or have reciprocal effects on the bonding-behavior relationship (Thornberry, 1987). The temporal sequence suggests that there is a cumulative effect of positive and negative bonding across domains that may influence gang involvement. Patterson and Dishion (1985), for example, found that poor maternal supervision weakened bonds in school and influenced bonding with delinquent peers.

Not only are gangs involved more often in illicit activity, but they also are adolescent groups. Accordingly, explanations of illicit behaviors among adolescents should be equally valid for gang and nongang youths. Because the relationship between substance use and delinquency is spurious and intrinsic to adolescent behaviors, these behaviors can be viewed as different manifestations of a general pattern of adolescent deviance and consequently share a common etiology. Shared explanations of deviance between gang and nongang youths also would portray gang participation as part of a continuum of adolescent peer networks that share parallel processes of learning and bonding, but differ in their behavioral norms (Schwendinger & Schwendinger, 1985). Accordingly, an integration of control and learning theories provides a testable set of hypotheses to examine the relationship between substance use and delinquency.

Methods

Samples

A general adolescent sample was constructed from three cities and neighborhoods: Chicago, Illinois (Wicker Park), Los Angeles, California (South Central), and San Diego, California (University Heights).[4] Fagan (1989) found no significant differences in types of gangs based on self-reports of gang members from these three neighborhoods. The research design employed two samples: a multistage cluster sample of high school students in each city, and a purposive, theoretical ("snowball") sample of high school dropouts (Biernacki & Waldorf, 1981). Samples included 200 students and 50 dropouts per study neighborhood. Respondents ranged in age from 13 to 20, were predominantly African-American and Hispanic, and included both males and females. Table 9.6, at the end of this chapter, provides details on the sample characteristics.

High school student samples were chosen from classrooms randomly selected from all classes in the schools that served youths from the target neighborhoods. Grades 9-12 were included in the survey. A random school day was selected within a two-month period for survey administration.

Ethnographic samples of school dropouts were recruited through chain-referral methods (snowball samples) within known dropout groups. The dropout sampling parameter, 25%, reflected a consensus of the high school principals in the three neighborhoods, though the reported rates varied from 15% to 45%. This strategy was used because none of the school districts kept accurate or comprehensive records of dropouts to allow specific sampling of individuals. The strategy ensured that no known or emerging dropout strata were either over- or underrepresented.

Chains were initiated through local social service agencies or community-based organizations to recruit dropouts from among known dropout populations: pregnant teens, working-class youth, non-English-speaking or foreign-born youth, and "official" (labeled) delinquents. Referrals were sought from social agencies that routinely dealt with dropouts. Advertisements were distributed through channels likely to reach them. For example, notices were posted and distributed in family planning clinics to teenage females who had sought services or advice. A short screening interview determined eligibility.

Both student and dropout respondents received stipends for their participation, in the form of either coupons from local record stores or T-shirts. These nominal stipends served as incentive as well as compensation for their time and participation. Participation was described as voluntary and anonymous. Neither names nor identifiers were recorded anywhere on the survey forms.

Gang Participation

Gang membership was determined by self-report. Gang members were asked whether they had belonged to a gang in the past year, and for how long. This strategy was chosen specifically to avoid the problems in definitions that have confounded gang research (see Klein & Maxson, 1989, and Chapter 3 of this volume; Morash, 1983, 1990; Spergel, 1989a). For example, official (police or social agency) definitions and rosters of gang membership often vary by city and agency, more often reflecting the organization of social control agencies than empirical realities about gang membership or gangs.

Self-selection avoided both these problems and the confounding of gang definitions with specific criminal or violent behaviors. This reduced validity threats due to subjective definitions and perceptions of gang crimes or violence. Because each neighborhood has had extensive and well-publicized gang activity for many years, youths from these neighborhoods were knowledgeable about and sensitive to the local gang scene. They arguably are the best judges of their own involvement in a constantly shifting gang scene, where official data are likely to lag behind actual events within gangs. The strategy, however, retained subjective definitions of *gang* and did not address varying types of participation in gangs.

The validity of respondents' self-reports of gang involvement was assessed through Pearson correlations of their reports of their behaviors and the behavior of their gangs, and Pearson correlations of their reports of gang behaviors and the behaviors of their "close friends." Reliability analyses showed comparable Cronbach's alpha scores (.70 or higher) for both gang and nongang youths.

Student and Dropout Survey Procedures

Student and dropout surveys were conducted twice: spring 1985 and fall 1985. Student surveys were conducted during regular study periods in classrooms in Chicago. In Los Angeles and San Diego, scheduling problems required that surveys be conducted immediately after school hours in an auditorium or large classroom capable of seating the 200 students. This procedure risked bias from exclusion of working youths or self-selection of participants with different motivations and interests. Ordinary least squares (OLS) regression analyses of delinquent involvement and substance use showed that the explained variance, univariate F tests, and order of entry of explanatory variables were comparable for the two survey procedures.

Dropout surveys were conducted in small groups of 10-15 youths in neighborhood facilities, with several scheduled time slots to accommodate youths with other commitments. To avoid repeats, volunteers from community groups familiar with neighborhood youth proctored the surveys and selected out repeaters. Together with members of the research staff, they kept informal logs of the number of each type (i.e., chain membership) of participant.

The survey schedule included demographic items, self-reported delinquency and drug use/sales measures, victimization items, and measures tapping social learning and control variables. For both student and dropout surveys, items were read aloud by research staff while respondents followed along on the survey form. The researchers also held up large displays of the response sets for sequences of items (e.g., self-reported delinquency items). In addition, proctors per session from the local neighborhood organizations walked through the classrooms or facilities to answer respondents' questions, provide other assistance, and randomly spot check for such errors as out-of-range codes.

Measures and Constructs

Self-reported delinquency (SRD) and substance use items were derived from the National Youth Survey items (Elliott et al., 1985), and included questions on delinquent behavior, alcohol and illicit drug use, and other problem behaviors. The original 47-item scales were modified in two ways. First, because the surveys were designed for adolescents in inner-city neighborhoods with high crime rates, adjustments were necessary to eliminate trivial offenses. Many behaviors in inner-city areas may be law violations but either would evoke no official action or are not perceived by local youth as illegal (Anderson & Rodriguez, 1984).[5] The items modified and retained were those that measured "high consensus" deviance (Thio, 1983), and included only acts that harm, injure, or do damage. Second, at the request of school officials, certain items in the original scales were eliminated, modified, or collapsed.[6] Other items—such as varying degrees of theft or minor assault—were collapsed to shorten administration time, again at the request of school officials.

The response set was a categorical set of frequencies, ranging from "never" to "once a year to monthly" to "2 to 3 times a week." [7] The recall period was 12 months, from "Christmas a year ago to this past Christmas" for spring surveys, and from "Labor Day a year ago until this past Labor Day" for fall surveys. Such anchoring techniques are consistent with other studies attempting to reconstruct behaviors for even trivial offenses (Speckart & Anglin, 1988). The items then were categorized into scales constructed from homogeneous crime types that are parallel with UCR categories.[8]

An index of delinquent involvement was constructed, called INDEX. Similar to ordinal scales developed and validated by Dunford and Elliott (1984) and Fagan et al. (1990), INDEX included dimensions of both severity and frequency of delinquent acts over the previous 12-month period. INDEX is a hierarchical typology in that less serious behaviors have been committed by those in successively more serious categories of offenders. Specific alcohol use, drug use, or drug-selling behaviors and incidents of intoxication are not considered in the typology. The categories range from petty acts (e.g., going to school high or drunk) to index felonies. Drug sales, a felony offense in all three study cities, was classified as a serious offense.[9]

The questions and response sets for alcohol and drug use items followed the same format and response sets as the SRD items. DRUG SALES was included as an SRD item, as was "driving while drunk or high" and "attending school while drunk or high." Questions about personal use of substances were included in separate items. Two alcohol items (beer or wine; whiskey, gin, vodka, or other liquor) and seven illicit drugs (marijuana, cocaine, heroin or opiates, hallucinogens, amphetamines or "speed," barbiturates or "downers," and inhalants or "glue-sniffing") were asked. The general format also asked, "How often in the past year, from [time anchor] a year ago until this past [time anchor] did you . . . ?" Categorical response sets again were employed.

Drug-specific scales involved the frequency of use of each substance. An index of the severity of drug involvement also was constructed, based on dimensions of the severity and frequency of drug use. Called DRUGTYPE, the scale specifies nonexperimental use (three times or more in the past year) of cocaine, opiates, or PCP as the most serious, with experimental use (less than three times) as the next level, followed by chronic use of marijuana or alcohol (more than 12 times per year) and other trivial use of marijuana or alcohol as the least serious category.

Explanatory variable sets were derived from the integrated theory described above. Sources of social development were hypothesized in three areas: social bonding to conventional norms and beliefs, social environments that influence the strength and direction of bonds and that may directly influence behavior, and psychosocial development of cognitive skills. The definitions of each scale are described in Table 9.7, presented at the end of the chapter.

Drug and alcohol problem scales were patterned after similar items in Jessor and Jessor (1977), Elliott and Huizinga (1984), and White et al. (1987). Self-reports of drug and alcohol problem behaviors were preferred to standardized scales or official records. These scales (DRUG PROBLEMS, DRINKING PROBLEMS) each included six items, reflecting negative social and personal consequences of alcohol or drug use. Each scale asked if the respondent "ever felt you had a drug (or alcohol) problem." Also, separate items asked whether in the past year "you have had a problem with your family, friends, girlfriend or boyfriend, in school, or with the police because of your drug use (or drinking)." Additional items asked if the respondent had gotten into fights or been arrested "because of drinking (or drug use)." Finally, respondents were asked if they had sought treatment, been in treatment, or been told to seek treatment for drinking or drug use in the past year.

Overall, these measures have strong explanatory power in both cross-sectional and longitudinal studies of serious delinquency, under a variety of sampling conditions. Fagan, Piper, and Moore (1986) validated these measures with samples of institutionalized and general-population male adolescents from inner-city neighborhoods, while Fagan and colleagues (Fagan, Piper, & Cheng, 1987; Fagan et al., 1990) validated the items with both males and females in inner-city neighborhoods. Validity was confirmed through selected bivariate correlations with theoretical variables whose independent relationships with drug use and delinquency also are well established.[10] The correlation coefficients were all significant and in the correct directions. Reliability analyses included calculation of consistency measures (Cronbach's alpha) for each scale, and again for theoretically important subgroups: males and females, students and dropouts, and site-specific calculations. In general, reliabilities were at least adequate (alpha = .70) or excellent (alpha = .90) for the total sample and for four delinquent types.

Results

Incidence and Prevalence Among Gang and Nongang Youths

Table 9.1 summarizes self-reported substance use and delinquency of gang and nongang youths during the past year. Three dimensions of each type of behavior are shown. *Prevalence* or *participation* is the percentage who reported at least one incident of the specific behavior measured. The significance of chi-square tests is reported for male-female differences among gang and nongang youths for each type of behavior. The *participation rate* for each behavior is the mean number of offenses in the past year for those who reported at least one incident. The *incidence* of each behavior is the mean number of acts for the specific population. For both participation rates and incidence, the results of two-way ANOVA tests are reported for effects of both gang involvement and gender.

Prevalence

The prevalence of self-reported delinquency and substance use was far greater for gang youths compared to nongang youths for all 12 behavior categories. Among nondrug behaviors, the highest prevalence rates were reported by male gang members (49.2%) for both FELONY and MINOR THEFT. The lowest prevalence rates were reported by female nongang members (4.4%) for ROBBERY. For drug- and alcohol-related behaviors, the highest prevalence rates were reported by male gang members (72.0%) for DRUG USE. The lowest rates were reported by nongang females (4.4%) for DRUG SALES. There were few differences between violent and nonviolent behaviors for each group.

TABLE 9.1:   Participation, Rate, and Past Year Frequency in Drug Use and Delinquency for Gang and Nongang Youths

Offense Type	Nongang			Gang			p(F)		
	Male	Female	p(χ)²	Male	Female	p(χ)²	Gang	Sex	Sex by Gang
FELONY ASSAULT									
%	11.0	7.2	n.s.	45.6	28.7	c			
λ	14.8	17.3		23.1	24.5		n.s.	n.s.	n.s.
x̄	1.6	1.1		10.1	5.8		a	n.s.	c
MINOR ASSAULT									
%	8.0	7.2	n.s.	37.8	23.0	c			
λ	10.3	11.1		13.0	20.1		n.s.	n.s.	n.s.
x̄	0.8	0.8		5.0	4.7		a	n.s.	n.s.
ROBBERY									
%	10.1	4.4	b	42.0	23.0	c			
λ	25.3	38.6		34.3	46.7		n.s.	n.s.	n.s.
x̄	2.5	1.5		14.1	10.9		a	n.s.	n.s.
FELONY THEFT									
%	16.2	7.4	a	49.2	27.6	b			
λ	19.2	20.6		46.1	44.5		a	n.s.	n.s.
x̄	3.0	1.4		20.7	11.1		a	b	b
MINOR THEFT									
%	17.3	16.4	n.s.	49.2	28.7	b			
λ	20.6	14.2		26.5	34.0		b	n.s.	n.s.
x̄	3.5	2.3		12.7	9.0		a	n.s.	n.s.
EXTORTION									
%	14.8	11.0	n.s.	45.6	34.5	n.s.			
λ	28.2	21.8		37.4	38.9		n.s.	n.s.	n.s.
x̄	4.2	2.4		17.1	13.6		a	n.s.	n.s.

(Continued)

Sex differences were reported more often for gang youths than for nongang youths. Male gang members were involved significantly more often in 8 of the 12 behaviors. Only for EXTORTION, PROPERTY DAMAGE, ALCOHOL USE, and DRUG SALES were sex differences not significant for gang members. Among

TABLE 9.1: (Continued)

| Offense Type | Nongang | | | Gang | | | $p(F)$ | | |
	Male	Female	$p(\chi)^2$	Male	Female	$p(\chi)^2$	Gang	Sex	Sex by Gang
PROPERTY DAMAGE									
%	12.4	7.6	c	37.8	24.1	n.s.			
λ	12.2	13.7		19.6	20.0		c	n.s.	n.s.
$\bar{x}$	1.5	1.1		7.5	4.9		a	n.s.	n.s.
WEAPONS									
%	17.6	14.0	n.s.	42.5	27.6	c			
λ	14.4	17.3		25.7	18.2		c	n.s.	n.s.
$\bar{x}$	2.5	2.4		10.0	5.0		a	n.s.	b
ILLEGAL SERVICES									
%	23.2	10.6	a	48.7	32.2	c			
λ	11.4	17.1		39.0	35.7		a	n.s.	n.s.
$\bar{x}$	2.6	1.8		19.0	11.5		a	n.s.	n.s.
ALCOHOL USE									
%	29.7	26.3	n.s.	67.4	59.8	n.s.			
λ	27.9	26.9		60.9	45.9		a	n.s.	n.s.
$\bar{x}$	8.4	7.1		41.2	27.7		a	n.s.	c
DRUG USE									
%	32.8	32.7	n.s.	72.0	56.3	c			
λ	42.4	34.5		77.2	66.8		a	n.s.	n.s.
$\bar{x}$	14.0	11.3		55.8	38.0		a	c	c
DRUG SALES									
%	8.9	4.4	b	33.7	23.0	n.s.			
λ	23.2	26.8		43.6	38.1		b	n.s.	n.s.
$\bar{x}$	2.1	1.2		14.7	8.9		a	c	c

a. $p < .001$
b. $p < .01$
c. $p < .05$

nongang youths, prevalence rates for males were significantly higher for five behaviors. Although females were involved less often in delinquency and substance use for each
group, prevalence rates for female gang members exceed the
rates for nongang males for all 12 behavior categories.

Participation Rates

The participation or offending rates for those involved at all in the past year also show that gang members are involved significantly more often in all behaviors except violence. Significant differences in participation rates between gang and nongang youths were found for all behaviors except FELONY and MINOR ASSAULT, ROBBERY, and EXTORTION. There were no significant sex-gang interaction effects for these or any other categories. Evidently, the frequency of violence for those involved at least once is independent of gang involvement. For example, the small number of nongang females involved in ROBBERY reported more than 38 events in the past year, a rate slightly higher than that for the males in gangs.

Drug and alcohol use behaviors were the most frequent events for both gang and nongang youth. Gang members had higher participation rates than nongang youths for DRUG and ALCOHOL USE and for DRUG SALES.

Table 9.1 also shows that there were no significant main effects for sex or significant sex-gang interactions for any category. Although participation rates were higher for gang members than nongang youth for nonviolent behaviors, there were no significant male-female differences within each group for any of the 12 categories. Accordingly, the effects of gender on drug and nondrug delinquency seem to influence the decision to participate in deviant behaviors rather than the frequency of participation.

Incidence

Table 9.1 shows that the frequency of drug and nondrug delinquent acts was significantly higher for gang members for each of the 12 behaviors. Significant sex-gang interaction effects were found for 6 behaviors. Overall, violent behaviors in the past year were less frequent than other behaviors, particularly felony theft and extortion.

The pattern for incidence rates more closely reflects the patterns for prevalence estimates than the participation or offending rates. These measurement distinctions reveal important differences in violent behaviors between gang and nongang youths. There was little evidence of offense specialization for gang or nongang youths. Although more gang members are involved in violence, the frequency of their participation apparently is no greater than that of nongang youths, and they also are involved extensively in several types of property crimes. When gang members are considered in the aggregate, however, incidence estimates portray gang members as a more violent group than nongang youths. Despite versatility in offending patterns for both gang and nongang youths, there appear to be a "violent few" within each group.

Whether inside or outside the gang, the frequency of violence appears to be similar for those involved at all in violence. Yet more gang members are involved in violence. The context of gang life may offer more opportunities for violence, thus explaining the higher prevalence rates of violence among gang members. At the same time, there may be a self- or social selection of violent individuals into gang life that contributes to more frequent violence within gangs. Group norms and status organizing processes also may explain the higher prevalence of violence among gang members. Nevertheless, these distinctions were not evident for other behaviors. Accordingly, individual differences between gang and nongang youths involved in violence may be less important than the context of gang involvement and microsocial interactions between gang members in explaining their higher aggregate rates of violence.

Severity of Delinquent Involvement and Substance Use

Gang members vary by role, reason for affiliation, and extent of participation in delinquent activities and substance use (Klein & Maxson, 1989; Spergel, 1989). Participation in gang activities may shift over time as members move in and out of various roles. Roles within gangs also may vary according to type of activity: Leaders for drug selling may differ from leaders or soldiers in "gang-banging" (Hagedorn, 1988; Moore, 1978; Vigil, 1988a). Spergel (1989a) refers to gang members who shift roles as "floaters." Despite the diversity and fluidity of gang affiliation and roles, there is consensus that core members are

TABLE 9.2: Severity of Drug Use and Delinquent Involvement for Gang and Nongang Youths

	Nongang		Gang	
	Males	Females	Males	Females
N	427	499	193	87
Delinquent involvement (%)				
petty	59.0	67.5	15.5	40.2
minor	12.6	12.2	13.0	16.1
serious	11.5	12.0	15.5	10.3
multiple index	16.9	8.2	56.0	33.3
Substance use involvement (%)				
nonuser	61.3	61.1	24.4	31.4
alcohol	5.5	6.0	3.6	11.6
marijuana	21.4	22.4	29.0	25.6
cocaine, heroin, PCP	11.9	10.5	43.0	31.4
Significance		Chi-Square	p	
Delinquent involvement by gang				
males		126.9	.000	
females		48.9	.000	
Substance use by gang				
males		99.7	.000	
females		38.7	.000	

involved in a wider range of more serious delinquent acts than are fringe or situational members. Table 9.2 shows the severity of delinquent involvement (INDEX) and substance abuse (DRUG-TYPE) for gang and nongang youths.

Delinquent Involvement

The severity of delinquent involvement was greater for both male and female gang youths. Chi-square tests comparing males and females by gang involvement were significant ($p = .000$). For both males and females, significantly more gang members had the most serious involvement in each behavior ($p = .000$). More than half (56.0%) of the male gang members were classified as MULTIPLE INDEX offenders, compared with

16.9% of the nongang youths. In fact, there were more male gang members classified in the most serious category than in the least serious category! One in three female gang youths (33.3%) was classified as a MULTIPLE INDEX offender, compared with fewer than 1 in 12 nongang females (8.2%). There also were diverse patterns among gang members, however, in the severity and frequency of their delinquent involvement.

The delinquent involvement of female gang members differed substantially from that of males. Among males, nearly three in five (59.0%) nongang youths were classified in the least serious category, PETTY DELINQUENTS, compared with only 15.5% of the gang youths. But more than 40% of the female gang members were classified in the least serious category, a substantial difference from their male counterparts. Among female gang members, there was a bimodal distribution, with nearly as many multiple index offenders as petty delinquents. Evidently, female gang members avoid more serious delinquent involvement than their male counterparts. Yet their extensive involvement in serious delinquent behaviors well exceeds that of nongang males or females.

Substance Use

Patterns of substance use involvement were similar to patterns of delinquent involvement. Chi-square tests comparing males and females by gang involvement were significant ($p = .000$). Table 9.2 shows that among both males and females, the percentage of gang members with the most serious involvement equaled or surpassed the percentage with the least serious involvement. Frequent cocaine, heroin, and PCP use was greater among both male and female gang youths, with relatively small differences between males and females.

Among both male and female nongang youths, the opposite pattern occurred: More than three in five youths (over 61%) were classified as nonusers. Among gang members, only 24.4% of the males and 31.4% of the females were classified as nonusers. Table 9.2 also shows diversity among all youths in their involvement in substance use.

The bimodal distribution of delinquent involvement was not evident for substance use—substantial percentages of gang youths were classified as nonusers and marijuana users (from 21.4% to 31.4%) as well as serious substance users. Although many more nongang youths were nonusers, gang and nongang youths differed little in their involvement in alcohol and marijuana use. Few youths confined their substance use to alcohol; if involved with any substance, they appeared to use other drugs as well.[11] Evidently, regular marijuana use is a natural social behavior among inner-city youths: over 32% of both gang and nongang youths were involved in marijuana use.

The Association Between Delinquency and Substance Use

Finally, the association between substance use and delinquency was analyzed. Among general youth populations nationally (Elliott et al., 1985), in local samples (White et al., 1987), and in inner cities (Fagan et al., 1990), serious substance use and serious delinquency were strongly—although perhaps spuriously—associated. If both delinquency and substance use are intrinsic to gang life, however, their association should be stronger for gang youths than for nongang youths. To examine this question, the INDEX and DRUGTYPE scales were cross-tabulated for gang and nongang youths and males and females. Table 9.3 shows the percentages of each group that were both nonusers and petty delinquents (the least seriously involved group), the percentages that were both multiple index offenders and serious substance users (the joint occurrence of the two most serious behaviors), the Pearson correlation and gamma coefficients, and the chi-square statistics for each analysis.

Table 9.3 shows that the percentage of gang youths who are both multiple index offenders and serious substance users far exceeds the percentage of nongang youths. Conversely, substantially more nongang youths were both nonusers and petty delinquents compared with gang youths. That is, far more nongang youths avoided all forms of deviant behavior than did gang youths. The table also shows that there is a bimodal distribution in the joint occurrence of these behaviors among nongang females. These trends were evident for both males and females. The relationships are statistically significant for all four groups.

TABLE 9.3: The Delinquency–Substance Use Association for Gang and Nongang Youths

	Nongang		Gang	
Statistic	Male	Female	Male	Female
Percentage nonuser and petty delinquent	48.7	50.3	9.8	25.3
Percentage serious users and multiple index	8.0	5.0	36.3	24.1
Gamma	.71	.66	.64	.69
Pearson R	.55***	.50***	.50***	.59***
Chi-square	119.4***	197.4***	68.1***	55.5***

***p = .000.

The joint occurrence of these behaviors is more common among gang youths than among nongang youths, as is their separate occurrence. Evidently, involvement in gang activities—or association with gang members—strengthens the drug-delinquency relationship. Other research, however, also shows the complexity and diversity of this relationship among gang youths and the importance of specific contexts in determining whether the relationship is causal or spurious (Fagan, 1989; Vigil, 1988a).

Social Development and Gang Participation

The validity of an integrated theory of social development to explain gang participation was assessed by analysis of theoretical variables for gang and nongang youth. Factor analyses with varimax (orthogonal) rotations were used to analyze patterns of covariation and to reduce the theoretical measures to a set of salient explanatory dimensions. Table 9.8 (at the end of this chapter) shows the rotated factor coefficients and explained variance for each factor. Factor scores were retained and serve as independent variables in analyses of gang participation, delinquency, and substance use.

Principal components analyses with varimax rotation yielded nine factors that explained 58.9% of the variance. The factors show convergence of individual and social environmental influences within specific social domains. That is, factors for family, peers, and neighborhood combine measures of both *integration* and *commitment* in single dimensions, as well as their perceptions of social norms for that domain.

The first factor, SUBSTANCE ABUSE PROBLEMS, explained 15.9% of the variance. It includes high coefficients for variables associated with substance use problems and behaviors while intoxicated. The second factor, VICTIMIZATION, explained 10.3% of the variance and includes measures of victimization experiences from both property and violent crimes. Both personal victimization and perceptions of the victimization of others are represented in this factor. The third factor, PEER AND GANG DELINQUENCY, includes items and scales that measured respondents' perceptions of delinquent behaviors among their close friends or "in your gang." [12]

FAMILY INTEGRATION includes measures of both family attachment and parental authority. Separate items for both mother and father are included. CONVENTIONAL BELIEFS represent variables concerning belief in the legitimacy of law, the rejection of attitudes supporting violence, and perceived control over the events in one's life. Perceptions of family violence and other criminal behaviors among neighbors are represented in the factor labeled NEIGHBORHOOD VIOLENCE. SOCIAL INTEGRATION and NEIGHBORHOOD INTEGRATION are factors that represent involvement in social domains such as school, work, and neighborhood. [13] SCHOOL AND GANG VIOLENCE reflects respondents' perceptions of violence within schools or violence by gangs in neighborhoods.

Table 9.4 shows results of univariate analyses for each factor to distinguish gang and nongang youths. Analyses of variance compared each of the nine factor scores by gang participation and gender. Covariates were included for age and the length of time in the gang. For those respondents who reported ever being in a gang, an item asked respondents how many years they had been in the gang. For nongang youth, this was scored as zero. Main effects were adjusted for the effects of covariates.

Main effects for gang participation were found for only three factors: VICTIMIZATION, PEER AND GANG DELINQUENCY, and CON-

TABLE 9.4: Social Development Factor Scores for Gang and Nongang Youths (Analysis of Variance)

| | Nongang | | Gang | | Significance (p[F]) | | | | |
| | | | | | Main Effects | | | Covariates | |
Social Factors	Males	Females	Males	Females	Gang	Sex	Gang by Sex	Age	Gang Time
SUBSTANCE ABUSE PROBLEMS	.03	−.20	.45	.06	n.s.	a	n.s.	c	a
VICTIMIZATION	.02	−.12	.22	.12	a	c	n.s.	c	n.s.
PEER AND GANG DELINQUENCY	−.29	−.31	1.19	.81	a	n.s.	b	b	a
FAMILY INTEGRATION	−.13	.15	−.15	.12	n.s.	a	n.s.	b	n.s.
CONVENTIONAL BELIEFS	−.12	.21	−.24	−.10	a	a	n.s.	a	a
NEIGHBORHOOD VIOLENCE	.03	−.05	.11	−.11	n.s.	n.s.	n.s.	c	n.s.
SOCIAL INTEGRATION	−.11	.11	−.09	.13	n.s.	a	n.s.	a	c
NEIGHBORHOOD INTEGRATION	.07	−.05	.05	−.19	n.s.	c	n.s.	n.s.	n.s.
SCHOOL AND GANG VIOLENCE	−.08	.11	−.13	.04	n.s.	a	n.s.	b	n.s.

a. $p < .001$
b. $p < .01$
c. $p < .05$

VENTIONAL BELIEFS. Differences are in the expected directions.
Age was a significant covariate for all factors that had significant main effects. Time in the gang was a significant covariate
for two of the three variables with significant main effects. Male
gang members again revealed their social distance from the
other groups. The factor scores were highest for SUBSTANCE
ABUSE PROBLEMS, VICTIMIZATION, PEER DELINQUENCY, and their
perceptions of NEIGHBORHOOD VIOLENCE. Their scores also
indicate the weakest FAMILY INTEGRATION and CONVENTIONAL
BELIEFS. Female gang members differ from male gang members
in several areas: They have stronger FAMILY and SOCIAL INTE-
GRATION and fewer SUBSTANCE ABUSE PROBLEMS, but weaker
NEIGHBORHOOD INTEGRATION. These differences suggest the
possibility of different etiological factors of gang participation
for male and female gang members.

Table 9.4 offers only partial support for the theoretical
integration in distinguishing gang participants from nongang
youths. The contribution of PEER AND GANG INFLUENCES suggests that gang involvement may reflect processes of differential association, because gangs are an important primary group
influence in the socially disorganized inner-city study locales.
The VICTIMIZATION factor suggests that gang members participate in a more dangerous milieu and routine activities with
higher risks. The significant effect for CONVENTIONAL BELIEFS
shows the generally weak social bonds among gang members
compared with nongang youths. The negative factor score for
CONVENTIONAL BELIEFS for nongang males suggests in turn that
inner-city youths are not well rooted in their beliefs in the law.
The weaker conventional beliefs among gang youths, however,
further illustrate their marginal status within an already marginalized adolescent population.

The remaining factors did not differ significantly for gang and
nongang youths. Participation in conventional social roles and
activities in families, schools, and elsewhere in the neighborhood did not differ significantly for gang and nongang youths,
suggesting that conventional values may coexist with deviant
behaviors for inner-city youths. The factors that distinguish
gang youths seem to reflect the norms and activities that
prevail in their social networks, rather than unique social

psychological processes that influence behavior. Other factors not included in these analyses, however, may also explain the decision of gang members to participate in that world.

Explanations of Delinquency and Drug Use for Gang and Nongang Youths

The inner-city youths in this study live in areas where social controls have weakened and opportunities for success in legitimate activities are limited. Nevertheless, participation in gangs is selective, and most youths avoid gang life. If the factors that explain substance use and delinquency differ for gang and nongang youths, then theories of gang participation and behaviors should incorporate unique factors to explain the behaviors of gang members compared with other inner-city youths. But if the correlates of gang delinquency among inner-city youths are approximately the same for nongang youths, then gang participation may not be a cause of delinquency, but a facilitator of it. In turn, the factors that explain the higher rates of delinquency among gang youths may lie in the social organization of gangs and their development in specific social and historic contexts.

Table 9.5 shows the results of OLS regression analyses comparing the predictors of substance use and nondrug delinquency for gang and nongang youths. Models were constructed with the frequency (total self-reported delinquent acts and substance-use occasions in the past year) and severity (INDEX, DRUGTYPE) of each behavior as dependent variables. Independent variables included the nine factor scores and dummy variables for gender (male), ethnicity (African-American and Hispanic), age, and (for gang youths only) time in the gang. All explanatory variables were entered into each equation as a set to facilitate comparisons across models.

All models were significant. Explained variance was greater for the models for gang members for all independent variables. For gang youths, explained variance was highest for the frequency of delinquent acts (42.3%) and least for both the severity of delinquent involvement (34.6%) and severity of substance use (35.4%). For nongang youths, explained vari-

TABLE 9.5: OLS Regression Models of Self-Reported Drug Use and Delinquency for Gang and Nongang Youths, Controlling for Gender and Ethnicity (standardized regression coefficients, significance of F)

Variables	Delinquent Involvement		Frequency of Delinquent Acts		Most Serious Substance Used		Frequency of Substance Use	
	Nongang	Gang	Nongang	Gang	Nongang	Gang	Nongang	Gang
Male	-.003	.124*	-.078**	-.018	-.111***	-.038	-.094**	-.021
Age	-.030	.017	-.026	-.059	-.056	.090	-.032	-.027
Time in gang	—	-.025	—	.226***	—	.006	—	.153**
Social Factors								
SUBSTANCE ABUSE PROBLEMS	.309***	.355***	.474***	.463***	.342***	.465***	.436***	.490***
VICTIMIZATION	.286***	.096	.215***	.051	.298***	.107*	.244***	.033
PEER AND GANG DELINQUENCY	.281***	.235***	.255***	.073	.183***	.165***	.198***	.088
FAMILY INTEGRATION	-.070*	-.203***	-.048	-.174***	-.081**	-.278***	-.061*	-.230***
CONVENTIONAL BELIEFS	-.212***	-.273***	-.163***	-.211***	-.137***	-.169*	-.159***	-.203***
NEIGHBORHOOD VIOLENCE	-.058*	-.027	-.064*	-.051	-.011	-.024	.004	.008
SOCIAL INTEGRATION	-.067*	-.214***	-.082**	-.094*	-.079**	-.225***	-.100***	-.095
NEIGHBORHOOD INTEGRATION	.078**	-.110*	.002	-.103*	.084**	-.024	.001	-.098*
SCHOOL AND GANG CRIMES	.009	-.078	-.029	-.148**	.010	-.068	-.008	-.075
Ethnicity								
AFRICAN-AMERICAN	-.093	.039	-.058	-.139	-.009	.027	-.090	-.194*
HISPANIC	-.171**	.045	-.031	-.158*	-.039	.052	-.067	-.158*
F (model)	26.1***	11.6***	28.4***	15.7***	19.3***	11.9***	24.0***	14.4***
Adjusted R^2	.261	.346	.278	.423	.205	.354	.244	.403

*$p < .05$; **$p < .001$; ***$p < .000$.

208

ance ranged from 20.5% for severity of substance use to 27.8% for frequency of delinquent acts.

Examining the four models, SUBSTANCE ABUSE PROBLEMS was the only consistent predictor, illustrating the strong association between substance use and delinquency for adolescents in inner cities. PEER AND GANG INFLUENCES were strong predictors for all variables for nongang youths, but only for the two severity indices for gang youths. Conversely, VICTIMIZATION experiences were strong predictors only for nongang youths. Gang and nongang youths differed for all models for FAMILY INTEGRATION, and for SOCIAL INTEGRATION for the two severity models. Predictors in the other models varied by both the dependent variable and gang participation. The coefficients for age, gender, and ethnicity were generally weak across models compared with the explanatory variables. Time in the gang was a salient predictor only for the frequency of delinquent acts.

The results suggest that the theoretical variables are relatively weak contributors to delinquency and substance use for gang and nongang youths, with the exception of the important contributions of SUBSTANCE ABUSE PROBLEMS and PEER INFLU- ENCES. The consistently high coefficients for these factors suggest that substance use and delinquency share common explanations and, for both gang and nongang youths, may be manifestations of a generalized pattern of deviant behaviors. The absence of high coefficients for age, gender, and ethnicity further illustrates the generality of deviance in this sample. The weak coefficients for all but one of the predictor variables suggests that the higher delinquency rates of gang youths may not result from differences in explanatory factors. That is, these rates do not seem to be attributable to social processes unique to gang members.

The involvement of both gang and nongang youths in serious substance use and delinquency suggests that gangs are only one of several deviant peer groups in inner cities. Among male gang members, Fagan (1989) found several types of gangs with varying involvement in substance use, drug selling, and other delinquency. Evidently, there are qualitatively different peer networks that exert parallel but independent influences of peer relationships and problems associated with delinquency and substance abuse. To understand why gangs differ from other youths in their participation in delinquency and substance use, while reflecting natural adolescent social processes and influences, we must look to the social and historic context of the gang itself.

Conclusions

Although gangs may be distinct social networks that are involved more extensively than other networks in substance use and crime, there appears to be diversity among gang members and gangs in their participation in these behaviors. Both gang and nongang youths are involved in serious delinquency and substance use, although perhaps fewer nongang youths participate in these behaviors and do so less often. Accordingly, "gangs" actually may encompass groups that are quite variable in their behaviors and represent one of several types of peer networks among inner-city youths with parallel network properties. Group processes are intrinsic to adolescent networks that encompass a wide range of behaviors, including such diverse groups as fraternities, the Guardian Angels, military groups units, athletic teams, street-corner groups, and youth gangs.

Nevertheless, gangs and gang members lie at the extremes of the distribution of deviant behaviors among inner-city youths. Rather than examine the individual characteristics of gang members to explain their behaviors, this chapter suggests that the natural organization and social processes of adolescent peer networks may explain their variable involvement in illegal activities. In turn, the processes that sustain gang formation and gang participation become the crucial factors in explaining differences between gang and nongang peer networks.

Over 50 years ago, Thrasher (1927) noted that gangs formed under conditions of social disorganization that in turn created social instability. More recently, Curry and Spergel (1988) linked these processes to residential mobility, poverty, and other social structural variables. Thrasher noted the isolation of "interstitial areas" from their surrounding society, where formal and informal social controls were either absent or attenuated. The social isolation of gangs from both legitimate economic opportunity and routine interactions with the larger society, and the absence of formal and informal social controls in their social areas, may launch social processes within gangs that contribute to their behavioral norms and the unique strength of their social networks.

The economic and social transformations of inner cities in the past 10 years have further closed the social systems within which gangs form and develop (Hagedorn, 1988; Moore, 1989a; Sullivan, 1989). As cities have changed, so too has gang change and variation occurred (Hagedorn, 1988; Huff, 1989a; Moore, 1989b; Spergel, 1989a). Since Thrasher's and other early studies in Chicago, and later gang studies in Chicago (Short & Strodtbeck, 1956) and other cities (e.g., Cloward & Ohlin, 1960; Cohen, 1955; Klein & Crawford, 1967), gangs may have become quasi-institutionalized. They compete for status and authority with other social institutions such as school and church, evidently with success. As inner cities have changed for the worse, street socialization also has become more important. The social networks of adolescents within schools and among neighbors have been weakened by the removal of social and economic capital over the past 25 years, tipping the balance of economic opportunities from the formal to the informal and from the legitimate to the illegal (Hochschild, 1989; Wacquant & Wilson, 1989). In this context, the socialization of adolescents becomes skewed toward processes where episodic and situational bonds to gangs evolve into lasting ties within the gang's social network.

How these temporary bonds develop into more lasting ones is a critical question. Delinquency is largely a group enterprise (Erickson & Jensen, 1977; Reiss, 1986), and the milieu of gangs may alter the semiotic meaning of group crimes. Gangs offer a wide variety of opportunities and services: status, economic opportunity, affiliation, and protection. If schools, families, and legal institutions are weak in inner cities, gangs have a near monopoly on status-conferring activities. Some also exert their own forms of social control to regulate behaviors among their members. The formation of alternative economies in inner cities also contributes to the salience of gangs as providers of opportunities, both social and economic.

In studies of initiation into gang life, it was apparent that participants did not carefully calculate the rewards and risks of participation, nor were they pressured by subcultural values (Fagan, 1989; Hagedorn, 1988; Horowitz, 1983; Keiser, 1969; Moore, 1978). Rather, gang members drifted into gang life, taking advantage of opportunities presented for money, status, protection, and social life. Their socialization into the gang reflected processes of social learning: the rewards of gang participation, the opportunities for practice of gang norms, and the teaching of functional value of gang participation. In addition, role engulfment within a network of relationships often serves to minimize attachments to people in other networks (Eckland-Olsen, 1982). These processes may explain the strength of the interpersonal bonds within gangs, and in turn the reification of the behavioral norms within their social networks.

Whether gangs have transformed in this decade from tenuous situational networks (Klein & Maxson, 1989; Spergel, 1989a) to deviant traditions is uncertain. As inner cities are changing, so too are gangs, which inevitably reflect the social disorganization and erosion of social controls that accompany the intensification of poverty. Lacking other opportunities, gangs may become a primary social influence, increase in importance, and in turn solidify their social networks. Research on gang members in jails or prisons suggests that they may play an increasingly important role in the maintenance of gang influence and strengthening of interpersonal bonds among their members (Moore, 1978; Skolnick et al., 1988). Understanding these processes may require research using the paradigm of network analysis to examine the size and stability of gang networks. Important questions should focus on how bonds form, are maintained, and disappear in gang networks; the social processes that sustain "groupness"; and the unintended contributions of social control to the hardening of network boundaries and social processes.

Future Research

The limitations of this research suggest directions for further research. The reports of "past year" behaviors overlook longer involvements and shifting patterns over time and by status or role within the gang. Rand's (1988) analysis suggests the importance of temporal order of onset of behaviors and gang affiliation. Self-reports of gang membership and involvement in collective and individual gang crimes and violence—always ambiguous and dependent on context and situational factors— also raise validity questions and avenues for future research. If new drug markets have skewed gang activities, for example, then the subjective meaning of "collective" gang behavior may have changed dramatically (see Taylor, 1990, and Chapter 4 of this volume).

Using life-event histories and ethnographic methods within the framework of network analysis, new research should examine the processes of gang affiliation and cohesion, and in turn the factors that explain how behavioral norms within groups develop and change over time. This is especially critical to the question of gang developments in response to new drug markets and the transformation of cities. The nature of collective violence may evolve as gangs evolve toward more instrumental goals and adapt to the changing social and economic climate in their cities. Analyses of gang and nongang networks should focus on the microsocial interactions within peer groups and their relation to external factors, especially the surrounding community, its economic opportunities, and its mechanisms of social control.

Females in gangs appear to be involved extensively in versatile patterns of illegal behaviors. Their involvement may indicate the changing status of girls within gangs, within illegal markets, within communities where male gang members frequently are incarcerated, or the evolution of female gangs within changing social and economic contexts. The nature of their affiliation with male gangs also may reflect on the social networks that emerge in the present context of inner cities. Whether the etiology of female gang participation and female gangs differs from that of male gangs evidently also is a valid question for future research (see Chapter 8 of this volume).

TABLE 9.6:   Demographic and Socioeconomic Characteristics of Gang
              and Nongang Youths

Demographic and Socioeconomic Characteristics (%)	Nongang		Gang		p (chi-square)	
	Male	Female	Male	Female	Male	Female
N	427	499	193	87		
Age					n.s.	c
14 or less	5.9	6.2	5.2	10.3		
15	20.4	15.2	17.6	25.3		
16	25.1	28.5	29.5	21.8		
17 or more	48.7	50.1	47.7	42.5		
Race					n.s.	c
White	2.3	1.2	4.7	3.4		
Black	71.9	76.1	65.8	78.2		
Hispanic	21.8	18.4	24.9	12.6		
Asian	3.0	3.6	2.1	4.6		
other	0.9	0	2.6	1.1		
School status					a	n.s.
student	82.9	94.6	61.7	89.7		
dropout	17.1	5.4	38.3	10.3		
Living with:					n.s.	n.s.
birth parents	31.4	30.5	24.9	21.8		
parent/stepparent	9.1	9.4	11.9	14.9		
single parent	48.7	51.7	54.4	57.5		
other adult/independent	10.8	8.4	8.8	5.7		
Parents' employment					n.s.	n.s.
none	22.7	24.6	24.9	17.2		
mother only	15.5	16.0	16.1	20.7		
father only	14.3	14.8	18.1	13.8		
both parents	47.5	44.5	40.9	48.3		
Parents' education					n.s.	n.s.
less than high school graduate	39.3	32.9	37.8	25.3		
high school graduate	18.7	25.1	22.3	24.1		
college graduate	41.9	42.1	39.9	50.6		

NOTE: Chi-square statistics for comparisons of gang and nongang youths within gender.
a. $p < .001$.
b. $p < .01$.
c. $p < .05$.

TABLE 9.7:   Definitions of Constructs and Measures

ATTITUDES TOWARD LAW: approval for law-violating behaviors

ATTITUDES TOWARD VIOLENCE: approval for violent behaviors, especially support for use of violence for instrumental gain or to exert personal power

CONVENTIONAL VALUES: an index of conformity based on the personal importance of attainment of social status and material goods

SCHOOL INTEGRATION: participation in school activities, achievement and performance in school, relationships with teachers and other students

ASPIRATION VS. REALITY: the extent to which respondent feels blocked in his or her efforts to achieve educational goals

PEER INTEGRATION: the strength of respondent's immersion in a peer group and personal involvement with his or her peers

FATHER ATTACHMENT: respect and emulation of parent figures, involvement of parent figures in respondent's emotional and social well-being (e.g., talking about school or personal problems)

MOTHER ATTACHMENT: same as father attachment for mother or mother figure

FATHER AUTHORITY: father or father-figure supervision practices, disciplinary practices, and rule setting in the home

MOTHER AUTHORITY: same as father authority, for mother or mother figure

NEIGHBORHOOD FAMILY VIOLENCE: violence within neighborhood families on the same residential block or in the same neighborhood

STUDENT DELINQUENCY: crimes in school by other students—percentage of students who commit specific criminal acts within schools

PEER DELINQUENCY: crimes by peers—percentage of peers outside of school who commit specific criminal acts

PEER JJS INVOLVEMENT: a scale including the percentage of friends who had been questioned, arrested, and charged with a crime, been on probation, or done time in detention or training school

---

(Continued)

TABLE 9.7: (Continued)

NEIGHBORHOOD CJS INVOLVEMENT: a scale including the percentage of adult neighbors (in the same residential block or neighborhood) who had been arrested by the police and charged with a crime, been on probation, done time in jail, been to state prison

GANG PERCEPTION: the extent of respondents' perceptions that gangs exerted influence of social control—whether they dominated social interactions in school or on the street, threatened or assaulted other youths, provided social or economic opportunities for other youths

GANG CRIMES: reports of "regular" collective involvement of gang members in six types of illegal acts

NEIGHBORHOOD VICTIMIZATION: a scale including respondents' perceptions of the percentage of neighbors who had been victims in the past year of one of seven different crime types, both violent and property offenses

VICTIMIZATION–VIOLENCE: a scale of respondents' reports of their own victimization in the past year for each of three types of violent crimes

VICTIMIZATION-PROPERTY: a scale of respondents' reports of their own victimization in the past year for each of four types of property crimes

LOCUS OF CONTROL: a standardized scale of internal-external controls and norm setting

SOCIAL SKILLS: respondents' self-assessment of their skills at filling out a job application, balancing a checkbook, resolving a dispute with a neighbor, talking with strangers about current events

DRUG PROBLEMS, DRINKING PROBLEMS: self-reports of negative social and personal consequences of alcohol or drug use; whether in the past year, respondent has had problems with family, friends, girlfriend or boyfriend, in school, with the police because of drug use or drinking; whether respondent ever felt he or she had a drug or alcohol problem

DRUG BEHAVIORS, DRINKING BEHAVIORS: self-reports of arrests because of drinking or drug use

TABLE 9.8: Rotated Factor Matrix

	Factor								
	1	2	3	4	5	6	7	8	9
School integration	-.386	-.055	-.099	.149	.213	-.168	.562	-.085	.007
School strain	.202	.103	.045	-.277	.309	.300	.232	.156	-.286
Teacher relations	-.083	-.029	.101	.081	-.176	-.031	.696	.025	-.025
Student delinquency	.063	-.050	-.009	-.080	-.062	.249	.050	.014	.682
Your social skills	-.086	.108	-.010	.061	.176	.006	.628	-.041	.040
Alcohol problems	.735	.104	.222	.064	-.182	-.125	.025	-.055	.006
Behavior while drunk	.805	-.106	-.041	-.120	-.131	.198	-.134	.041	.029
Drug problems	.774	.138	.274	-.080	-.024	-.091	.008	-.006	.006
Behavior while high	.779	-.101	.018	-.193	-.057	.246	-.157	.037	.003
Peer integration	.158	-.132	-.214	.007	.074	.102	.445	.150	.015
Peer JJS records	.218	.283	.444	-.134	-.354	-.024	-.062	.042	.016
Presence of gangs	-.020	.199	.199	.035	.041	.039	.010	.165	.684
Crimes by gangs	.140	.017	.836	-.049	-.048	.083	-.050	.067	.085
Gang social activity	.009	-.016	.814	-.018	-.011	.061	-.008	.089	.014
Peer delinquency	.249	.235	.643	-.076	-.161	.057	-.017	-.007	.095
Locus of control	.028	.151	-.056	.103	.640	-.027	.071	-.026	.092
Attitudes toward law	-.182	-.023	.134	.136	.640	.003	.129	.080	-.017
Attitudes to violence	.249	.065	.045	.047	-.597	.119	.047	.125	.133
Neighborhood ties	.050	-.041	.026	.121	-.008	-.048	.105	.746	-.099
Neighborhood quality	.096	.074	.090	-.021	-.241	.141	-.149	.604	.198
Neighborhood needs	-.197	.186	.106	.159	.189	-.014	.083	.585	.228
You victim—property	.040	.601	.300	-.092	-.106	.072	-.064	.192	-.120
You victim—violence	-.066	.681	.141	.035	-.035	.003	-.021	.162	-.099
Others victim—property	.054	.809	-.018	.080	.102	.118	.038	-.074	.180
Others victim—violence	.023	.803	-.058	.099	.109	.073	.010	-.091	.167
Conventional values	-.331	.023	-.089	.365	.189	-.198	.339	.146	.217
Father attachment	-.056	.009	-.004	.715	-.177	.007	.122	.189	-.200
Mother attachment	.010	.026	-.039	.760	.159	-.026	.001	.030	-.058
Father authority	-.192	.078	-.087	.678	.025	-.027	.198	.068	.049
Mother authority	-.064	.037	-.055	.588	.345	.120	-.052	-.050	.210
Neighbor family violence	.039	.137	.085	.029	-.032	.847	.002	.006	.136
Neighbor CJS records	.099	.077	.077	.002	-.072	.845	-.052	.023	.135
Eigenvalue	5.09	3.29	1.97	1.87	1.63	1.47	1.23	1.18	1.08
Percentage variance	15.9	10.3	6.1	5.9	5.1	4.6	3.9	3.7	3.4
Cumulative percentage	15.9	26.2	32.3	38.2	43.3	47.9	51.8	55.5	58.9

Notes

1. Few adolescent substance users, however, are involved in serious delinquency. Because the drugs-delinquency relationship is skewed, knowledge of drug use is better predicted by delinquency than knowledge of delinquency is predicted by drug use (Fagan et al., 1990).

2. The empirical evidence suggests otherwise. Klein, Maxson, and Cunningham (1988) found that gang participation in "rock" cocaine (crack) trafficking, although frequent, was no greater than nongang participation and had not increased significantly, at least for the first two years after crack appeared in Los Angeles. In New York, Fagan and Chin (1989) found that few adolescents participated in crack selling, and the few teenage participants worked in organizations that bore little resemblance to the youth gangs of Los Angeles, Chicago, or other U.S. cities with long-standing youth gang activity.

3. Cohen (1969) and Tracy (1979), for example, relied on a definition of gang membership and gang offenses based on designations from the Philadelphia police department. Rand (1988) used self-reports of gang membership. Friedman, Mann, and Friedman (1975), however, confirmed the findings based on official definitions using other classification procedures for gang crimes and gang membership.

4. Controls for intercity differences were introduced into OLS regression analyses using dummy variables for each city. Only for Los Angeles was the univariate F significant, but the standardized coefficient and simple R were weak. Accordingly, the influence of local context appeared minimal.

5. For example, removal of pipes from an abandoned building is not considered illegal activity in several urban areas, and is viewed as a legitimate economic opportunity. These adjustments resulted in the refinement and specification of items regarding weapon use, specification of victims (e.g., teacher, student, other adult), and elimination of trivial items such as "ran away from home" or "made obscene phone calls."

6. For example, items on family violence were deemed by school administrators to be "sensitive" or "intrusive" and were eliminated. In their place, items were developed to measure respondents' perception of violence among "neighbors' families." Still others were eliminated because of their reference to "excessive" violence or self-incrimination for major offenses: homicide and sexual assault.

7. These procedures are particularly important for high-rate offenders because of the psychometric properties of open-ended versus categorical response sets, making them particularly well suited for theoretical tests.

8. Offense-specific scales of narrow homogeneous crime types parallel with UCR categories, such as robbery or felony theft, were derived by summing the reported incidence scores for nonoverlapping items within the scale. See Fagan et al. (1987) for an item-scale map.

9. The categories include the following:

multiple-index offenders: those reporting at least three index offenses (felony assault, robbery, or felony theft) within the past year

serious delinquents: those reporting one or two index offenses (felony assault, robbery, or felony theft) in the past year, or three or more incidents in the past year of extortion or weapon offenses

minor delinquents: those reporting no index offenses and one or two incidents in the past year of extortion or weapon offenses, or four or more incidents in the past year of minor theft, minor assault, vandalism, or illegal activities (buying or selling stolen goods, selling drugs)

petty delinquents: those reporting no index offenses and three or fewer incidents in the past year of minor theft, minor assault, vandalism, or illegal activities (buying or selling stolen goods, selling drugs)

10. For example, involvement with delinquent peers is strongly associated with several deviant behaviors under various sampling and measurement conditions (Hirschi, 1969; Wiatrowski, Griswold, & Roberts, 1981). Accordingly, the Pearson correlation coefficients for PEER DELINQUENCY and several SRD scales were compared, controlling for gender and school status.

11. The DRUGTYPE scale is hierarchical: Youths involved in a higher classification also meet the criteria for the lower classification. Thus marijuana users used both alcohol and marijuana at least three times in the past year.

12. For nongang youths, items concerning "your gang" were scored as zero.

13. Neighborhood integration includes respondents' ties to the neighborhood and the evaluation of its quality and needs.

PART IV

Assessing the Changing Knowledge Base

10

New Wine in Old Bottles?
Change and Continuity
in American Gangs

JAMES F. SHORT

For the most part, criminology's "new issues" represent new urgencies to old issues. This is almost certainly true with respect to gangs. The great majority of gang-related issues and the directions we are taking with respect to them are not really new. They are, rather, continuing trends—albeit some are now more serious—and controversies among contending interests in delinquency and crime and their control. This essay, therefore, is about recent empirical advances and the challenges they present for the manner in which we go about our business. My focus is on a small set of studies that I believe have special significance for what we do.

Let us stipulate that evidence bearing on the issues is by no means clear or unequivocal. Evaluation of human behavior, including the effects of delinquency control programs (whether directed to individuals, groups, or communities) is

AUTHOR'S NOTE: This chapter is a revision of the keynote address presented to the Western Society of Criminology, on February 24, 1989, in Orange, California. The theme of the meetings was "New Wine in New Bottles: New Directions for New Issues." Portions of the chapter are drawn from Short and Moland (1976) and Short (1990).

extraordinarily difficult. Given the complexity of human behavior, and of explanatory forces and processes, precise determination of neither the causes of behavior nor the effects of control programs is possible. This much is clear, however: No matter how successful efforts to punish, rehabilitate, or otherwise control delinquents may be, unless the forces and processes that produce delinquent behavior are changed, new delinquents will continue to be produced. Given this fact, it is especially important that control programs be based on sound theoretical principles. The course of human history in this regard is not encouraging. The hope, if not yet the promise, is that we can do better.

Communities and Crime

Recent research on communities and crime (Reiss & Tonry, 1986) and on youth groups in their local settings demonstrates the importance of *local* communities and conditions in determining the behavior of young people (see, e.g., Hagedorn, 1988; MacLeod, 1987; Schwartz, 1987; Sullivan, 1990). The concept of the criminal or delinquent career also has become popular as an indication of the relationship of participation in delinquent activities, the frequency of offending, the seriousness of offenses committed, and the period (time) of active offending. Communities, too, have careers in delinquency. Here the primary causal forces are macro-level, ranging from the global to the neighborhood in scope (Sullivan, 1990). This chapter focuses on the nature of relationships among individual, group, and community careers in delinquency, with illustrations from my own work (Short & Strodtbeck, 1965) and from more recent studies of juvenile gangs.[1]

The Vice Lords and the Nobles

The Vice Lords and the Nobles were located in very different community areas of the city of Chicago. The Vice Lords' turf initially was in Lawndale, on the west side of the city, while that of the Nobles was in Douglas, in the traditional "Black belt" on the south side. Henry McKay's analysis of delinquency rates demonstrated that between 1934 and 1961 (the latter at the midpoint of our most intense research activity with the Vice Lords and Nobles), Lawndale experienced the greatest *increase* in rates of delinquents of all 75 Chicago communities (Shaw & McKay, 1969). During this same period, delinquency rates in Douglas, though still high, experienced the greatest *decrease* of all Chicago communities.

The Nobles' and Vice Lords' communities also differed in other ways. For several decades the great majority of Douglas residents had been Black. In contrast, Lawndale had only recently, and rapidly, undergone the classic ecological pattern of invasion, followed by succession of a Black population. This change was accompanied by the now-familiar pattern of severe economic loss and institutional disruption.

The fact that most readers of this chapter will recognize the Vice Lords' name, while few will have heard of the Nobles, is a good indicator of the nature of the two gangs. The Nobles were a neighborhood play group that became a delinquent gang, "solidified" by conflict (Thrasher, 1927). A dozen years after our initial contact with the gang, we asked a former member of the Nobles to reflect on the history of the gang. A casual observer, he said, would not be able to distinguish between members and nonmembers. When boys from the Nobles' turf left the area "for a party or something and they would get into a humbug [gang fight], they would send somebody around to . . . the hanging place for the whole area" for reinforcements. The area was plagued with drugs (it was widely known as "Dopeville") and there was a good deal of interpersonal violence and other types of crime.

When we first became acquainted with the Nobles, 25 boys and 1 girl belonged to the gang. Three years later the Nobles numbered 45, and the group had become less cohesive. Older members had begun to drift away from gang life. The young woman had entered nurse's training, and many of the young men had turned their attention to jobs and families.

We sought information on former members of both gangs by means of interviews and informants. The Nobles no longer existed, and, despite the efforts of key informants, we were able to obtain information on only 27 former Nobles, including 19 of the original gang. Of these young people, 4 (15% of those on whom information was available) were dead by the summer of 1971. Of the 23 living and known Nobles, 19 were employed and none incarcerated, but 2 of the 3 who were unemployed were involved in drug abuse.

The lack of information on so many Nobles is instructive. They never completely lost their play-group orientation, despite heavy involvement in delinquency. As members aged, they left the gang, and most led conventional adult lives.

By several accounts, the Vice Lords began in 1958, two years before our initial contact with the gang (see Keiser, 1969). Our chief informant, its president and strongest leader, told us that the Lords began when several residents of a cottage in the Illinois State Training School for Boys decided to pool their affiliations with different gangs on Chicago's west side to form the Vice Lords and to make the group the toughest gang in the city.

In that resolve, the Vice Lords were notoriously successful. They were also aggressively expansive. At the time of our initial contact, 66 boys were identified as members of the Vice Lords. In less than two years that number had risen to 311, constituting five Vice Lords branches.

This was only the beginning. The Vice Lords became one of the "supergangs" of the late 1960s, incorporating under the laws of the state of Illinois as a nonprofit organization claiming some 8,000 members in 26 divisions (see Sherman, 1970). The "Vice Lord Nation" initiated a variety of economic and community service enterprises, none with notable success.

The instability marking the original Vice Lords (we focused on our list of 66 members for the follow-up study) was overwhelming. Most remained in Chicago when they were not incarcerated. We lacked information on only 4 of the early group. Of the remaining 62, 12 (19%) were dead, most as a result of criminal violence. A total of 27 (43.5%) were working. Among the unemployed, at least 6 and probably more were involved in a drug distribution network. Another 10 were in prison. Nearly all had served time in correctional institutions.

Many factors doubtless contributed to the observed differences between the Nobles and the Vice Lords: their communities, founding conditions, and the supergang status of the Lords, as well as individual differences among gang members. The community context seems especially important, however. Chicago's supergangs emerged in communities characterized by recent and rapid population turnover. The most notorious of these, the Black P. Stone Nation, began in the community of Woodlawn, which, like Lawndale, had recently and rapidly undergone racial transition. Others arose in communities of recently arrived immigrants from Puerto Rico and Mexico.

Communities that produce supergangs lack stable populations and institutions, though instability may have less to do with ethnic invasion than with other destabilizing factors. In the 1960s, with the help of well-meaning persons from outside their communities (in some instances including funding from private foundations and the federal government), the supergangs emerged as multipurpose institutions. For the most part they were unsuccessful in both business and social service enterprises. Expectations held by gang members and by those who funded their efforts or tried to help in other ways were largely unfulfilled, and there was much bitterness in the aftermath. There was naïveté on all sides, among those who wanted to help and among the gangs. The gangs did not possess the necessary skills for the enterprises undertaken, and there was little involvement of other community residents and institutions in the supergang projects. There was, in addition, considerable fraud in the administration of large grant funds. Projects were poorly monitored, and little technical assistance was provided. Official opposition, particularly by the police, undermined some of the programs (see Short, 1976).

Much has changed today, largely for the worse. A few gangs have become more sophisticated in crime than their counterparts 20 or more years ago, as jailed gang members returned to their communities disillusioned with mainstream social, economic, and political goals (see Hagedorn, 1988). Many of these young men have remained active gang members. There are more, and more lethal, guns available. Drug abuse and trafficking have become more widespread, contributing to the devastation of community life (see Anderson, 1989, in press). More important, the political and economic structure of many U.S. cities has changed.

Urban Poverty and the Underclass

William Julius Wilson (1987) has demonstrated the rapidity with which poverty has become urbanized in this country. Together with demographic and structural changes in the economy, the economic downturn of the 1970s resulted in the emergence of a ghetto underclass. "Urban minorities," Wilson (1987) argues, "have been particularly vulnerable to structural economic changes, such as the shift from goods-producing to service-producing industries, the increasing polarization of the labor market into low-wage and high-wage sectors, technological innovations, and the relocation of manufacturing industries out of the central cities" (p. 39). Black unemployment rates more than doubled between the end of World War II and the 1970s, remaining approximately twice those of Whites in both good and bad economic years since the mid-1950s. The increase in numbers of the most crime-prone population (the young) in the country as a whole was especially pronounced in the inner cities and among the minority poor.

Although historical and continuing patterns of prejudice and discrimination against Blacks exacerbated all of these problems, Blacks were not the only affected minority (see Lieberson, 1980; Wilson, 1987). Between 1970 and 1984, Black and Hispanic families headed by women increased by 108% and 164%, respectively, compared with an increase of 63% for Whites. Out-of-wedlock births to Black teen-age mothers increased greatly, rising by 89% in 1983. The pattern was similar, but the numbers smaller (39%), among White teenagers. The result was that nearly half of all Black children under 18 years of age were in families with less than poverty-level income in 1983, and three-fourths of these families were headed by females. These changes left in their wake a large population of the "truly disadvantaged" who were mired in poverty and ill equipped to participate in opportunities provided by civil rights advances, or by Great Society or affirmative action programs. Those who could moved out of the inner-city ghettos, thus removing from these communities their most economically successful and politically capable residents (see Anderson, 1989, in press; Hagedorn, 1988). The effects on minority communities have been devastating.

The next generation of community-oriented delinquency prevention programs emerged even as problems of the ghetto underclass were becoming more apparent.

Recent Innovations

On the face of it, James Coleman and Thomas Hoffer's (1987) *Public and Private High Schools* would seem to have little to do with delinquency prevention. The book details research on the performance of students in public, Catholic, and other private high schools, comparing academic success, school dropout rates, continuation in college, and other matters. In sum, students in Catholic private schools performed better on almost all counts than did public school students. Students in other private schools also fared better than those in public schools. Most important, *disadvantaged students—minorities and the poor—in Catholic schools did particularly well, compared with their counterparts in public and other private schools.*

To explain these findings, Coleman and Hoffer draw upon the notion of functional communities. In functional communities institutions present a consistent pattern of norms and sanctions, reinforcing one another. Perhaps most important, *intergenerational relationships,* like other relationships between segments of the community, "arise out of the social structure itself" (p. 7). The down side of functional communities has often been documented—their tendency to stigmatize and exclude those who are "different," for example. Coleman and Hoffer stress more positive qualities in such communities, noting that they augment resources available to parents in their relationships with school authorities, in child supervision, and in monitoring their children's associations (with adults as well as with peers). Feedback from friends and associates is an additional resource for parental monitoring of both schools and children.

The truly disadvantaged lack education, organizational skills, self-confidence, and "social capital"—the intangible, but very real, qualities consisting of "*relations* between persons." Coleman and Hoffer argue that social capital facilitates productive capacity just as physical and human capital do (see also Coleman, 1988). Indeed, without social capital, the relevance for children of human capital (e.g., education and technical skills possessed by their parents) may be diminished severely, as when parents employ their human capital exclusively at work or in other activities not related to their children's lives.

Functional communities provide opportunities for, but do not guarantee, the development of social capital. The stigmatizing and self-serving qualities of social relationships in slum communities (hustling as a way of life, for example; see Valentine, 1978) make social capital development especially difficult. Structural differences among families also pose barriers. It is more difficult to build social capital, for example, in single-parent families than in two-parent families, and more difficult still when the single parent is a teenager.

Coleman and Hoffer attribute the advantages achieved by students in Catholic schools to the embeddedness of youth and their parents in the religiously based functional communities of these schools. They argue that intergenerational functional communities are lacking in most contemporary urban communities as a result of structural changes in the family and media influences. To these must be added the structural economic changes noted above.

The challenges posed by these changes occur at many levels. Here the focus is on promoting positive relationships between the generations as a basis for functional communities in order to create social capital. Is it possible to create and maintain functional communities in which social and human capital can be stimulated among the underclass? Recent innovations in community delinquency prevention and rehabilitation are promising. Some of these programs seek to create "functional extended families," while others focus on entire communities. The goal in each case is essentially the same, however: to create a community of values in which institutions and programs are mutually supportive. Ethnic and social class ties, individual needs for nurturance and boundaries regarding acceptable conduct, employment skills and opportunities, and access to the levers of community power all are of critical importance. Many of us recognize in these themes echoes of the Chicago Area Project and the Industrial Areas Foundation, associated long ago with the names of Clifford Shaw, Saul Alinsky, and others.

"Crime prevention programs" tend often to focus narrowly on persuading community residents to *protect* themselves from crime by "target hardening" and other means of reducing opportunities for the commission of crime, while ignoring the causes of crime. Lynn Curtis (1987) notes that many of these programs focus primarily on public relations and fear of crime rather than on crime reduction. He argues that grass-roots initiatives that address the causes of crime as well as opportunities for crime demonstrate both greater success and greater cost-effectiveness.

A number of "natural experiments" have grown out of the concerns of local people and their attempts to create a sense of family and/or community, and to minister to special problems of youth. Unlike the supergangs, which often are viewed by local residents as a threat to personal property and safety, they have been supported by their communities. They incorporate the gangs, rather than the reverse, so that the community and the gangs become more acceptable to one another (see Curtis, 1987; Woodson, 1981). These programs emphasize local participation and control, and indigenous rather than professional leadership. Most rely to some extent on expertise from outside the community for consultation and/or training in skills relevant to program goals. They raise financial support from both public and private sources, but incentives are provided for continued funding through economic enterprise and local institutional support. Most are multipurpose, but job placement and recreational opportunities for youth are given high priority. Several have created job opportunities by initiating economic enterprises such as product manufacture and distribution, and service businesses. Most reach out to young people who have been referred by juvenile courts or released from incarceration, as well as those who have not yet been caught up in the juvenile and criminal justice systems.

A few carefully designed community programs have been inspired by these natural experiments, some of them based on more abstract principles drawn from research and theory. Some of these have been the object also of extensive and intensive monitoring and evaluation (see Curtis, 1987).

A Note on Community-Based Police Research and Innovation

Their frontline exposure to the social ills of the community provides unique opportunities for the police to identify emerging problems and to place choices before the community with respect to many problems, as well as to work aggressively with other agencies and the private sector in proposing solutions to identified problems. "Problem-oriented policing" is a proposal to do just that, by focusing on the nature of complaints, their location, and the relationship between reported incidents, noting the behaviors, people, and places that generate calls for police assistance. In the long run, Herman Goldstein (1987) suggests, the police role could change dramatically, from dealing directly with crime problems to focusing primarily on supporting and strengthening community norms and helping citizens to solve their problems. Rather than attempting to *solve* so many problems *for* the community, police would be helping them to develop and promote a sense of community.

Should police forces emphasize skills in mediation and community organization, research methods, and interpretation, both police and community responses to delinquency would be affected profoundly. Police might become community advocates, for example, rather than community adversaries, as is so often the case in high crime areas.

This vision of the police role is similar in important respects to the role of the Chicago Area Project community workers and that of community organizers and other consultants in the community-oriented programs noted above (i.e., as a resource for the community, aiding local residents and working with indigenous leaders to solve community problems with special focus on problems of young people). The goal, to return to my major point, is to promote social capital through the achievement of "functional communities"; that is, communities in which family life, work, religion, education, law enforcement, and other institutional areas reflect and reinforce common values.

Communities and Individual Careers in Crime

Even in high-delinquency communities some individuals do not engage in delinquent behavior, and some individual delinquent careers stop short of prolonged involvement in serious crime (see MacLeod, 1987, pp. 146ff.; Sullivan, 1989, pp. 62-63). It is difficult to generalize from such cases, however, because contingencies affecting individual cases are so varied and complex. The point can perhaps be illustrated by comparing the lives of two young Black men who lived in the same west-side Chicago community, but whose careers differed greatly. One of these was the aforementioned "founder" and strongest leader of the Vice Lords. The other, when I knew him, was about to graduate from a prestigious university and was applying for admission to the best graduate schools in the United States.

There is much that we do not know about the early lives of these two young men (e.g., about the quality of their family experiences). They were physically similar: tall and muscular, each with a commanding appearance. Both spent a portion of their youth in Vice Lord territory on Chicago's west side. The gang leader became embroiled with the law and a gang member at an early age, eventually being sent to the state training school for boys.

Although much remains unclear, we know that this young man so impressed leaders of various youth programs that special efforts were made to work with him in order to prevent his continued participation in crime. For a time these efforts seemed to be successful. He worked in a variety of ways with the YMCA program with which our gang research was associated (see Short & Strodtbeck, 1965). Shortly thereafter he was recruited to another program that offered him the opportunity to attend a small but prestigious eastern college, located in a large rural setting. He did so and became for a short time a member of the football squad.

It would be hard to imagine a greater contrast than that between the social world of Chicago's west-side gangland and that of the elite eastern college. By his own account the college experience was dull for this young man. He did not do well in academic course work and soon became involved in selling drugs to other students. He left the college before completing his freshman year. When he returned to Chicago he picked up where he had left off, peddling drugs and playing a prominent role in the Vice Lords.

Because this young man was knowledgeable about the Vice Lords, John Moland and I hired him to assist us in contacting members and former members of the gang, and in informing us concerning those who could not be contacted. He told us that he wanted to return to college, this time in Chicago. He readily agreed to assist us in our research, and at first he performed well. It soon became apparent, however, that the small funds we were paying him could not compete with the income he derived from his thriving drug business. He began to lose interest in the research, and after a few months we could no longer depend on him.

The second young man, the university student, was a few years younger than the gang leader. The discovery that he was from Chicago and had grown up on the west side prompted me to ask that he tell his story as part of a course requirement. He reported that his uncle was a member of the Lords. I had known the uncle and several other Vice Lords members whom this young man professed to know. Other details of his story concerning the Vice Lords also were consistent with data from our research, lending credibility to his story.

Though "Jay" was "drafted" into several gangs, he never became an active member of a gang. As a young boy he greatly admired members of the Vice Lords. He would sneak out on the front porch late at night to listen to his uncle and other members of the gang talk about their exploits; he noted "without a doubt that *if my parents had decided not to move I would have become a Vice Lord.*"

The fact that Jay was never an active gang member did not prevent him from extensive involvement in delinquent behavior. With his best friend, Jay stole car batteries and stripped auto parts. The practice was lucrative because a local fence purchased nearly everything they stole. These activities and his association with gang members drew Jay to the attention of the police, but his account fails to mention ever being arrested. He reports that as he grew older much of the prestige that he had associated with the Vice Lords "faded away."

The fact that Jay's family moved during his early years, first out of Vice Lord territory and then again later, helped to insulate him from the influence of gang members and from full participation in a delinquent subculture. Another important difference in the two careers arises from an apparent similarity. Jay, too, was favored by being sent to a prestigious university, but his academic promise had been recognized earlier and he had been sent to an eastern prep school.

It is not possible to determine with precision the basic intelligence of these two young men. Those who knew them were impressed with their high intelligence and potential. But Jay was prevented from strong identification with a delinquent subculture, and he was removed completely from the social world of lower-class delinquents when he was a sophomore in high school. His academic success propelled him into still other opportunities. His social capital clearly was superior to that of the gang leader.

The gang leader was firmly embedded in the gang world; he was rewarded by his peers and by others as a result of his prominence in the gang. Intervention to remove him from this world occurred only after his established life-style made it virtually impossible for him to adjust to a social world so alien to his experience. To conclude in Jay's words: "I suppose I was one of the lucky ones. *I was able to go away to school . . . and, unlike [the gang leader, whom he knew], I was . . . able to adjust to a totally different way of life.*"

Timing clearly was important to both of these cases. So also, perhaps, was the fact that Jay was able to avoid entanglement in the juvenile justice system and the labeling experience. Yet others have been able to survive such experiences without extensive careers in crime. Clifford Shaw's (1930) "Jack-Roller" managed to live an essentially law-abiding adult life, after considerable involvement in crime as a child and in young adulthood and extensive and painful experience in both juvenile and criminal justice systems (see Snodgrass, 1982). Waln Brown's (1983) autobiographical account of a disturbed childhood, trauma, and delinquent behavior in a variety of institutional contexts documents his recovery and successful adult adjustment.

Conclusion

I close this essay by making more explicit another theoretically based principle of intervention. For this purpose I return to the focus on the ghetto underclass. This is where the problem is the most serious and intractable.

Wilson's policy agenda includes provision of child-care services and subsidies to working-poor parents. Illustrative of the innovative and experimental child-care programs required in ghetto underclass communities is the Center for Successful Child Development in Chicago. Better known as the "Beethoven Project" because it serves the Beethoven Elementary School catchment area in Chicago, the project is centered in six units of Chicago's Robert Taylor Homes, allegedly the largest public housing project in the world. Stretched out along a two-mile section of a major expressway (which effectively isolates the project from the rest of the city), Taylor Homes consists of 28 high-rise buildings housing approximately 20,000 people. Nearly all Taylor Homes residents are poor and Black. More than 90% of the households receive public assistance, and three-quarters are headed by women.

Taylor Homes is plagued by every poverty-related problem: high rates of drug abuse, crime, delinquency, unemployment and dependency, educational deficiencies that begin as early as the first grade, school dropouts, and health and nutrition problems. The Beethoven Project focuses on preparing mothers for parenthood and on the child's earliest experiences with his or her environment. The goal "is to prevent social, psychological, and physical dysfunction among . . . [a cohort of] children so that they will be fully prepared to enter kindergarten" (Center for Successful Child Development, n.d.). Like the family- and community-oriented projects discussed above, the Beethoven Project is multifaceted: a variety of health and social services aimed at both parents and children are provided, including a "family drop-in center" that is the project's physical base; a neurological, physiological, and psychological assessment and referral program for infants; parent-child relationship screening and parenting education; and home visitation and day-care services. The most immediate targets of the project are the annual cohorts of children born between January 1, 1987, and January 1, 1992, in the designated housing units, and their mothers (who will have been identified prior to the births of the children). Others benefit, too, because many project personnel are themselves residents of Taylor Homes, including the home visitors who are trained specifically for this work. The project is designed to provide a "Head Start on Head Start," as a *New York Times* editorial proclaimed.

The project thus seeks to remedy social, physiological, and psychological deficits that result from the operation of macro-level forces affecting the lives of the target population. In a broader sense, however, the approach is experimental, with the clear expectation that lessons will be learned that can be applied on a larger scale.

More will be required, of course, if this cohort of infants and their parents are to break out of the cycle of poverty, dependency, delinquency, and other social ills. It will be important to evaluate carefully what happens to these children and their parents, and to study the impact of the project on other Taylor Homes residents. More than this, attention must be given to family and community maintenance beyond the kindergarten years. It will be important to build on the social capital opportunities created in the course of the project if others in the larger community, as well as those who are its primary targets, are to benefit. Attention to kindergarten cohorts may have little impact on older children or on their elders unless changes also occur in job opportunities and in other institutional areas (see Hagedorn, 1988; Sullivan, 1989). The basic point seems clear, however: Projects that are able to create and sustain functional families and communities are more likely to promote conventional learning and achievement opportunities and bonds to conventional persons and life-styles.

Most youngsters do not become seriously involved in delinquent behavior. Those who do too often become society's criminals, wards of the criminal justice system, the specter of public fears, and a major drain on the public purse. Yet despite the best intentions of reformers and the best efforts of scholars, the combination of the uncertainty of knowledge, the continuous need for socialization of the young, and social change ensure that there will always be youth problems and delinquents. Increasingly we are discovering that uncertainty is a problem in all fields of knowledge, even in the most advanced sciences and technologies. Although this may be small comfort to those who suffer as a result of these uncertainties and the many flaws in social systems, it should strengthen our resolve to understand these problems and address them with intelligence.

Much of this essay is meant to suggest that doing good and doing justice are not always—and certainly not necessarily—incompatible. As Stan Cohen (1985) notes, "The ideology of doing good remains powerful. . . . [It] is the essence of a humanistic civilization to exert power and to do good at the same time" (p. 86).

Critics of positivism and of doing good focus on their preemption and abuse by the powerful, especially in the form of state power. Yet, as the Beethoven Project and many others demonstrate, the state has no monopoly on justice, nor is it necessary that control efforts directed at chronic delinquents and others in high-risk categories be the province solely of the criminal and juvenile justice systems. When criminal opportunity reduction and doing good are based on sound theoretical principles, delinquency prevention and rehabilitation programs can be both humane and successful.

Note

1. I define a *gang* as a group whose members meet together with some regularity, over time, on the basis of group-defined criteria of membership and group-determined organizational structure, usually with (but not always; see Hagedorn, 1988) some sense of territoriality. This definition includes neither delinquent nor conventional behaviors, since these usually are what we wish to explain. It does not include characteristic dress, names, or types of organization, each of which varies in myriad ways that may help to understand gang behavior, and that may be important to gang identity and behavior, for members and for others.

11

Back in the Field Again: Gang Research in the Nineties

JOHN M. HAGEDORN

> *Q. If the governor came in here now and said, "Marcus, I'm going to give you a million dollars to deal with the gang situation," what would you do with it?*
>
> *A. First, I'd do some research like you're doing now, talk to everybody and try to understand . . .*
>
> Marcus, 1-9 Deacons

What do we know about modern gangs? I don't think we know that much. We simply haven't done the research.

We do have a substantial academic literature on gangs dating back to the 1920s. Recently the media have been filled with stories of gangs, drugs, and violence. In the last few years, a few articles on gangs have appeared in professional journals, mainly analyzing crime statistics or surveying public officials. This volume you are reading speaks to a renewed academic interest in gangs. But do we possess accurate descriptions of today's gangs on which to ground theory and base public policy? What kind of data do we need to disentangle academic and popular gang stereotypes from the underlying reality?

Some believe there's little need for new field studies. They see gangs as generated by a culture of poverty and by persisting "focal concerns" of an ethnically neutral lower class. They believe the vast economic and social changes of the past decades have had little impact on youth gangs. Because "lower-class culture" changes only slightly over time, variations in gangs are only "elaborations of existing forms, rather than genuinely original additions to or changes in traditional features" (Miller, 1974).

However, others contend that deindustrialization and changes in the structure of labor markets have drastically altered the way of life for the urban poor, their families, neighborhoods, and institutions (Kasarda, 1985; Wilson, 1987). These structural changes have created a minority underclass, and contemporary gangs may be a "fraction" of that class (Moore, 1985).

Our concern as social scientists should be with variation in how new conditions may alter familiar forms. If in fact a new class is emerging in urban ghettos and barrios, how has the familiar form of youth gangs been affected? This question can be answered only through investigation into how gangs and gang members lead their lives. This essay is a straightforward call for more field studies to be conducted to investigate gangs in their urban environments. It makes a case for such new field studies, looks at the limitations of other types of gang research, reviews objections to undertaking fieldwork, and concludes with a call for collaborative and innovative forms of empirical research.

Why We Need New Field Studies

We need new field studies for four reasons.

(1) First of all, we need these studies because times have changed and there is very little recent empirical research on

modern gangs. The 1990s look very different from the 1920s or 1960s, when most gang fieldwork was done. We need to ask whether or not today's largely African-American, Hispanic, and Asian gangs are different in significant respects from the European immigrant gangs studied in the past. Have the lack of "good jobs" within central cities, the influx of illegal drugs, and the predominance of a ghetto welfare economy significantly influenced modern gangs? Aside from the field researchers participating in this volume, only a few others (e.g., Moore, Padilla, and Sullivan) have headed out toward urban street corners to investigate these questions. I believe the 1990s require an emphasis on empirical research to find out what is the same and what is different about today's gangs.

(2) We need more field studies because some recent research is suggesting that gangs have changed fundamentally. Many recent studies conceptualize gangs not as part of transitory delinquent subcultures, but as persistent structures with long-term social control and economic functions within poor minority neighborhoods. William Julius Wilson's concept of an "underclass" plays a central role for much of this new gang research.

For example, the Chicano gangs Joan Moore has studied in East Los Angeles have persisted within their barrios for more than 40 years and contain both juvenile and adult members. Moore (1987) has suggested that such persisting gangs should be understood as underclass "quasi-institutions." Moore sees the gang as one factor in "reproducing" an underclass by trapping delinquents in unconventional life-styles.

Our Milwaukee research looked into the relationship between deindustrialization and the occupational and educational careers of gang members (Hagedorn, 1988). Tracking the careers of the 260 founding members of Milwaukee's 19 major gangs, we found that the overwhelming majority of the male gang members were not "maturing out" of the gang, but rather were unemployed, uneducated, and still involved with the gang as young adults. Gangs in Milwaukee have persisted now for a decade and have filled a neighborhood institutional void.

Carl Taylor (1990, and Chapter 4 of this volume) focuses on economic functions of gangs in Detroit. He suggests a typology of gangs with a natural progression from "scavenger" to "territorial" to "corporate." The success and charisma of Detroit's Young Boys Incorporated prompted a widespread emulation of this organized crime ring by youth gangs. Taylor contends that a new, amoral outlaw culture has emerged, different from the have-not culture of most of the African-American community.

Taylor's work raises many more questions. Are the Detroit gangs he studied typical of a transformation of gangs in large cities into organized crime? What different types of gang-related economic organizations exist, and what roles within gangs have been produced? If most gangs are not big businesses, do they resemble small businesses, with a high failure rate and many employees working part-time for less than subsistence wages? Do persisting gangs have noneconomic functions within underclass neighborhoods? To answer these questions, empirical investigation, not abstract theorizing, is needed.

(3) We need more field studies because existing contemporary research makes a strong case for wide variation in gang types, structures, activities, and roles in the illegal economy. Taylor's gangs are quite unlike Moore's and most of the gangs I studied in Milwaukee. Milwaukee gangs and Los Angeles gangs have both similarities and differences (Hagedorn & Moore, 1987). Gangs today vary widely by gender (see Chapter 8 of this volume) and ethnicity (see Chapter 7 of this volume). There also are differences between small-city and big-city gangs (Hagedorn, 1988).

Mercer Sullivan's (1989) comparative ethnography reintroduces to gang research the study of neighborhood-level differences made famous by Cloward and Ohlin. Sullivan looks at individual and group variation in "youth crime and work" within and among three Brooklyn neighborhoods. Needless to say, Sullivan's Brooklyn gangs are quite different from Taylor's, Moore's, or those I studied in Milwaukee. For all this diversity, we still have a limited number of descriptions of contemporary gangs. Thrasher's (1927) 60-year-old pointer may still be true: "No two gangs are alike." Developing a new typology requires more case studies.

(4) Finally, we need more field studies because gangs will be portrayed differently when studied in their natural environment than when studied as homicide statistics, interviewed in prison, or described by public officials or other self-interested parties.
Gangs may seem irrational to many conditioned by sensational media reporting and law enforcement opinion. But historically, community studies by Thrasher, Whyte, Suttles, Horowitz, and Moore found patterned behavior where outsiders saw only pathology and disorganization. In Milwaukee, the widespread notion that gangs were transplanted from Chicago was dispelled by a careful history of local gang origins based on interviews with gang founders. Recent research in Ohio came to similar conclusions, disputing media stereotypes (Huff, 1989a).

Gang problems are a prime modern example of what C. Wright Mills termed "official definitions of reality": public issues framed by the powerful to serve their own interests. In order to get beneath and behind media images—to see in what ways they may be true, in what ways false, and in what ways they serve those with something to gain—we need studies that see the world as gang members see it. Methods of research that rely on official statistics or official channels of access are necessary but not sufficient if we are to fully understand the reality of modern gangs. Routine academic research methods, which I call "courthouse criminology" and "surrogate sociology,"[1] seldom do more than reinforce popular stereotypes.

Courthouse Criminology

Courthouse criminology refers to the analysis of official statistics and data gathered on gangs by surveys of law enforcement or other public sources. Gangs are counted and crime statistics tabulated, but gang members are not interviewed or described by direct observation. Good examples of gang "courthouse criminology" are the nationwide surveys of Walter Miller in the 1970s, and, most recently, the Spergel and Curry study (see Chapter 13 of this volume). These surveys asked public officials to report on the number, size, and type of gangs and particularly their "law-violating" activities.

There are two basic problems with such surveys. First, gang survey data are notoriously unreliable. Walter Miller (1975) gives an honest portrayal of the problems of his own famous survey: "Much of the base data from which conclusions are derived—single interviews with local respondents, press accounts of uneven detail, in-house descriptions of agency operations, statistical tabulations compiled under less-than-ideal circumstances—fail to reach the level of quality necessary to sound research" (p. 4). Data gathered in these surveys must be seen more as a tabulation of *perceptions* by public officials than as accurate descriptions of gangs.[2]

Local data compiled on gangs can be very imprecise. Gangs don't keep membership rosters, and police often are accused of labeling kids as "gang members" just because they live in certain neighborhoods. Police estimates of gang membership are often far off the mark.[3] Gang members also pride themselves on a "code of silence" (Taylor, 1990), actively concealing information from authorities.

And gang members aren't the only ones who lie. Information given by public officials in surveys is also subject to distortion based on politics and organizational needs. For example, in organizing a Midwest conference on gangs, we encountered disagreements among public officials within individual cities about whether or not their cities even had any gangs. In Indianapolis, after repeated denials of the reported presence of gangs, one exasperated official told us, "Look, we do not have a gang problem here. We do have a slight problem in the summer with groups of youths running around with shotguns. But we don't have a gang problem." The official said admitting they had a gang problem was impossible while Indianapolis was preparing to host the Pan American Games and a possible Olympic bid. How would a survey filled out by those officials report the nature of their city's "gang problem"?

The reporting of a gang problem varies with the needs for city officials to promote a respectable image of their city, for police officials to make a case for hiring more officers, for community agencies to lobby for funds for "outreach," and for other reasons.[4] Given all the above conditions, information on gangs from surveys of public officials must be treated with extreme caution.

The second problem with courthouse criminology is its one-sided focus: Gangs are defined primarily as a law enforcement problem, and are analyzed in those terms. The two most recent surveys, Miller's and Spergel's, both were funded by the Justice Department and looked at gangs basically as a crime problem. In this volume, Spergel and Curry (Chapter 13) say about their survey, "Our interest in youth gangs was defined primarily in law enforcement terms. Therefore our study deals mainly with high-profile youth gangs who have come to police attention usually for violent, but sometimes for various other kinds of criminal behavior."

We certainly need information on gangs as a crime problem. Most gang research, including my own, takes note of criminal actions by gang members and endemic violence. Both gang-related homicides and the involvement of gangs in the sale of drugs are serious problems, no matter how *gang-related* is defined (see Chapter 3 of this volume) or whether gang drug sales are mainly by individuals or organized by the gang.[5]

On the other hand, in analyzing homicide or other crime statistics we may forget that gangs are problems of neighborhoods controlling their own youth and consequences of structural economic changes. We also may forget that the vast majority of gang members likely have very little connection to violent behavior. Stop! Is that last sentence true? Read it again. How would we find out if the vast majority of gang members have little connection to violence? Tabulating crime statistics only gives us data on gang members who commit crimes. The only way to get a rounded picture of gang activities is to study the gang as a whole, what its members do each day, what different roles exist, and how the gang functions within its neighborhood.[6]

The point is *not* that gangs are nice groups of boys and girls waiting for a social worker to save them and seldom are violent drug dealers. Some gangs may run organized drug sales in a city and be destructive to their communities (Taylor, 1990), some may sell drugs and enjoy conditional community support (Sullivan, 1989), and some may be extremely violent with no use of drugs (see Chapter 6 of this volume). The point is that if the sole focus of the study of gangs is on homicide statistics or drug arrests, we will inevitably be one-sided in our understanding.

Miller (1975) points out that accurate information on gangs can be obtained only "by trusted persons who maintain close and continued contact with gang members" (p. 2). Courthouse criminology needs to be cross-checked by ethnographic research or other on-site field studies. This is precisely the point of this chapter. But how should such studies be undertaken? One type of empirical study, surrogate sociology, is especially problematic.

Surrogate Sociology

Many academics understand the limitations of courthouse criminology and seek to get closer to their research subjects for a better look—but not too close. A brief peek at the exotic world of gangs, crime, and drugs is enough to publish an article and claim to be an expert. "Surrogate sociology" uses intermediaries to identify gang members and allow the researcher to gain temporary access to gangland.

There are three common types of gang surrogate sociology: (a) interviews with incarcerated gang members identified by correctional officials, providing both the thrill of personal contact and the safety of a nearby guard; (b) a softer version, utilizing probation and parole officers to identify "at-large" gang members and to provide introductions for interviews; and (c) hiring community agencies to identify and even interview gang members in a one-shot survey. All these methods provide useful data but have severe limitations.

One obvious problem is sample bias: Interviewing gang members who have been incarcerated or are on probation tells us something about gang members who broke the law and got caught, but may not be representative of their gang. It yields information about gangs drawn solely from failed lawbreakers.

Information from incarcerated gang members may confuse the prison gang with the community gang. Although many gangs in prisons or jails today maintain contacts with their gangs in the community (Jacobs, 1977), prison gangs usually have quite separate origins and histories (Camp & Camp, 1985). Gang members put into prisons often have to develop quick loyalties to prison gangs, if only to defend themselves against their enemies. An inmate may give information about his preprison community gang that may be distorted by the prison experience and that may confound two different gangs.

Information gathered from gang members locked up in day-to-day contact with rival gang members, having confrontations with authorities, and assimilating the inmate culture will undoubtedly produce information reflecting these intense realities. Milwaukee gang founders reported that members of their gangs were almost always "more involved" with the gang while in prison than when in the community. Moore (1989b) points out that an incarcerated gang member "is so removed from the everyday realities of the gang-home-community web and so concentrated on his-her own beef and the gang-in-prison that distortions are bound to occur even if the kid were motivated to be truthful."

Another problem is that an incarcerated gang member has good reasons to lie. Whyte (1969), in an incisive article on participant observation, demands that researchers constantly ask themselves whether there are any "ulterior motives" (p. 107) respondents might have that color their comments. An incarcerated gang member often has pressing ulterior motives (i.e., to get out from behind bars or to plead the merits of his case or character to a respectable person who might be helpful in front of the judge). Prisoners have strong incentives to tell researchers only what the researchers want to hear. Gang members on probation have similar ulterior motives—to say or do nothing that might get their probation revoked.

Utilizing community-based agencies to select a sample of gang members is also problematic (see, for example, Chapter 9 of this volume). First, a sample selected by a community agency may be just as biased as a sample of incarcerated or paroled gang members. Gang members selected by community agencies may be representative of gang members involved with agency programming, but are they representative of the entire gang? Agency-selected gang members may have left the gang, and their own attitudes toward the gang may have become quite hostile. Moore (1989b) points out that "repentant or 'redeemed' gang members in a program may overemphasize the evils of the gang they have just left, and program staff—usually embattled in any local government—may have even stronger selective and interpretive biases, trying to justify their own programs." Gang members may attempt to deceive a naive researcher or may be "so caught up in their own mythologies that a researcher has a hard time extricating self-aggrandizing myths from the often grubby realities" (Moore, 1989b). Agencies may only pretend to know "active" gang members and easily fool outsider researchers, selecting neighborhood non-gang kids for interviews, particularly if the kids will be paid.

The problem is compounded because of the wide gulf that exists today between gangs and community agencies. Carl Taylor (1990) quotes young Detroit gang members as calling community agencies "fake-ass programs." Our Milwaukee interviews are filled with vituperative comments of gang members about community agencies. For example, if given a million dollars, Mike of the Black Gangster Disciples would

open of a lot of centers for, you know, teens who can just go there and be theirselves, just be theirselves. Like . . . Silver Spring [a youth center], all of them, I'd tear them down and rebuild some for them. I'd ask for a whole new staff, man, they are all on the wrong wavelength. When there's no communication there, don't nobody get nowhere.

Tony of the Vice Lords sees agency staff as setting a bad example:

'Cause they ain't helping nobody. They sittin' on their
butts. . . . They ain't doing nothing. Half the motherfuckers
in there is alcoholic. . . . They ain't thinkin' about us . . . all
this money they be getting for running them programs and
grants. . . . Ain't no telling how much they be using. . . . I'd
shut them phony agencies and get to the real ones.

Even though most of the agencies gang members criticized
were run by African-Americans or Hispanics, the agencies were
still perceived as exploiting gangs for grant dollars, but not
really helping. Mike sums the problem up as a class difference:

They got Ph.D.s and bachelor's and, you know, master's—
they not really down to our lives, they don't really live our life.
They upper middle class, you know.

Certainly there are good community programs and agencies
that do their job with gangs. But using community agencies—
particularly those with "respectable" reputations—as intermediaries, may be a very bad sampling strategy to get data from
less-than-respectable gangs.

In the final analysis, courthouse criminology and surrogate
sociology give us questionable data. They are methods best
suited to reinforcing the outlook of law enforcement and community agency bureaucrats. Although such information is
important, it has value only insofar as it is balanced by field
studies attempting to understand how gang members and
other neighborhood residents see the world. But there have not
been many researchers heading for the field to study modern
gangs. Why not?

Objections to Undertaking Field Studies

There have been numerous technical and professional objections raised against undertaking field studies in gang neighborhoods. The technical objections center on the difficulties of
access and of getting informants to tell the truth. Race also
surfaces as a reason White academics are unwilling to do gang

research. Like Ned Polsky (1967), I think such reasons are cop-outs. I'm convinced much more good field research on gangs is both desirable and possible. Let's consider a few of the commonly voiced objections.

Technical Objections

"It's too hard to get access to gangs." Nonsense. Any good field researcher, committed to learning about gangs and willing to spend the long hours necessary to develop good informants, can solve the problem of access. Polsky (1967), in his study of career criminals, points out, "Most difficulties that one meets and solves in doing field research on criminals are simply the difficulties one meets and solves in doing field research." He concludes that the problem isn't access; it is "the inability to do field research" (p. 119).

There have been a variety of ways recent field researchers have solved the problem of access to gangs. Joan Moore (1978) founded a Chicano Pinto Research Project that has utilized former gang members as full participants in community re-search for the past 20 years. Carl Taylor (1990, and Chapter 4 of this volume) recruited researchers from a security firm he headed and investigated gangs that developed from Taylor's childhood neighborhood. Mercer Sullivan (1989) utilized contacts from a prior research project at Brooklyn high schools to develop an ethnography of groups of young people in three different neighborhoods. Terry Williams (1989) did 1,200 hours of traditional fieldwork in observing a teenage cocaine ring at work. Felix Padilla has been developing contacts with Chicago gangs for the past several years through a community agency. I gained access to Milwaukee's gangs through contacts I made as a gang program director and developed a collaborative methodology with several gang founders. Although some researchers have utilized police to provide contacts (e.g., Campbell, 1984), that practice has obvious drawbacks. Unlike surrogate sociology, gaining genuine access to gangs is not a one-shot deal and requires patience, careful work over a long period of time, and mutual respect.[7]

"How do you know if they are telling the truth?" How does any researcher know if a respondent is telling the truth? Do gang boys lie more than police officers? Obtaining valid and reliable data is a problem for all research. There are many methods of checking for reliability and validity (e.g., Bogdan & Taylor, 1975; White, 1969).

For example, in my own research in constructing a history of Milwaukee's gangs, I utilized a series of cross-checks. I interviewed more than one gang founder from each gang, and rival gangs were interviewed. All parties were asked about the same events to provide repeated descriptions. Often conflicting versions of events were given, usually about who started a fight, who escalated gang warfare, or how the gang adopted its name. At times I would confront an answer clearly at variance with other information and challenge the respondent. Through cross-checking answers from several informants and challenging data that didn't "sound right" (White, 1969, p. 110), I began to have a clear picture of how Milwaukee gangs actually formed.

"Gangs don't trust researchers." And for good reasons. Poor minority communities deeply distrust academic research. If a researcher's sole purpose is to do some quick-and-dirty interviews and publish an article, then trust will of course be difficult and the data will be suspect. A part of winning trust is convincing young gang members they should have their stories told honestly. But more important, it requires a commitment by the researcher to the needs of the research subjects along with gang/community participation in the research (Moore, 1979).

For example, Joan Moore's (1978) Chicano Pinto Research Project was initiated out of a California prisoner self-help movement. This project combined research with the demands of Chicano *pintos*, or ex-cons, for changes in narcotics laws and enforcement practices. Moore's long history of work with Chicano movement organizations gave her credibility in Chicano neighborhoods and particularly with *pintos*.

Our Milwaukee research began as a result of my experiences as a gang diversion program director. The research was designed to "tell the truth" in order to change public policy, particularly on the need for more central-city jobs. A former gang leader, Perry Macon, participated in all stages of the research and is a contributing author to *People and Folks* (Hagedorn, 1988). Perry and I also spent countless hours helping our informants with court problems, getting them back into school, or into employment programs. Winning trust requires honesty, a rather unscholarly commitment to informants' needs, and dedication to social change.

"White researchers can't do research with minority gangs." Clearly minority social scientists are best suited to do gang research today. For Carl Taylor (1990),

> Race was an important factor because this was a predominantly black neighborhood. Outsiders, in particular non-blacks, were treated like foreigners or negative authority figures such as bill collectors, process servers, social workers, or police. The mention of research, pretest, or other academic labels meant little, if anything, in this community.

The problems minority researchers may have—"overrapport" or withholding tendencies[8]—are minor compared with the barriers White researchers must face in gaining access to and trust of African-American, Hispanic, Asian, or other minority gangs. But although racial barriers are difficult, they are not insurmountable. Joan Moore developed a collaborative methodology that trained Chicano ex-gang members to interview other Chicano ex-gang members. The Milwaukee Gang Research Project was also a collaborative project, with former gang members participating as paid staff, informants, and data analysts. Acceptance of White social scientists in minority communities is contingent on the motives of the research, the degree of community participation in the research, and an honest sharing of any research benefits—what Blauner and Wellman (1973) call the "decolonization of social research."

To be White is to be an outsider to gang members. Trying to act like an insider, trying to be "one of them," is phony, and the data reported will inevitably be phony (Polsky, 1967). The trick is to understand that being an outsider can have value, both to the informants and to the research. Value can be demonstrated through reciprocity: Gang members give you interviews or allow your observation, and in return you pay them (Blauner & Wellman, 1973). Commitment to the informants and their community is also valuable. Unless the researcher is perceived as being "on the community's side," information will be distorted consciously and the researcher misled.[9] Why should gang members care about research that benefits only the professional careers of White academics?

If the principles of commitment and reciprocity are met, White researchers can gain access to minority gangs and produce good social science. Although we clearly need more minority fieldworkers, White researchers in whose minds "two worlds can meet and fuse" (Park, 1969) are also invaluable.

Professional Objections

Technical problems can be overcome, but I believe the more potent objections to doing fieldwork are linked to the structure of the academic profession. Again, let's consider several commonly heard arguments.

"There's no money in field studies." This objection is literally "on the money." The real dollars are in courthouse criminology and other methods dominated by the assumptions of those who fund it—that is, the Justice Department and others who are interested primarily in more efficient prosecution strategies (Horowitz, 1983b). If it's big grant money you want, ethnography, collaborative projects, and long, intensive field studies are not the way to go.

Our Milwaukee research received a total of $18,000 from Milwaukee foundations. For that $18,000 we designed the research and pretested it, identified and interviewed 47 founding members of Milwaukee's 19 major gangs and paid them $20 each, tabulated and analyzed the data, prepared a final report, and then wrote *People and Folks* (Hagedorn, 1988). The process took more than three years. Perry Macon was paid part-time out of the $18,000 while he worked and went to school, I took what I could and tried to support myself with some part-time consulting and teaching, and we paid for hundreds of pages of transcription and other costs. Although not exactly a "labor of love," our research didn't produce a living wage, either.

"Field studies take too long." This is also true. Gaining access to gangs is time-consuming, and publishable findings often take many years to develop. As Whyte (1943) points out, *Street Corner Society* took so long because he could "understand a group only through observing how it changed *through time*" (p. 357). Field studies disrupt the daily academic routine (Polsky, 1967), force the researcher to keep long hours (Becker, 1963; Horowitz, 1983b), and aren't conducive to writing the numerous journal articles necessary to get tenure or academic promotion. And if it is true that proven involvement in community issues is a prerequisite of trust, as suggested earlier, this may be too much to ask of most professional academics. Observing and talking to gang members on run-down playgrounds and solving problems of late welfare checks wasn't what most sociologists or criminologists had in mind when they embarked on an academic career.

"Fieldwork is dangerous." There is clearly more danger of getting shot on urban streets than in a university library. With violent behavior associated with cocaine, there is risk involved in doing this kind of research. Carl Taylor (1990) was forced to utilize "indirect" methods to obtain some of his field data. He felt "traditional up-front (open) research methodology could not be used in such risky conditions." Today's mean streets are not the ghettos of Thrasher, Whyte, or Suttles (Wilson, 1987).

Though I normally felt safe in our Milwaukee research, there were many uneasy situations. One time, rumors spread that I was a cop and Howard, a leader of a neighborhood gang, was my snitch. Howard was threatened with violence and called me urgently one night to "come through for me like I did for you." I went down to Howard's neighborhood and we calmly walked around together, Howard introducing me to everyone he knew—including local drug dealers. Howard reasoned no one would believe that I was a cop, and he was informing, if we were seen together so openly. He was right. The threats on Howard ceased. All the same, I must admit I was more than a little nervous on our late-night stroll.

Danger in gang field research comes from two sources. First, the very introduction of research into suspicious and law-violating communities creates problems. No matter how careful researchers are, there are people and events beyond his or her control. Random violence, or violence prompted by paranoia over the presence of researchers, may occur despite the most stringent precautions.

Second, violence can occur because of mistakes in technique. There are clearly some situations to avoid. Joan Moore instructed her *pinto* researchers to stay away from drug transactions, knowing they were likely scenes of violence. In Milwaukee, we took pains to interview gang leaders first, knowing that their participation would legitimate the research for others in their gang. Where the gang leadership was hostile to our requests for interviews, we backed off, fearing a "set-up" or confrontation. Although gang research is more dangerous than literature reviews, honest relationships with informants and sound methods of collecting data will reduce the probability of violence.

Technical objections to doing gang field research may be cop-outs, but the professional objections above *have* inhibited good gang fieldwork in the last decades. For aspiring academics, field research is not a good method to advance their careers, get fat government research grants, and sit back and enjoy the fruits of their long years of schooling. When these technical objections are added to the sparse numbers of minority social scientists, the scarcity of recent gang research becomes more comprehensible.

Conclusion:
Gangs and Underclass Research

But now we're back to where we started. This essay aims to persuade minority and White social scientists, students, and practitioners that undertaking gang field studies, though difficult, is not impossible. We can and must do more than tabulate crime statistics or interview incarcerated gang members. What kind of studies do we need?

James Short and Fred Strodtbeck (1965), in their impressive 1960s testing of gang theory, confessed that to do gang research properly they "were forced to be inventive." They called their method "retroductive"; they sought to expose themselves "to data not specifically relevant to existing hypotheses concerning gang delinquency and thereby to stimulate new perspectives and hypotheses" (pp. 24-25). I think we need such "retroductive" studies today, both to test the hypothesis that some gangs are underclass structures and to discover the unexpected.

We need bold people to take on the task of new social science descriptions of modern gangs. We need many forms of direct observation. We need life histories, like James Diego Vigil's recent book; we need ethnographies and participant observation, like Mercer Sullivan's or Felix Padilla's; we need collaborative projects like Joan Moore's; and more unique forms, like Carl Taylor recruiting researchers from his security firm. We need "involved observers" with gangs; people like Kenneth Clark, actively involved with community organization while using the tools of social science to describe, understand, and recommend.[10] We need research that sees underclass communities as participants, rather than just as data. Most of all, we need researchers—both from academia and outside it—who are not afraid to see for themselves, uncover stubborn facts, rethink old paradigms, and become advocates for new policy directions. We need a renewal of the 1920s Chicago school, which forced its students to go "from the library to the streets" (Kirk & Miller, 1986, p. 39).

The emergence of an underclass in our nation's cities poses questions that cannot be answered by courthouse criminology or surrogate sociology. Without more genuine fieldwork, all the surveys and SPSS-analyzed quantitative studies may be valid on their own terms, but they fail to help us understand what is really happening and what to do about it.

Notes

1. Ned Polsky coined the term *courthouse criminology*. Paul Elitzik of Lake View Press is to be blamed for coining *surrogate sociology*. For my unique definitions of these two terms, see the next sections.

2. Spergel and Curry's chapter in this volume (Chapter 13), based on data from the most recent national gang survey, is concerned *solely* with perceptions of mainly law enforcement officials.

3. Even keeping an accurate roster of a city's gangs may be problematic. Gangs come and go or change their names, merge with others, or fade away and then return. And sometimes public officials are just plain wrong. For example, many gangs in Milwaukee named themselves after the streets where they hung out. Milwaukee police listed the "2-7 Gang" (27th Street), "3-4 Mob" (34th Street), and so forth in their gang roster. When they arrested a bunch of kids on 19th Street, they wrote down they arrested the "1-9 Boys." The problem, one of those arrested in this sweep told us, was his 19th Street gang already had a name, the Deacons. The *real* 1-9 Boys hung out a few blocks away. Police never realized that their "1-9 Boys" were in fact two separate gangs.

4. For several years in Milwaukee, there was one set of grass-roots community agencies insisting there was a major gang problem and another set insisting there weren't any gangs at all. Was it coincidence that the first set of agencies received funding for "gang outreach" and the second set did not? Reporting of gang problems even within individual cities often proceeds in stages that may have nothing to do with variations in gang behavior, but more to do with the political needs of various actors with a stake in the problem (Hagedorn, 1988; Huff, 1989a).

5. Moore (1989a) and Hagedorn (1988) stress the distinction between the prevalent practice of individual gang members dealing drugs and less frequent drug dealing by organized criminal gangs. Taylor (1990) gives evidence to the contrary in Detroit.

6. In an old, but still interesting, field study, Miller (1958) does a time-study analysis and insists violence and crime occupy only a small portion of gang members' time. Even courthouse criminology can yield some surprises. In a 1983-1985 study of Los Angeles gangs and their relationship to crack cocaine, Malcolm Klein and Cheryl Maxson analyzed LAPD arrest data and found that while crack sales did dramatically escalate over that time, gang involvement in those sales did not, gang members were no more likely than nongang youths to possess firearms, firearms possession by gang members *decreased* over the period of study, most crack sales were small scale, and well-fortified rock houses were the exception rather than the rule in the household sale of crack. They sum up that the world of crack cocaine belongs to everyday drug dealers and not principally to street gangs (Klein, Maxson, & Cunningham, 1988).

7. Another classic example of genuinely gaining access to gangs is Short and Strodtbeck's (1965) comprehensive study of 1960s Chicago

gangs, which used YMCA "detached workers," gang members, and direct observation by field researchers over three years (see also Short, Chapter 10 of this volume).

8. For a discussion of "overrapport," or overidentifying with respondents because of shared characteristics such as ethnicity, see S. M. Miller (1969). For discussion of tendencies of minorities or liberals to withhold negative data considered stigmatizing, even if truthful, see Wilson (1987, p. 6) and Sawyer (1973, p. 367). White researchers could concentrate on White gangs, but there are fewer White gangs in cities than ever before. Class differences also create problems for minority researchers. See Vigil and Long, Chapter 2 of this volume, on etic and emic perspectives.

9. To be committed in this way to one's research subjects does not require adopting their viewpoint or values, or "going native." Rather, I believe, it is necessary to hold to your own values and "draw a line" between yourself and those you are studying. See, for example, Gouldner (1968) responding to Becker's (1963) *Outsiders*.

10. My own field studies have been "applied research," concerned with the altering of public policy. I have tried to apply Clark's role of "involved observer" to my studies of gangs and, currently, the welfare bureaucracy.

PART V

Public Policy Issues

12

Why the United States Has Failed to Solve Its Youth Gang Problem

WALTER B. MILLER

In the 1950s youth gangs were widely recognized as a serious problem in major U.S. cities. The image of the fighting gang was disseminated widely, and New York gang conflict was the subject of a play that became a classic of the American theater. Millions of dollars in federal, state, and local money were spent on scores of projects and programs aimed at the prevention and control of youth gang crime.

Three decades later, youth gangs still are widely recognized as a serious problem in the United States. But there is a major difference. Youth gangs of the 1980s and 1990s are more numerous, more prevalent, and more violent than in the 1950s, probably more so than at any time in the country's history.[1]

It is obvious that the United States not only has failed to solve the problem of youth gang crime but also has failed to keep it from getting worse—much worse. How can this failure be understood? The United States is one of the richest and most powerful nations in the world, with abundant resources in money and human talent. Why has its ability to secure a reasonable degree of safety and stability to millions of citizens in thousands of communities been frustrated for so long by a relatively small group of youthful males? This chapter will suggest some answers, however incomplete, to these questions.

But before addressing the major question of this chapter, it is necessary to ask whether the question itself should even be asked. Even to suggest that the problem of youth gangs might be ameliorated—let alone "solved"—could easily be seen as naive, disingenuous, or both. The United States faces and has faced a wide range of domestic problems, and although it has "solved" or dealt quite successfully with some (e.g., the Depression, elderly poor living in poverty, infectious diseases such as polio and scarlet fever), others remain unsolved, including a set of problems called "social problems." These include alcoholism, drug abuse, homelessness, illiteracy, public education failures, child abuse, welfare dependency, and others.

Prominent among social problems are problems of crime. Crime resulting from the use and marketing of drugs is a dominant national concern. High levels of homicide, particularly in certain urban centers, are endemic and persisting. Prison overcrowding in many states has reached unprecedented proportions. The United States has had limited success in mitigating, let alone solving, these and other serious crime problems. Why, then, is it legitimate even to imply that a long-standing problem such as youth gang crime might be more susceptible to a solution than the others?

In fact, it is quite possible to make a case that, unlike other persisting crime problems such as robbery, burglary, racketeering, white-collar fraud, and political corruption, crime by groups or gangs of youths—and particularly violent crimes—do in fact have a much better chance, not of being "solved" by elimination, but of being reduced substantially in frequency and severity. There is little doubt that there are powerful influences in many communities that undergird the formation and perpetuation of youth gangs, and that gang youth engage in more serious crimes than their nongang counterparts (W. B. Miller, 1969a; Tracy & Piper, 1981). But there are also certain characteristics of gangs and gang crime that suggest that these problems have a good potential for being mitigated by well-designed strategies.

First is the well-established finding that gang problems in particular localities wax and wane. Serious problems in some cities have diminished substantially or disappeared.[2] *Something* has happened that has caused dramatic reductions. This indicates that there do exist potentially identifiable factors associated with particular gang control programs, "natural" community developments, or both that cause gang problems to diminish or disappear. Efforts to focus specifically on identifying these factors could provide major policy guidelines for future control programs.

A second and related characteristic is the fact that there are some communities with demographic characteristics generally associated with serious gang problems (e.g., low-income inner-city areas, high concentrations of "minorities") but where gang problems are mild or absent. This again suggests that there are discoverable factors associated with the absence of gang problems.[3]

A third characteristic is the relatively young age of gang members—particularly of the "midgets," "pee wees," or "wanna-bes" in their early teens. Despite the appeal of the gang and the influence of older adolescents and young adults as role models, most gang members simply have not made the degree of commitment to crime found in older career criminals such as mafiosi or bank robbers. For many gang membership is a passing phase, and youths "mature out" to become law-abiding adults. Pressures to leave or not to join gangs are in many cases supported by community antigang pressures—sentiments that gang membership is foolish or ill advised, articulated not only by adult females, but also very often by ex-gang members. Younger individuals are more likely to be crime novices and less likely to escape detection and arrest than older and more experienced offenders. In addition, adolescent groups generally are less integrated into established crime networks that provide protection for members through payoffs, influence with politicians, and other connections with both legitimate and illegitimate organizations.

A fourth characteristic of youth gangs lies in the positive functions they serve in the lives of their members. Youth groups designated as "gangs" because their members customarily engage in crime are one subtype of a prevalent social form—the adolescent peer group.[4] These groups in the United States play a major role in the socialization of youth, and in this sense are not a problem but a solution, despite perceptions to the contrary by many adults. All but a small percentage of the activities of youth gangs consist of customary and legal forms of adolescent behavior—boy-girl contacts, group participation in recreation, entertainment, dancing, music, and the like. Gangs, like other adolescent groups, enable youths to learn important social skills in a group context.

It is important to note that as individuals with a proven capacity to function in a group context, gang members do not engage in either legal or illegal activities because of physical compulsions, as is the case, for example, for many drug and alcohol users. Crime by gang members is largely a product of social and cultural learning; it lacks the element of physiological addiction that makes the rehabilitation of drug addicts and alcoholics so difficult.

A final characteristic of youth gangs affecting prospects for gang control is the degree of visibility of gang activities. A major reason that efforts to control crimes such as drug dealing, robbery, burglary, computer fraud, and illegal financial manipulations is so difficult is that major operations are conducted in secrecy by people who go to great lengths to hide their identities and activities.

Youth gangs, by contrast, are for the most part highly visible, often ostentatiously so. Members of adult crime syndicates do not wear sweaters bearing the legend "Manhattan Mafia," nor do they list the names of syndicate members as graffiti on neighborhood walls. This is not to deny some element of secrecy in gang activities, but it is minor relative to their visible activities and the secrecy of most other kinds of collective crime. Both criminal justice and social service personnel throughout the years have had relatively little difficulty in identifying members of local youth gangs and tracking their activities. This characteristic greatly facilitates the task of locating and dealing with gang crime.

History of Gang Control Efforts

The nation's failure to remedy its gang problems is not attributable to lack of effort. Scores of programs have been implemented and millions of dollars spent in efforts to cope with gang problems. A historical examination of approximately 60 such enterprises reported between 1920 and 1985 can be summarized by citing five of its conclusions (Miller, 1985). First, programs were based on a limited number of basic philosophies and methods; most programs used one or some combination of five major approaches. Second, with the exception of a small number of innovations, the great majority of programs could be described as pedestrian and unimaginative. Third, procedures were used repeatedly during the 65-year period independent of evidence on their effectiveness. Nor did the fact that a number of the most popular methods had been evaluated as ineffective keep them from being used again. Prominent among approaches showing poor results were those based on the philosophy of attempting to change gangs by changing the overall character of their communities. Finally, since the 1920s, methods based on a set of popular rallying cries—including those of "prevention" and "coordination"— have been advocated repeatedly despite little evidence of their feasibility or potential effectiveness.[5]

If one accepts the proposition that youth gang problems are less intransigent than many other persisting crime problems, one might have expected a better record of success than appears from the historical review. In fact, it is possible that some of the programs did have a more positive impact than can be demonstrated, but the poor quality of available evidence makes it very difficult to determine which of the methods used were better and which were worse. As a consequence, those who face today's serious gang problems do not have at their disposal reliable information on a set of methods with a proven capacity to produce positive results. This is one reason for the low rate of success in coping with gang problems. This chapter discusses this and other reasons under four major headings: strategy, resources, implementation, and social context.

Strategy

A central reason for the failure of the United States to deal effectively with youth gang problems lies in its failure to develop a comprehensive national gang control strategy. This task poses major problems of conceptualization as well as implementation, but the absence of either a guiding plan or any serious intention to develop one is a critical defect. With some exceptions, most current efforts are localized and parochial, unrelated to programs in other localities or to past experiences in their own or other communities.

What form would such a strategy take? Visualizing its character is not as difficult as one might suppose. A major precedent is provided by going back three decades to the experience of President John F. Kennedy's Committee on Juvenile Delinquency and Youth Crime (PCJD), authorized under the Juvenile Delinquency and Youth Offenses Control Act of 1961.

Although this program was aimed at the broader problem of juvenile delinquency, its general approach is directly applicable to the more specific problem of youth gang crime. Conceptually the strategy was relatively simple. It comprised nine major steps or phases, some of which could run currently with others:

(1) Establish an office at the federal level to support and oversee the national effort.
(2) Select a variety of sites throughout the country that manifest the problem at issue.
(3) Develop, adopt, or adapt explanations on a general theoretical level for the problem at issue.
(4) Develop remedial programs whose basic procedures are derived logically from the basic tenets of the general explanation.
(5) Implement the programs.
(6) Do careful evaluation research on program results.
(7) Use the evaluation findings to judge the relative effectiveness of the various local programs.

(8) Develop program "models" by refining program procedures and adapting them to other locales and/or situations.

(9) Keep experimenting until methods are developed that work better or, at least, fail less.

Looked at in historical perspective, this approach might appear wildly idealistic, and in fact the implementation of the program encountered major obstacles. In contrast with the simplicity and clarity of the conception, its implementation required those who ran the programs to confront extremely difficult political, procedural, and practical problems, only some of which were accommodated successfully.[6]

But despite these problems, 12 major cities—including New York, Los Angeles, Chicago, Philadelphia, Detroit, and Cleveland—formulated and implemented major prevention and control programs on the basis of national guidelines. All of these cities implemented steps 3, 4, and 5, and a few implemented step 6. The overall program was aborted not by the obstacles it faced but by the assassination of President Kennedy and a policy decision by the succeeding administration to direct the programs and resources of the PCJD into other channels.

Nothing in the experience of the program negated its basic assumption that a rational, systematic, national-level remedial program incorporating major elements of theory formulation and evaluation was workable and potentially effective. Comparing the conduct of present-day gang control programs to the conduct of the PCJD gives the impression that there has been a major step backward. The sophistication of national efforts to cope with gang problems has not kept pace with the increasing seriousness of the problem, and seems instead to have diminished. It is difficult to conceive of any current agency, public or private, proposing a gang control strategy with the scope and conceptual breadth of the PCJD.[7]

Using the PCJD procedures as one model of a systematically developed strategy makes it possible to identify several elements that appear to be weak or absent in most current efforts. Three of these will be discussed briefly: national perspective, theory, and evaluation.

National Perspective

In approaching the problem of juvenile delinquency, the PCJD took as its major arena the whole of the United States, viewing the problem from a broad national perspective. By contrast, for most current efforts the arena of consideration is a single city, county, or, rarely, state.

By failing to conceptualize the youth gang problem as a national rather than a local phenomenon, the enterprise of gang control loses the advantage of powerful tools for developing better information and more effective strategies. There is at present no centralized source of national information on the most basic and fundamental facts about gangs, let alone information on the location, character, and effects of gang control efforts. No one knows, for example, how many gangs and gang members there are in the United States, the location and seriousness of gang problems, how much crime and what kinds of crime gang members are responsible for, or the social characteristics of gang members. Data-collection operations such as the routine collection of unemployment information by the Bureau of Labor Statistics or of arrest data by the Federal Bureau of Investigation have never been considered seriously, let alone implemented. The absence of this kind of basic information makes it virtually impossible to ascertain with any accuracy the scope and seriousness of gang problems, and thus the priority to be assigned to gang control efforts. Nor is there a central resource available either to cities facing new gang problems or to cities that might want to review their own past efforts—efforts for which the historical record is often lost or ignored.

Further, the failure to conceptualize the problem as a national phenomenon deprives program efforts of the power of a major analytic instrument—the comparative method. Physical science uses the device of experimental variation as a major tool; for complex social problems like youth gang crime this method is generally impractical, politically unfeasible, or both. In its place investigators have developed a technique that starts by identifying as wide as possible a set of existing variations of the phenomenon at issue, and using this observed variation as a kind of natural experiment that can provide—among other things—important clues to critical questions of cause and of program effectiveness. Youth gangs, with their immense variety of sizes, types, and circumstances, are tailor-made for the application of the comparative method, but in the absence of a national perspective its potentially rich yield remains untapped.

Theory

It would seem logical that the prospects for developing more effective methods for dealing with a difficult social problem like youth gang crime would be enhanced greatly by the availability of an acceptable explanation of what causes that problem. What factors and conditions are associated with the emergence and persistence of law-violating youth gangs? Which of these are most susceptible to change through planned strategies, policies, and programs? Current answers to these questions are poor. One might expect that as youth gang problems have become more serious and more prevalent during the past two decades that there would have been a commensurate increase in research on basic causes—as, for example, in the case of AIDS. But in fact the opposite seems to have happened.

During the 1950s a brief period of concern with theories of youth gangs, mostly by sociologists, produced a number of theoretical formulations based on the circumstances of that period. Among these were Albert Cohen's delinquent subculture theory, Cloward and Ohlin's blocked opportunity theory, and Walter Miller's lower-class subculture theory. Since that period efforts to refine old theories and/or develop new ones have decreased significantly. Some 30 years later, these formulations, along with the Chicago school explanations of the 1920s and 1930s, still constitute the major set of sociological explanations available for explaining youth gang behavior. One of the few recently developed explanational frameworks centers on the concept of *underclass*, and there have been efforts to relate this notion to youth gang problems (Hagedorn, 1988; Moore, 1985). This concept will be discussed in a later section.

There have been hundreds of gang control operations and programs during the past several decades, but few of them have been based on explicitly developed theoretical formulations as was the case for the PCJD programs. Of course there have been rationales for these efforts, but for the most part these have been based largely on implicit and unexamined premises, many derived from political philosophies rather than research-based explanations.

Two positions have been particularly influential: an "individual responsibility" position favored by conservatives and a "social injustice" position favored by liberals. The first blames youth gang problems on personal failings of gang members, their families, and their communities, related to a general decline in public morality. The second blames gang problems on discriminatory and exploitative policies by the larger society that foster inequality, race discrimination, and blocked opportunities.

It is unrealistic to expect the development of general explanations that are free of political philosophies, but it does seem reasonable to advocate a renewed effort to develop explanations that present their basic premises openly and rationally, and are derived as much as possible from conclusions based on careful research.[8]

Evaluation

The PCJD required its programs to include an evaluation component on the assumption that without systematic evaluation it is impossible to present credible evidence on program impact. Evaluation research on social programs is a highly developed field with an extensive literature that describes specific techniques and specifies in detail research designs for a variety of evaluation contexts and objectives.

The execution of a sound evaluation design poses difficult problems, technical and political. In the 1960s serious efforts were made to identify and overcome these problems. As a result, a number of successful evaluations of gang programs were completed. Wright and Dixon (1977) describe six gang program evaluations conducted between 1959 and 1971, along with 12 evaluations of Area and Youth Service projects, some of which included gang components.

In recent years, as gang problems have increased, the conduct of program evaluation has decreased. A bibliography of juvenile gangs prepared in 1983 by the U.S. Office of Juvenile Justice cites 115 documents; of these, only two are evaluation studies, and only one of these reports results (Seidman, 1983). Irving Spergel's 1989 survey of 45 cities with gang programs found only two evaluation reports, neither of which—according to Spergel—constitutes a comprehensive outcome evaluation (Spergel, Curry, Ross, & Chance, 1989).[9]

The virtual abandonment of sound evaluation of gang control efforts is a major reason for our failure to reduce gang problems. Evaluation research permits rational, systematic progress in developing more effective methods by making it possible to decrease the use of methods that are shown to be less effective and to refine and increase the use of more effective methods. In the absence of the kind of outcome evidence provided by sound evaluation, officials can and often do make exaggerated claims of success without credible supporting evidence.[10] Without evaluation the choice of gang control methods is speculative and inefficient. Any hope of developing more effective methods requires that evaluation research on gang programs be resumed.

Resources

Those who have access to financial and human resources must be willing to direct those resources to the solution of particular social problems if effective remedial methods are to be developed and implemented. Despite the popular slogan that social problems are not solved by throwing money at them, progress in coping with difficult problems such as youth gang crime is next to impossible without adequate financing. Resources available to youth gang control in the 1990s are meager in both absolute and relative terms.

Accurate information on the exact amounts of money allocated to gang control is difficult to obtain. One reason for this is that most gang control activity is conducted on the local level by criminal justice agencies as part of their overall crime control operations. Calculating the proportion of a general operating budget that goes to support gang control as such, while theoretically possible, is in most instances difficult in practice.

But what limited information is available strongly suggests that if the importance of a social problem is measured by the amount of money allocated to it, youth gang problems rank very low in the nation's priorities. Some evidence on the importance of gang problems at the federal level is provided by the *Catalog of Federal Domestic Assistance Programs.* The 1989 edition lists 1,139 grant programs under approximately 535 major subject categories, including alcoholism, crime, and juvenile delinquency. Youth gangs are not listed as a major or minor category. Of the 1,139 listed programs, the term *gang* appears in descriptions of four programs, or about one-third of 1% of all programs; of these, two involve gang control as such, another a conference on gangs, and a fourth a program of drug abuse prevention and education as it relates to youth gangs. By contrast, there are 23 grant programs for alcoholism, 37 for narcotics, 16 for recreation, and 19 for youth programs not involving gangs (U.S. Office of Management and Budget, 1989).

The 1990 federal budget allocates about $10 billion to drug programs administered by the Office of National Drug Control Policy. There is no Office of National Gang Control Policy, and a generous estimate of the amounts allocated at the federal level to all gang-related enterprises produces a figure that is less than 1% of this amount. This follows a year that recorded the highest number of gang-related homicides in history for a single county—at least 570 gang homicide victims in 1989 in Los Angeles County (Hormell, 1990).

How can one explain why the federal government places such a low priority on youth gang problems? Some see it as one consequence of a general reluctance by recent conservative administrations to allocate needed funds to domestic social programs; this is particularly evident, the argument goes, during periods of severe budget constraints. But this factor alone is not enough to account for the low priority. As just shown, another domestic problem, drugs, is granted a very high priority at the federal level. In addition, low funding for gang control has prevailed during both conservative and liberal administrations.

The difference between the priorities accorded to gangs and to drugs raises the issue of what it is that determines the priority of social problems. This complex issue cannot be examined here, but one important element is the role of victimization. Groups such as the homeless, abused children, or battered women are readily perceived as pitiable victims and thus more easily command higher priorities. Victimization in connection with gang crime is more ambiguous. There are thousands of individual victims of gang violence each year, but most of these share the same social characteristics as their victimizers; the same people are often both victims and assailants. It is hard to enlist the degree of sympathy evoked by a homeless mother with three small children for an 18-year-old minority youth shot in a gang dispute.

Even further, there are those in public positions who privately consider youth gang violence as a solution, not a problem (see Miller, 1982). Priority considerations are affected by a cynical "let them kill each other off" philosophy. This position obscures the issue of victimization in its broader sense, and illuminates the differences between federal authorities and lower-class communities with respect to priorities. Few middle-class communities are victimized by gangs; it is in the nation's slums, ghettos, and barrios that one finds the principal victims of gang activity. In these communities are many residents whose dominant concern is the security and stability of community life—a security that gangs seriously jeopardize. Prominent among these residents are mothers whose children are at risk. These are the Americans who are most directly victimized by gangs, and it these Americans for whom gang control is a major priority.

Here one finds a serious disparity between priorities and resources. In most cases these communities have limited political power, and hence little access to potential resources. Gang control is a low national priority in large part because those with good access to resources put a low priority on gang problems and those who put a high priority on gang problems have poor access to resources.

Implementation

There is not a single organized agency in the United States, public or private, that takes specific responsibility for youth gangs as a national problem. There are thousands of organizations and associations conducting programs and advocating remedial measures for such problems as alcoholism, firearms use, abused children, or race relations, but there is no National Organization for Gang Control and no federal Office of Gang Control.

As in the case of street crime in general, the traditional position of federal authorities is that youth gangs are a local problem and should be handled at the local level. There is no doubt that there are essential gang control tasks that can be performed only at the local level, but it is also true that there are other important tasks that locals are in not in a position to perform. Previous sections have described a variety of elements needed for the development of more effective methods. These include the formulation of a comprehensive national strategy, basic research and theory development, evaluation research, and conducting operations in the context of a national arena.

By and large, workers at the local level are concerned primarily with conducting agency service operations, and some regard activities such as evaluation or theory development as irrelevant if not harmful. And even those who do see value in such elements are seldom in a position to act on their beliefs. Without local efforts a national strategy has no substance, but without a national strategy local efforts are denied the potential of powerful operational assets.

What type of organization should assume primary responsibility for youth gang problems? Organizations that in the past have played a major role are private foundations, universities, and the federal government. All have conducted important gang control activities, often in conjunction with one another.

For a variety of reasons, including its organizational continuity and access to resources as well as its constitutional obligation to ensure domestic tranquility, the federal government appears as the most appropriate locus of responsibility. But throughout the years federal agencies have shown little inclination to assume major responsibility for gang problems, and have even—in some instances—evinced antagonism to the idea.

In 1978, for example, the Subcommittee on Juvenile Delinquency of the Judiciary Committee of the U.S. Senate held hearings on serious juvenile crime. A witness had submitted a detailed proposal for the establishment of a federal gang control operation, and cited that proposal in his oral testimony. The idea was rejected decisively and unconditionally by the committee chairman, a liberal Democrat (Miller, 1976).

Federal agencies have in the past and still do support programs relevant to gang control, but these have been sporadic, unrelated to any coherent strategy, and scattered among various agencies without effective coordination.[11] There is nothing like a federal Office of Gang Control, analogous to the Office of Drug Control Strategy, located in a cabinet-level department or in an office with the responsibility for coordinating programs in several departments. Without a center of responsibility at the federal level—an office with the authority and resources to develop a national strategy and monitor efforts at the national, state, and local levels—the enterprise of gang control is severely handicapped.

Social Context

A particularly vexing reason for the nation's failure to solve its gang problem lies in a pervasive reluctance to face squarely the issue of the social context of gang crime. The social context of gang life and the social characteristics of most gang members entail a set of extremely sensitive issues involving social class and ethnicity that are highly charged in U.S. society, and evoke strong passions.

During the 1950s most sociologists studying gangs were in essential agreement that there was a special relation between youth gangs and the population at lower social levels. There was less agreement on how to refer to this population and exactly what characteristics to use to define it, and even less agreement on how it came into being and was sustained over time (Cloward & Ohlin, 1960; Cohen, 1955; Miller, 1958; Rodman, 1963).[12]

But beyond these differences there was a fair consensus that there was an American lower class, and that most youth gangs were in some way a product of the life circumstances of that class. In the succeeding years the existence and special characteristics of the lower class have become more firmly established, and the link between gangs and the lower class has grown even stronger. But during this time the willingness of most policymakers and planners to utilize this link as a central key to gang control strategy has diminished.

My own position in the 1950s was based on three major premises: that there are identifiable social classes in the United States; that one of these classes, centered on the circumstances of low-skilled labor, can be called the lower class; and that this class, in common with others, has a subculture with distinctive characteristics as well as characteristics shared with other class subcultures (Miller, 1958, 1959).

During the last 30 years few public figures have agreed with the last two premises. The terms used to refer to this population reveal a deep reluctance to characterize it in social class terms, let alone perceive the class as having a distinctive subculture. Commonly used terms include *the disadvantaged, the underprivileged, inner-city residents,* and *the culturally deprived.* Even during the height of national concern with this population, in the War on Poverty in the 1960s, the primary term used to refer to the population was *the poor,* a term based on income rather than on class.

What had been a virtual taboo among public figures against characterizing low-status populations as a class finally came to an end in the 1980s, with the surprisingly rapid acceptance and spread of the term *underclass.* Most analysts in the 1980s who examined the links between youth gangs and the lower class utilized the underclass concept—a concept whose connotation in the 1980s derived largely from a seminal study of young Black males in the Watts district of Los Angeles in the 1960s (Auletta, 1982; Glasgow, 1980; Wilson, 1987).[13]

The gangs and underclass position is essentially a variant of Cloward and Ohlin's blocked opportunity theory of the 1960s. Underclass theory postulates a new social class created by a new set of demographic, technological, and economic conditions whereby the demand for low-skilled workers in an increasingly service-oriented high-tech economy has been reduced drastically, permanently locking them out of the labor market and cutting off upward mobility routes available to earlier generations. At the same time, the sense of community formerly found in lower-class neighborhoods has weakened, alienating inner-city minorities not only from the society at large but from higher-status members of their own ethnic groups. The formation of gangs is a response by alienated minority youth to the unavailability of legitimate employment and potential for fulfillment in their local communities.

Briefly, the underclass is a product of technological and economic changes coupled with persisting racism in U.S. society. In common with Cloward and Ohlin, underclass theorists see economic forces and their impact on the availability of jobs as the primary forces that generate and sustain the underclass.

The subcultural position views the contemporary lower class quite differently. It is not outside the system, it is not new, and it is sustained by important subcultural influences that arise from a variety of social forces in addition to economic circumstances. Unlike the underclass position—which depicts the underclass as not only outside of, but permanently excluded from the existing social class system of the United States—the contemporary lower class is seen as an intrinsic part of that system, sharing countless cultural characteristics with members of other social classes as well as manifesting distinctive characteristics. Lower-class citizens are as much a part of American society as their fellow citizens in other classes.

Rather than representing a "new" social class that manifests a sharp break with the past—a difference in kind, not degree—

the contemporary lower class represents a logical historical development of a traditional population category. Major features used in the past to characterize this class, such as prevalence of female-based households, limited involvement in formal education, reliance on public welfare, and prevalence of births out of wedlock, have not disappeared or diminished significantly. On the contrary, many have become more prevalent. The contemporary lower class is not a new class, but a further developed and more distinctive version of a traditional class.[14]

Despite differences in conceptions and definitions of the lower class, underclass theorists agree with other analysts on the "special link" noted earlier between gangs and the lower class. If the existence and importance of this special link is accepted, the question of its policy implications for gang control becomes relevant.

One logical policy option can be stated simply, but raises very complicated issues. If youth gangs are a product of the circumstances of the lower class, eliminating or substantially changing these circumstances will eliminate or substantially reduce gang problems. This position is seldom stated this baldly, but the general notion has served on some level as a rationale for many programs, past and proposed. If characteristics such as female-headed households, limited educational background, intermittent employment and low-skilled jobs, poor housing, inferior health resources, and others contribute to the persistence of the lower class, then successful efforts to raise job skill levels, ensure steady employment, and improve education, housing, health, and other services will change its essential character and ameliorate its major social problems—including high crime rates and youth gang crime.

There are serious problems with this formulation. As noted in the historical review of gang programs, major programs based on this approach were not successful. An important reason is that the major premise, that gangs arise out of the circumstances of lower-class life, is inadequate. It is almost always true that where you find youth gangs you will find lower-class communities, but the obverse does not obtain. As noted earlier, there are numerous lower-class communities that do not have youth gangs. This suggests that there are certain critical features of lower-class life whose presence enhances the development of gangs, and whose absence inhibits that development; what these are is not known (Delaney & Miller, 1977).

Taking the position that it is the totality of lower-class life that produces gangs and that this totality must be changed to affect gangs is like trying to kill a gnat with a pile driver. However desirable such change might be, if gang control is in fact one's objective a policy of effecting major changes in the character of lower-class life and the complex set of societywide forces that sustain it is misdirected, inefficient, and uneconomical. Even if prospects for success were far better than they now appear, it would take many years to achieve results that would affect gangs; meanwhile, millions of lower-class citizens continue to suffer bitterly because of youth gang violence.

As suggested by Spergel and his colleagues (1989b), what is needed are carefully targeted programs focused on specific objectives and based on explicit explications of how achieving specific program objectives will affect gangs. How can we know which elements are most critically associated with the presence or absence of gangs? As suggested earlier, we can use the fact of the absence of gangs in many lower-class communities and their intermittent absence in others as a key to research aimed at detecting and identifying these critical elements—elements known to be changeable because they have changed—and use this knowledge as a basis for devising more focused programs and policies. As noted earlier, compared to such "core" characteristics of lower-class life as female-headed households and low-skilled labor, youth gangs are less intrinsic to the subculture, and thus less resistant to change.

The social class status of contemporary youth gang members is close to that of their counterparts in the 1950s; the same cannot be said of their ethnic status. In the 1950s a substantial proportion of gang members were Caucasian; in the 1990s almost all gang members belong to a category designated as "minority."[15] This has made the task of developing solutions to the gang problem more difficult, both conceptually and tactically.

Present-day lower-class populations, as in the past, comprise a wide variety of subtypes. Differences among subtypes are based on ethnicity (e.g., Black, Hispanic), region (southern, northern), location (urban-rural), religion, and other bases of subcultural differentiation. Of particular relevance to youth gang policy are subtypes based on recency of immigration. Today, as in the past, one can divide these populations into two gross categories—newcomers (more recently arrived) and established minorities (less recent).

It is likely that youth gangs belonging to these two categories come into being and are sustained by different kinds of causal influences, and would require significantly different remedial strategies. In the 1990s the established minority category consists primarily of youth of Puerto Rican, Mexican, and African backgrounds; the newcomer category is much more heterogeneous, comprising a variety of Latin American groups (Panamanians, Nicaraguans, and others) and about 10 different Asian nationalities.

Youth gangs in the newcomer populations show many similarities to the gangs of the 1910s and 1920s described by Frederick Thrasher (1927), and can be seen, now as then, as occupying a transitional status as part of the process of Americanization (Launer & Palenski, 1989). A major difference between the newcomers and the established minorities is their potential for upward social mobility. If history is any guide, gangs in most of the newcomer groups will cease being a problem after a few generations of normal acculturation and upward mobility. The underclass explanation for gangs, which postulates little or no mobility for its minorities, has limited relevance to the newcomer gang phenomenon.

It is the problem of gangs among the established minorities that raises the most complicated and painful policy issues, because it taps into one of the most divisive and intractable issues in the history of the republic—that of race relations. There is deep concern in minority communities over tendencies in the media and elsewhere to stereotype gangs as a minority phenomenon. Programs aimed at controlling gangs in minority communities may face opposition from one community faction for unfairly stigmatizing minorities or violating their civil liberties while being supported by another faction as a necessary measure for protecting the safety of law-abiding citizens. For some the explanation that minority gang problems are a product of racism is so compelling and complete as to obviate the need for further research into causes.

Another issue is that of the ethnic status of personnel involved in gang programs. In the 1950s there was a fair amount of cross-ethnic involvement in gang work. In some cases Black adults provided services and guidance for White gangs, and Whites worked with Black gangs (W. B. Miller, 1969a). In the 1990s this kind of relationship is rare. Many minority workers claim a special competence and a special right to work with youth of their own ethnic status, and are inhospitable to the involvement of persons of different backgrounds. There are certainly good grounds for the claim of special competence, but there is also a danger that capable and dedicated people of other ethnic statuses will be discouraged from contributing to an enterprise that needs all the help it can get.

Conclusion

This chapter has explained the nation's failure to solve its youth gang problems as a consequence of major procedural and policy deficiencies. The following reasons for the failure have been presented: The nation has failed to develop a comprehensive gang control strategy. The problem is viewed in local and parochial terms instead of from a national perspective. Programs are implemented in the absence of demonstrably valid theoretical rationales. Efforts to systematically evaluate program effectiveness have been virtually abandoned. Resources allocated to the gang problem are incommensurate with the severity of the problem. There is no organizational center of responsibility for gang problems anywhere in the United States. There is a deep-rooted reluctance to face up to the implications of the social context of gang life.

But such a catalogue of deficiencies becomes valuable only insofar as it provides the basis of proposals for more effective policies. A comprehensive national gang control strategy must be developed. Efforts in local communities should be informed by policies based on a national-level perspective. Gang control operations should be undergirded by sound theoretical rationales. The determination of which methods are most effective must be based on carefully conducted evaluation research. Serious efforts must be made to convince those who control resources that gang control should be granted a much higher priority. A federal office of youth gang control should be established. Accurate information on the social class and ethnic characteristics of gang communities should be used as a major element in the development of more effective gang control strategies.

This is admittedly a very ambitious set of recommendations, and there is little likelihood at present that even a few might be considered seriously. But they will have served some useful purpose if they can be seen as indicating general directions for developing a more effective national youth gang policy.

Notes

1. In the absence of accurate national data for the current period as well as for previous periods, trends in the number of gangs, of gang members, the volume and forms of gang crime, and other indices of gang problems can only be estimated. Evidence presented in the most recent national-level gang survey presenting these kinds of data, however, supported the conclusion that problems in 1980 were more serious than at any previous time. In the succeeding decade all available evidence strongly suggests further worsening of gang problems (see Miller, 1982).

2. The two cities whose gang problems received most national attention in the late 1960s and early 1970s were New York and Philadelphia. Philadelphia reported a record 47 gang-related homicides in 1970; New York, a record 57 in 1972. In 1978 only one gang-related homicide was reported for Philadelphia, and in 1988, none. In 1988 the Philadelphia police had no unit or officers with a specialized gang function. New York in 1971 had an active gang intelligence unit with special gang officers in Manhattan, Queens, Brooklyn, and Staten Island. In 1988 there were two gang officers in the police department, and gang homicides—no longer separately tabulated—were estimated by police at less than 5.

3. A preliminary attempt to identify measurable characteristics associated with the level of seriousness of gang problems in different cities is

reported in Delaney and Miller (1977). Twenty-three cities were ranked according to seriousness of gang problems, and data on 426 demographic and other variables were collected for each city; a subset of 90 variables was used for analysis. A variety of statistical techniques, including clustering and factor analysis, was used. A few variables such as population density were associated with differences among cities, but in general the techniques used were unable to identify the critical elements associated with more serious gang problems.

4. Terms used here follow the usage recommended in Miller (1989). The term *gang* is applied only to groups that engage routinely in illegal activity.

5. Discussions and general recommendations with respect to prevention and coordination have shown a high degree of continuity over the last 60 years. See, for example, Peyser (1932), National School Safety Center (1988), Rubinow (1954), and Bryant (1989).

6. The President's Committee on Juvenile Delinquency and Youth Crime is discussed in Moynihan (1969) and in Maris and Rein (1967). Outcomes of PCJD programs are discussed in Miller (1966b).

7. There is one contemporary gang control project whose design incorporates many of the elements of the PCJD—the National Youth Gang Suppression and Intervention Project, directed by Irving A. Spergel under the auspices of the University of Chicago's School of Social Service Administration and the Department of Justice's Office of Juvenile Justice and Delinquency Prevention. The major objective of the project is to locate those current gang control efforts in the United States that appear most effective or most promising, analyze their techniques, and construct program models that could serve as a basis for more effective programs throughout the country. The project has conducted a wide variety of activities in connection with this objective, including the production of what is probably the best general review of the youth gang literature ever compiled. Like the PCJD, Spergel's project takes the whole nation as its arena, examines a wide variety of sites with differing conditions, and ties its programmatic proposals to a specific theoretical explanation for the existence of gang problems. One difference between the PCJD and Spergel's project in this respect is that the PCJD utilized a number of different theories as the basis for different kinds of program strategies; Spergel's project uses a single theory—community disorganization—one of the principal gang theories, but still only one.

8. Outside of the PCJD, no known project has used the technique of indirectly testing the validity of particular theories by measuring the effectiveness of programs developed out of or corresponding to those theories. One major project, however, did take a significant step in this direction by designing a research program explicitly as a test of several competing theories of gangs (see Short & Strodtbeck, 1965).

9. Exceptions to the dearth of evaluation studies include Dahmann (1981) and Klein, Maxson, and Gordon (1984).

10. Following the decline in gang activity in Philadelphia in the 1970s, representatives of more than a half dozen agencies or programs, including the police department, claimed primary credit for the outcome. It is still impossible to know which programs or combinations of programs, if any, were responsible for the change. A recent example of unsubstantiated claims of effectiveness appears in *Gangs in Schools*, which states that "there is unanimous agreement that this type of early prevention is the most effective way to stem gang delinquency" (National School Safety Center, 1988). In addition to the problem of demonstrating that no one in the country disagrees with this proposition, there has been no systematic evaluation research showing that this method is effective at all, let alone the most effective of all known methods.

11. There have been some attempts to organize gang control efforts on other than a strictly local basis. California has a statewide organization for police officers working in gang control. A national-level data base on street gangs was initiated in 1989 by the U.S. Drug Enforcement Administration and the National Association of Chiefs of Police. The data base, however, is not intended to serve the general purposes of gang control throughout the nation but rather as a specific aid to law enforcement agencies engaged in drug control activities. Gang-related programs are conducted by different federal agencies, including the Family and Youth Service Bureau of the Department of Health and Human Services, the Office of Juvenile Justice and Delinquency Prevention, and the Drug Enforcement Administration of the Department of Justice, but there are no organizational arrangements for coordinating these efforts.

12. Cloward and Ohlin, Miller, Rodman, and others used the term *lower class* to refer to the population at issue; Cohen used the term *working class*, but in effect the population he was concerned with was similar to that of the other writers.

13. In earlier years the term *underclass* was classified along with terms such as *lumpenproletariat* as a pejorative term. See W. B. Miller (1969b).

14. Accurate data on historical changes in the subcultural characteristics of the U.S. lower class are difficult to obtain. W. B. Miller (1969) defined the lower class in subcultural terms as manifesting "a characteristic set of life conditions and customary behavioral practices" and discussed 10 of these, including involvement in low-skilled labor, prevalence of female-headed households, and limited educational attainment. Data on these conditions and practices available through routine data collection operations are rough surrogates at best. Some available information, however—such as the Census Bureau data on the "population below the poverty level," a population that overlaps to a considerable degree the subculturally defined lower class—provides some relevant evidence. The data suggest that during the past several decades many lower-class subcultural practices have become more firmly established and more distinctive when compared with equivalent practices by other social classes. For example, in 1959 the percentage of female-headed households in the poverty-level population was about 23%; in 1966,

about 30%; and in 1984, about 48%. Other characteristics show analogous trends. One exception relating to formal education involves the practice of dropping out of high school. In 1975 about two-thirds of poverty-level youth left high school before graduation, but by 1982 this figure had fallen to about 54%. This could indicate a weakening of the "limited concern with formal education" characteristic. It could also reflect an easing of requirements for graduation in some areas.

15. The term *minority* has been and is still used to refer to a wide variety of different population categories. At the turn of the century, the term was used primarily to refer to ethnic populations of Irish, Italian, Jewish, and Slavic backgrounds. In recent years the term has been used to designate a variety of different populations, ethnic and nonethnic, including women, although women in fact constitute a majority of the population. In contemporary usage the term *minority* is used most commonly to refer to populations of Hispanic and Black African background, along with some of the more recently arrived ethnic populations.

13

Strategies and Perceived Agency Effectiveness in Dealing with the Youth Gang Problem

IRVING A. SPERGEL
G. DAVID CURRY

A major objective of the National Youth Gang Suppression and Intervention Research and Development project in cooperation with the Office of Juvenile Justice and Delinquency Prevention is to identify promising approaches to dealing with the youth gang problem. In this excerpt from the National Youth Gang Survey (Spergel, Curry, Ross, & Chance, 1989), we examine the relationship between youth gang program strategies and perceived program effectiveness as well as

AUTHORS' NOTE: This chapter was prepared under grant 87-JS-CX-K100(S-1) from the Office of Juvenile Justice and Delinquency Prevention, Office of Justice Programs, U.S. Department of Justice. Points of view and opinions in this document are those of the authors and do not necessarily represent the official position or policies of the U.S. Department of Justice. We are indebted to Ron Chance, Ruth Ross, Amy Chak, Alba Alexander, Candice Kane, Phyllis Garth, Dawn Isis, Michael Hyatt, Robert Caldero, Paul Hamada, Pamela Rodriguez, and Janet Curry for varying levels of assistance in the research from which this chapter is drawn. Also of considerable value to us were the comments of Malcolm Klein, Walter Miller, and Cheryl Maxson on earlier versions of the report of the research.

reduction in the problem. The survey was part of the assessment stage and is to be followed by prototype development, technical assistance and training, and prototype testing stages.

National Youth Gang Survey

We were interested not simply in the scope and character of the youth gang problem but in the response to it at the organizational, and especially the community, level. It was likely that the youth gang problem was structural since it was pervasive across a variety of institutions and communities. Based on earlier research, we were sensitized to the possibility that agency response patterns might be indicative of social disorganization and poverty/underclass or anomie explanations of the youth gang problem (see, for example, Kornhauser, 1978). At the same time we were aware that most organizations that deal with the youth gang problem usually do so out of a general organizational mission, and not necessarily through an exclusive or primary focus on the youth gang problem.

Our interest in youth gangs was defined primarily in law enforcement terms. Therefore, our study deals mainly with high-profile youth gangs who have come to police attention usually for violent, but sometimes for various other kinds of criminal behavior, including drug use and trafficing. Youth gangs tend to be better organized than delinquent groups, with established traditions in some of the larger cities where the problem is chronic. Youth gangs also tend to have a communal and more complex functional character probably serving a greater variety of interests and need than ad hoc delinquent groups. The two concepts, youth gangs and delinquent groups, are overlapping and distinctive rather than categorically different. Moreover, the definition of the youth gang also varies within cities by different kinds of agencies and especially across cities, and probably by sizes of cities. The term *youth gang* refers often (but not always) to youths, mainly males between the ages of 12 and 25, in various organizational forms. Race/ethnicity, region or city, economic opportunities, and traditions appear to influence organizational forms and behavioral patterns.

The data were obtained from 254 respondents in 45 cities and six institutional agencies (mainly correctional sites) selected through a process that began with the screening of approximately 100 cities. Selection criteria included the following: presence and recognition of a youth gang problem; the presence of a youth gang program; the existence of a program for at least a year, whether operating currently or in the recent past; an articulated set of program goals; evidence of more than a simplistic unitary response to the problem, such as either only police arrests or youth gang recreation programs; and some capacity to describe the impact of the program. Our response rate was 70.5%, with noncompletion most commonly associated with an agency determining that the respondent did not fall within the aims of our study. Our response rate on a city basis was much higher. We received questionnaires from one or two agencies in all but one of the eligible cities. The nonrespondents were mainly in the very large cities, where we already had ample respondents.

Table 13.1 classifies the 254 respondents in 10 major categories and six subcategories: law enforcement (police) (20.5%), prosecutors (10.2%), judges (5.5%), probation (12.6%), corrections (3.1%), parole (4.3%), schools (13.3%) subdivided into security and academic personnel, and community service agencies and organizations (24.4%). This last category was subdivided into youth service, youth and family service/treatment, comprehensive crisis intervention, and grass-roots groups. Two other categories were community, county, or state planners (4.7%) and other (0.8%).

The focus of our analysis is the city, or urban area, with its formal organizations addressing youth gangs or some aspect of the problem. Still, we do not clearly have a sample from a known population of eligible cities, urban areas, or constituent or related agencies or local community organizations. What we have in the study is a fairly large group of cities and agencies generally recognized, respectively, to have youth gang problems and organized programs to address them.

TABLE 13.1:   Respondent Categories

Category	Major Categories No.	%	Subcategories No.	%
Law enforcement	52	20.5		
Prosecutors	26	10.2		
Judges	14	5.5		
Probation	32	12.6		
Corrections	8	3.1		
Parole	11	4.3		
School	35	13.3		
academic			26	74.3
security			9	25.7
Community/Service	62	24.4		
youth service agency			46	74.2
youth and family service			8	12.9
grass-roots			5	8.1
comprehensive			3	4.8
Community planning	12	4.7		
Other	2	0.8		
Total	254	100.0		

Our survey analysis is concerned with the youth gang problem and organized response to it in two types of areas or cities: chronic youth gang problem cities, which often had a long history of serious problems; and emerging youth gang problem cities, often smaller cities that recognized and began to deal with the problem only after 1980. Of the 45 cities or areas, 21 are classified as chronic and 24 as emerging youth gang problem cities (Table 13.2). A relatively greater proportion of our chronic gang problem cities have large or very large populations, but there is a sizable number of smaller cities as well. Most of the cities classified as emerging youth gang problem cities have populations that are smaller, although some have populations of over 500,000. We were also able to classify the correctional schools and special agency programs or sites under these two rubrics, but our analysis here focuses on the 45 cities/counties or county sectors and the California Youth Authority (regarded as a single large jurisdiction with many sites, equivalent to a city or urban area for our present analytic purposes).

TABLE 13.2: Type of Gang Problem by Area (City, County, Site)

Chronic Problem Cities/Areas (n = 21)	Emerging Problem Cities/Areas (n = 24)
Albuquerque, NM	Atlanta, GA
Chicago, IL	Benton Harbor, MI
Chino, CA	Cicero, IL
Detroit, MI	Columbus, OH
East Los Angeles, CA	Evanston, IL
El Monte, CA	Flint, MI
Inglewood, CA	Fort Wayne, IN
Long Beach, CA	Fort Worth, TX
Los Angeles City, CA	Hialeah, FL
Los Angeles County, CA	Indianapolis, IN
New York, NY	Jackson, MS
Oakland, CA	Louisville, KY
Pomona, CA	Madison, WI
Philadelphia, PA	Miami, FL
Phoenix, AZ	Milwaukee, WI
San Diego, CA	Minneapolis, MN
San Francisco, CA	Reno, NV
San Jose, CA	Rockford, IL
Santa Ana, CA	Sacramento, CA
Stockton, CA	Salt Lake City, UT
Tucson, AZ	Seattle, WA
	Shreveport, LA
	Sterling, IL
	Tallahassee, FL

Chronic Problem-Institutional Sites (n = 2)	Emerging Problem-Institutional Sites (n = 4)
California Youth Authority[a]	Ethan Allen School (WI)
Sunrise House (CA)	Glen Mills School (PA)
	McClaren School (OR)
	Paramount School (CA)

a. In much of the analysis, only the California Youth Authority is included as an area along with cities or county areas. It has also dealt with the youth gang problem since before 1980.

Program Strategy

Agencies and community organizations respond to a problem such as gang crime in terms of their general missions, goals, and objectives. Most respondents in our study represent organizations established to deal with issues and problems and to carry out activities broader than confronting youth gangs and gang crime. Based on our research focus, however, we have attempted to develop a set of measures of the goals and objectives, key programs, or activities that underlie the organizations' efforts to deal specifically with the youth gang problem. We have termed these measures *strategies of action.* At a conceptual level, they are situated between the idea of broad mission or goal statements and specific or discrete program activities.

Social problems wax and wane, but our responding organizations have to sustain themselves whether a youth gang problem is present or not. The relationship between gang problem and program strategy, however, must be made sooner or later for the sake of logic or common sense (as well as public relations) and more often to justify requests for additional funds for gang program initiatives. In order to understand and evaluate the organization's or community's response to gangs, we believe it is important to describe and analyze the nature of the specific strategy or set of strategies developed within and across agencies and communities and to assess the effectiveness of these strategies in reducing the problem.

Our survey respondents answered five open-ended questionnaire items intended to give us information on program activities, priority of strategies employed, and estimates of effectiveness of agency efforts. These items are as follows:

- *Item IV-1:* What is your unit's or organization's goals and objectives in regard to the gang problem?
- *Item VI-2:* What has your department (or unit) done that you feel has been particularly successful in dealing with gangs? Please provide statistics, if relevant and available.
- *Item VI-3:* What has your department (or unit) done that you feel has been least effective in dealing with gangs?
- *Item VI-6:* What do you think are the five best ways employed by your department or organization for dealing with the gang problem? (Rank in order of priority.)
- *Item IV-14:* What activities do gang or special personnel in your organization perform in dealing with the problem?

[Probe to determine how they are tied to the problem as described in goals/objectives.]

We used the answers of respondents to these items to construct an empirically based and theoretically sensitive set of five underlying strategies. Our analysis relies most heavily on the responses to Item VI-6. The strategies are conceptualized as *community organization, social intervention, opportunities provision, suppression,* and *organizational development.* The strategies are defined and their indicators or statements or program activities are classified as follows.

Community organization: local community organization or neighborhood mobilization. Spergel's (1989b) literature review (see also Shaw & McKay, 1942) lists community organization as one of four major strategies that have been employed historically in dealing with the youth gang problem: "Community organization is the term used to describe efforts to bring about adjustment, development, or change [in or] among groups and organizations in regard to community problems or social needs" (p. 142). The term *interorganizing,* a key dimension of community organization or community organizing, also is used to refer to "efforts at enhancing, modification, or change in intergroup or interorganizational relationships to cope with a community problem" (Spergel, 1969).

Key words and phrases were employed by the respondents that at times could be included clearly in this community organization category, and at other times not. Much depended on the context and intent of the key words used. Decisions for placement of items in a category had to be made based on some appropriate rationale. For example, the contemporary term *networking* was classified under the strategy of community organization, unless it referred to networking among law enforcement agencies. (When networking involved only law enforcement agencies, it was classified under suppression; see below.) References to prevention, when they implied (and they usually did) intervention efforts across agencies, were coded as community organization. When prevention referred primarily to a service activity such as counseling by a specific agency focused on at-risk youth prior to full-fledged gang membership, the reference was placed in the category of social intervention. All references to attendance at meetings of community organizations or with community leaders were regarded as pursuing a community organization strategy. After much consideration, we included advocacy for victims under the general strategy of suppression rather than community organization, because it can be viewed as part of a more basic strategy of crime control and justice system processing. Additional goals or activities encompassed by the community organization strategy included the following:

cleaning up graffiti in the community
involving the schools
mobilizing the community
building community trust
involving parent groups in community programs
educating the community
changing the community

Social intervention: youth outreach and street work counseling. Spergel (1989b, pp. 144ff.) lists youth outreach and street work as a second major gang program strategy. Street work is

the practice variously labeled detached work, street club, gang work, area work, extension youth work, corner work, etc. It is the systematic effort of an agency worker, through social work or treatment techniques within the neighborhood context, to help a group of young people who are described as delinquent or potentially delinquent to achieve a conventional adaptation. This requires the agent to work with or manipulate the people or other agency representatives who interact critically with members of the delinquent group. (Spergel, 1966)

The traditional notion of street work may be somewhat outdated or limited and can be regarded as part of a larger, more contemporary strategy of social intervention that focuses on individual behavioral value change or transformation (Klein,

1971). Therefore, we place street work under the more general category of social intervention. Recreational and sports activities also are encompassed by this strategy. Social intervention includes mainly counseling or direct attempts—informational or guidance—to change the values of youths in such a way as to make gang involvement less likely. References to knowledge improvement or general education, however, especially for certain groups or populations of youth, are included under opportunities provision, below. Social advocacy for individual gang members is classified as a social intervention goal. The following key words or indicators fall into the social intervention category:

    crisis intervention
    service activities
    diversion
    outreach
    providing role models
    leadership development
    intergang mediation
    group counseling
    temporary shelter
    referrals for services
    religious conversion
    counseling of gang members
    drug use prevention/treatment
    all psychological approaches
    all social work approaches
    postsentencing social services
    work with the gang structure
    helping members leave the gang
    tattoo removal

Opportunities: jobs, job training, and education. Spergel (1989b; see also Cloward & Ohlin, 1960) lists opportunities provision as a third major gang strategy. This approach emphasizes "large scale resource infusions and efforts to change institutional structures, including schools, job opportunities, political participation, and the development of a new relationship between the federal government and local neighborhoods in the solution not only of delinquency but of poverty itself" (p. 146). Here are included efforts to stimulate the development of new and improved school, special training, and job programs, and business and industry involvement in the social and economic advancement of people, including and targeting gang youth. Key words or phrases under opportunities provision include the following:

job preparation
job training
job placement
job development
school tutoring
education of gang youth

Suppression: arrest, incarceration, and supervision. Spergel (1989b) lists suppression as the fourth major gang program strategy. Under this approach gang members may be "arrested, prosecuted, and removed for long prison sentences" (p. 147), although the strategy may be employed in less drastic form by non-justice system personnel, as well. Tactical patrols by police gang units, vertical prosecution, intensive supervision and vertical case management by probation departments, legislation targeted at gang members, and interagency task forces involving criminal justice actors are placed in this category. Also included are the development and implementation of information systems (i.e., gathering/collecting and maintaining information), as well as information sharing or publishing of information on gangs that facilitates law enforcement. Other key words or phrases included are the following:

enforcement
neutralization
investigation
adjudication

apprehension
monitoring
restraint
arrest
discipline
intelligence
identification of suspects
legal consequences
removal from community
correctional placement
law enforcement liaison

Organizational development and change: institutional and policy adaptations and mechanisms. A fifth category has been added that has a modifying or limited organizational development quality. This strategy refers to organizational adaptations and changes that mainly facilitate the achievement of the other strategies. Especially characteristic is organizational structure and process specialization in order to deal with the gang problem—for example, forming a special gang unit in the police department for gang information, investigation, and enforcement purposes. Other activities or key words under this strategy are as follows:

internal agency coordination
improving organizational efficiency
program development
advocacy for legislation
specialized training
additional resources
case management
use of media

Coding Method

Using these written guidelines, the two senior members of the research team separately interpreted and classified key

TABLE 13.3: Distribution of Strategy Rankings

| | Strategy Rank | | | | | |
	1	2	3	4	5	Total
Community organization						
number	22	58	35	5	1	121
percentage	8.9	23.4	14.1	2.0	0.4	21.2
Social intervention						
number	78	46	19	3	0	146
percentage	31.5	18.5	7.7	1.2		25.5
Opportunities						
number	12	38	15	4	0	69
percentage	4.8	15.3	6.0	1.6		12.1
Suppression						
number	109	35	16	4	1	165
percentage	44.0	14.1	6.5	1.6	0.4	28.8
Organization change						
number	27	21	18	5	0	71
percentage	10.7	8.5	7.3	2.0		12.4

words or activities and the ranking strategies of each of the 254 respondents. We agreed independently on approximately 70% of the classifications of the hundreds of separate items. After hours of case-by-case discussion, agreement was reached on all item classifications and priority rankings. We note that not all respondents provided items for the five separate strategies. Each item was ranked into one strategy only. If an item provided by a respondent repeated a particular strategy already ranked, it was eliminated.

Distribution of Strategies

Table 13.3 shows the distribution of strategies by rank for all of the respondents. As can be seen, the most common first or primary strategy of agencies in our survey is suppression (44%), followed by social intervention (31.5%). Organizational change (10.9%) and community organization (8.9%) are comparably less common as first or primary strategies. Provision of opportunities as a primary strategy is most infrequent (4.8%). Over the total listing of strategies regardless of rank, suppression was still the most often chosen, and opportunities and organizational change or development the least frequently selected. Because the majority of respondents are from criminal justice agencies, this distribution is not surprising.

Type of Gang Problem and Strategy

Here we are interested in analysis at the city or area rather than the agency level. For simplicity, we initially concentrate on each agency's primary strategy. Our city- or area-level measure is the proportion of agencies in an area exhibiting each of our five strategies as their primary strategy. There are significant differences between chronic and emerging youth gang problem cities in the incidence of three of the five primary program strategies. The mean proportion of respondents drawing primary strategies of social intervention and opportunities provision is significantly higher in chronic gang problem cities or areas, but the proportion of respondents exhibiting a primary strategy of community organization is significantly higher in emerging gang problem cities (see Table 13.4).

Furthermore, a multivariate analysis of variance for these differences across city or area by youth gang problem type is significant at the .05 level. Use of discriminant analysis to generate a function that separates cities by youth gang problem type on the basis of these three primary strategies produces a function that can be used successfully to reclassify two-thirds (66.5%) of the cities or areas by youth gang problem type. There is, therefore, some empirical support for the notion that primary strategy choices vary by type of youth gang problem city. Whether these variations in strategy are associated with differences in perceived program effectiveness is our next concern.

Measuring Perceived Program Effectiveness

In the absence of comparable and reliable concrete measures of program effectiveness, we examined three measures of perceived program effectiveness—perceived improvement in the

TABLE 13.4: **Mean Proportion of Respondents per City or Area Exhibiting Primary Strategy by Gang Problem Type**

	Chronic Youth Gang Problem Cities (n = 20)	Emerging Youth Gang Problem Cities (n = 22)
Community organization	.065	.160*
Social intervention	.283	.142*
Opportunities provision	.071	.017
Suppression	.454	.573
Organizational change	.107	.085

*Student's *t* test significant at .05 level.

gang situation between 1980 and 1987, perceived agency effectiveness, and perceived community-level effectiveness in 1987. We also tested, to some extent, the validity of our measure of perceived improvement in a later separate collection of "hard" data on gang crime changes in 21 of 42 cities over the same period.

We used the following items to generate these three original measures:

- *Item III-18:* Has the gang situation changed since 1980?
- *Item III-19:* If yes, how?
- *Item V-1:* How effective do you think your unit was in 1987 in dealing with the gang problem?
  very effective _____ moderately effective _____
  hardly effective _____ not at all effective _____
- *Item IV-8:* Are there any interagency task forces or communitywide organizations that attempted to coordinate efforts to deal with the gang problem in 1987?
- *Item IV-9:* If yes, were these efforts
  very effective _____ somewhat effective _____
  hardly effective _____ not at all effective _____ ?

The item concerning change in the youth gang problem since 1980 was content analyzed to produce a dichotomous variable of improvement versus nonimprovement. Each of the three measures is significantly related to the other at the .01 level of

TABLE 13.5: Normalized (PROBIT) Scores for Three Gang Program Effectiveness Measures

Improvement Since 1980   yes = −1.63   no = 0.24

Evaluation of Effectiveness of 1987

	Agency Level	Community Level
Very effective	−0.86	−1.02
Moderately effective	0.48	0.30
Hardly effective	1.52	1.22
Not at all effective	2.37	1.88

statistical significance, using a tetrachloric test of correlation. In transforming these three measures into a single evaluation measure, we chose not to give equal weight to each of these three variables because we believed that the variables merit separate weights. We feel that these weights should be derived empirically from the structure of their covariation in this particular set of respondents. At the agency level, one of these variables is dichotomous and the other two are sets of ordered categories. We chose to normalize these measures at the agency level using PC-PRELIS to generate normalized (PROBIT) scores for each of our categorical variables (see Table 13.5). A principal components analysis of the normalized (PROBIT) scores for the three measures results in three eigenvalues, none of which approaches zero. We used the first and largest of these eigenvalues (accounting for 45.5% of the variance) to generate the set of principal components coefficients to be used as weights for our three normalized measures (Table 13.6).

The score that is generated for improvement in the gang situation since 1980, a very effective agency rating, and a very effective community-level program rating is −2.18001. This value can be transformed easily so that it is equal to 1.0 and all subsequent values are positive by adding 3.18001 to each score. The result is a set of general effectiveness scores ranging from 1.0 to 5.87. It must be remembered in the analyses that follow that the lower the value of this measure of

TABLE 13.6:   Coefficients for First Principal Component

	Coefficient	Percentage of Variance Explained
Improved since 1980	0.411	31.5
Agency effectiveness	0.531	52.5
Community program effectiveness	0.531	52.4
Variance attributed to first principle component		45.5

perceived general effectiveness, the greater the perception of effectiveness.

Validity Check

In our external validity check of the "perceived improvement" component of our measure of general effectiveness, we recontacted law enforcement representatives in a sample of 21 cities or counties of our original survey. We randomly selected 11 of the locations from the 15 with the highest general effectiveness scores and 10 of the locations from the 15 with the lowest general effectiveness scores. We obtained information on five empirical indicators: number of gangs, gang members, gang-related homicides, gang-related assaults, and number of gang-related narcotic incidents in 1980 and in 1987. Most of the law enforcement respondents had access to a data base. Sixteen had access to a data base at both points in time.

We find general agreement comparing perceptions of improvement or deterioration and the five empirical indicators per city or county. Problems of full congruence occur for only 3 of the 21 locations. In one case, perception by the police officer and eight other nonpolice informants in this very large city indicated a worsening of the youth gang situation. Three other nonpolice respondents, however, perceived an improvement. More important, the perception of the police officer is not supported by any of the empirical indicators. We observe, nevertheless, that the official police data system in this city is flawed seriously because data collection is based on unclear definition, unclear identifying procedures, and unreliable recording of gang incidents, particularly for youths 16 years and older.

In the second case, a county, the perceptions of law enforcement and empirical indicators show an absence or a low point in the youth gang problem in 1980, with a peaking of the problem in 1987 but a rapid and sharp decline in 1988, when the law enforcement officer was interviewed. All of the available empirical indicators signify an increase in the problem for 1987, although the law enforcement officer's response probably reflected the improvement in the youth gang situation that occurred only in 1988. In the third case, a county, adequate data were available for only two of the five empirical indicators at the two points in time. Data on the other three indicators, however, were available for the later period. The perception of the law enforcement officer that the youth gang situation has worsened was consistent with all of the available empirical indicators, except one (gang-related homicides), which showed a 23% decline between 1980 and 1987.

If we use the most rigorous standards for comparing change in the youth gang problem based on the perceptions of improvement and empirical indicators between 1980 and 1987, we find the association is perfect for 18 of 21 randomly selected cities or counties for a general correspondence rate of 85.7%. A Fisher's exact test reveals that the hypothesis of no correspondence between perception and the set of empirical measures can be rejected at the .05 level of statistical significance. Therefore, we regard the "perceived improvement" component of our measure of general effectiveness as valid.

Program Strategies and Perceived Effectiveness

We are able to compare relationships between perceived effectiveness and primary strategy by regressing our measure of perceived general effectiveness on the proportion of agencies within each city or area exhibiting a particular strategy as

TABLE 13.7: Analysis of Covariance Results: General Effectiveness Score by Youth Gang City Problem Type with Primary Strategy as a Covariate

Primary Strategy Covariate	Regression Coefficients		Group Comparisons
	Chronic Gang Problem City	Emerging Gang Problem City	
Community organization	−2.14	−3.01*	***
Social intervention	0.34	2.03	*
Opportunities	−3.62**	−2.70	
Suppression	0.48	0.67	
Organizational change	0.89	1.84	

*significant at the .05 level;
**significant at the .01 level;
***significant at the .001 level.

primary. Table 13.7 presents the results of an analysis of covariance for each strategy by type of youth gang problem city. It should be remembered that a negative slope (as indicated by the sign of the regression coefficient) shows a positive relationship between the proportion of agencies in each city or area exhibiting a strategy and perceived general effectiveness. Conversely, a positive regression coefficient indicates a negative relationship between the proportion of agencies in each area exhibiting a strategy and perceived general effectiveness. Table 13.7 provides answers to two statistical questions: First, are the regression lines significantly different from zero? Here we are not comparing chronic and emerging youth gang problem settings. Second, are the regression lines for each group or type of setting different from each other?

Caution in interpreting these findings is further merited by several conditions of the results. The two sets of areas or types of settings are regarded as samples rather than as populations. In this case, only two of the regression slopes as indicated by the regression coefficients—priority of community organization in emerging youth gang problem settings and priority of opportunities provision in chronic youth gang problem settings—are significantly different from zero. Also, given the structural dependence that is built into the creation of the primary strategy measures (i.e., only one primary strategy choice is possible per respondent) and the assumptions of statistical techniques that decompose variance, it is inevitable that some primary strategies will have the appearance of a negative effect on our measure of general effectiveness. Hence we limit our conclusions to identifying those primary strategies that appear to be positively associated with enhanced perception of general effectiveness.

With these cautionary prerequisites in mind, we may tentatively conclude from Table 13.7 that community organization as a primary strategy appears to be associated with *greater* perceived general effectiveness in emerging youth gang problem areas and also is relatively more important in emerging than in chronic gang problem cities. Social intervention as a primary strategy is associated significantly more often with *lower* perceived effectiveness in reducing the problem in emerging than in chronic gang problem cities. Opportunities provision as a primary strategy is associated with *greater* perceived general effectiveness only in chronic youth gang problem settings. We already know from Table 13.4 that opportunities provision is seldom exhibited as a primary strategy in emerging gang problem settings.

The final step in our analysis is the construction of regression models of perceived general effectiveness. We considered a wide range of types of variables in our extended analyses of the data (Spergel et al., 1989); however, primary program strategy dominates all regression models of perceived general effectiveness regardless of problem type setting. Table 13.8 shows the multiple regression models for predicting perceived general effectiveness based on the proportion of agencies in a city exhibiting a particular primary strategy.

We find that in cities or areas with chronic youth gang problems, agencies perceive there is a significant reduction in the problem mainly when the primary response strategy is the provision of social opportunities. Community organization or community mobilization is also significant, but only in the presence of the provision of social opportunities. In the chronic youth gang problem cities, we can explain a considerable amount of the variance (almost 50%) on the dependent vari-

TABLE 13.8: **Multiple Regression Models for Perceived General Effectiveness at the Area Level Based on Particular Primary Strategy**

Problem Setting Type	Independent Variable	b	Beta	R^2
Chronic cities	proportion of agencies exhibiting opportunities provision as primary strategy	−4.18**	−0.634	0.497
	proportion of agencies exhibiting community organization as primary strategy	−2.91*	−0.450	
Emerging cities	proportion of agencies exhibiting community organization as primary strategy	−3.01**	−0.558	0.311

*significant at the .05 level;
**significant at the .01 level.

able—perceived general effectiveness in lowering the gang problem—when these two strategies are employed together. In the emerging youth gang problem cities, only community organization or mobilization shows up as a significant variable, explaining 31% of the variance on the dependent variable (perceived general effectiveness).

Conclusions and
Implications for Policy

We conducted a survey of 45 cities or urban areas and six institutional sites to determine the scope of the youth gang problem and especially to examine the relationship of the response of different types of agencies and cities to the problem. We were interested mainly in discovering what promising patterns existed for reducing the problem, or at least its perceived reduction. Strategies for dealing with the problem seemed to vary, particularly in terms of priority, across different kinds of agencies and cities. We identified five sets of program strategies: community organization, social intervention, opportunities provision, suppression, and organizational development and change. We were also able to measure effectiveness of agency and city or area approach in terms of four variables: perceived improvement in the gang situation (also with a data validity check as to actual reduction of gang crime), perceived agency effectiveness, perceived interagency or community-level effectiveness, and finally a perceived general effectiveness measure based on the former three measures.

Our findings demonstrated that although suppression and social intervention were the most prevalent strategies used by agencies and cities in addressing the problem, in fact strategies of community organization and social opportunities were associated clearly and strongly with perceptions of agency effectiveness and a reduction of the gang problem, particularly in terms of perceived greater effectiveness of city or urban area efforts.

Our analysis of the relationships between five primary program strategies and perceived general effectiveness suggests that community organization as a primary strategy is strongly associated with and explains perceived general effectiveness of the youth gang problem in those cities where it is emerging. Opportunities provision rarely is tried in these settings, where probably a modicum of social resources is still present although the community is undergoing considerable population and class change.

Community organization as a primary strategy is relatively less significant and appears only in the context of some degree of commitment to a primary strategy of opportunities provision, which in association is then highly significant with perceived effectiveness by agencies in reducing the youth gang problem in chronic youth gang problem cities. Chronic gang problem cities tend to be larger, probably with more severe problems of poverty as well as community disorganization. Thus community mobilization, per se, in these settings would appear insufficient to deal with the youth gang problem. A major infusion of resources, particularly through development of such social institutions as the educational system and improved job opportunities targeted at youth gang or potential youth gang members, would seem to be most appropriate in the reduction of the youth gang problem.

It appears that primary strategies of social intervention, suppression, and organizational change or development do not contribute to perceived effectiveness of agencies in the reduction of youth gang problems in cities or areas where the problem is either chronic or emerging. This is not to deny the essential importance of social intervention, suppression, and organizational change approaches, but these may be beneficial only when community organization and opportunities provision are dominant strategies.

In other words, the implication of our finding is that more resources alone for police or even human service programs would not contribute much to dealing effectively with the youth gang problem. It is more likely that community mobilization and more resources for and reform of the educational system and the job market, targeted at gang youth or clearly at-risk youth, would be more cost-effective as well as more effective in the reduction of the problem.

Policy recommendations emanating from these findings would not necessarily require a renewed war on poverty, but rather a series of programs targeted specifically at the youth gang problem addressing not only issues of economic deprivation and lack of opportunities but social disorganization and the mobilization of community institutions in a concerted attack on the problem (Curry & Spergel, 1988). Distinctions in policy emphasis also would have to be made depending on the nature and the level of severity of the problem in particular cities.

14

Denial, Overreaction, and Misidentification: A Postscript on Public Policy

C. RONALD HUFF

The title of this chapter reflects the process by which most U.S. cities have reacted to the formation of youth gangs. My own research (Huff, 1988a, 1988b, 1989a) and that of others (see especially Hagedorn, 1988, and Chapter 11 of this volume) suggests that the first official reaction on the part of city officials is to deny the existence of gangs. In my own state, for example, the three largest cities (Columbus, Cleveland, and Cincinnati) have all had youth gangs and have experienced youth gang violence. Yet, for quite some time, Columbus (now joined by Cleveland) was the only city whose officials publicly acknowledged the existence of youth gangs. Why?

In the case of Columbus, our public officials were also in the "denial stage" until several "high-visibility" gang-related events occurred in 1984 and 1985:

(1) A local gang leader appeared on a local television news program and challenged other gangs to "stay off his turf." Several days later, he was killed in a drive-by shooting carried out by a rival gang.

(2) The daughter of Ohio's governor was assaulted by a gang at a local fast-food restaurant.

(3) The son of Columbus's mayor was assaulted by gang members at a high school football game.

These events forced Columbus officials out of the denial stage, while little more than 100 miles to the north and to the south, both Cleveland and Cincinnati officials continued to talk only about "youth groups" (see Chapter 11 for a parallel discussion concerning Indianapolis officials).[1]

This sort of denial on the part of public officials is not surprising. After all, their intuitive and reflexive reaction is to protect their city's image and keep it competitive with respect to economic development and, in some cases, tourism. The city of Honolulu, for example, has been experiencing problems with youth gangs, including both local (especially highly marginalized Samoan and Filipino youths) and mainland (Los Angeles gang members who use some of their drug profits to travel to Hawaii for a little "R and R") gangs. Although officials there have begun intensive law enforcement and prosecutorial efforts to address the gang problem, there is great reluctance, for the most part, to acknowledge the problem publicly or to commit the kind of resources necessary to engage in effective prevention programs directed at providing expanded opportunities for underclass youths. Tourists are essentially unaware of the problem, because they don't see (nor would they recognize) gang members—so why tell them about it and perhaps scare them off?

But are these intuitive assumptions accurate? Are they functional for the cities involved? Consider the case of Los Angeles, widely acknowledged as the "gang capital of the world" (a phrase that is not to be found in any Chamber of Commerce literature, I might add). Has the widespread publicity concerning Los Angeles gang violence deterred people from moving to or visiting Los Angeles? The lines at Universal Studios and Disneyland don't seem to suggest that. And have Los Angeles's economic development and growth suffered from this terrible image of a gang-infested city? Hardly! Instead, feverish attention is being devoted to how to build more freeways to keep up with the massive in-migration that continues to choke the Los Angeles metropolitan area.

In fact, the evidence suggests that cities probably *could* publicly acknowledge that they have gangs, and that some violence in those cities is gang-related, without causing undue damage to the economic infrastructure. And doing so is important, because denial tends to be associated with a sort of paralysis on the part of officials—a leadership vacuum that *facilitates* the victimization of citizens in the schools, on the streets, in public transit vehicles, and elsewhere. What is needed is public (and private sector) leadership that acknowledges the problem but keeps it in the proper perspective, recognizing (a) that gangs are essentially dependent variables whose existence is attributable to social structural and sociocultural independent variables; (b) that the amelioration of the gang problem will require an in-depth *understanding* of the social and economic contexts of gangs; and (c) that coordinated communitywide and systemwide strategies will be necessary, rather than isolated programmatic efforts, and that sufficient resources will be required to implement those strategies.

As Miller suggests in Chapter 12, those with a concern about this problem (especially victims) tend to be people with little political power, while those with political power and access to the necessary resources tend not to be concerned about the problem because they don't see it as affecting them or their affluent constituents, who tend to live in suburbs distant from these problems.[2] In fact, public attention to gangs often is spurred by some catalytic event—as often as not, the victimization of an affluent or high-profile resident (the daughter of Ohio's governor, the son of Columbus's mayor, an affluent woman in the Westwood theater district of Los Angeles).

If the denial stage is problematic because of the paralysis of leadership associated with it, what usually follows is just as bad, if not worse. Spurred by some catalytic event, such as the aforementioned high-profile victimizations, city officials often *overreact* and define the problem as "a law enforcement problem." This is, of course, in keeping with the American tradition of holding the police accountable for increases in crime—somewhat analogous to holding physicians responsible for outbreaks of influenza! What often happens in this stage is that the police form a "gang unit" and the gang problem is met almost entirely by a suppression response (see Chapter 13 for data demonstrating the relative ineffectiveness of this approach, particularly in isolation from community-based and systemwide strategies).

This response often backfires when marginal gang members and "wanna-bes" (those who may be considering gang membership or may just be "groupies" who hang around with the gang) are lumped together with leaders and hard-core followers in the police "gang profile" approach. This labeling process often leads to the kind of secondary deviance described by Lemert (1951), because these marginal members often react by saying, "Well, the police believe I'm in this gang and treat me as if I am, so I might as well be in it." Also, because Gang A may be in conflict with Gang B, spreading the word that a marginal member is "affiliated" with Gang A means, in effect, that he or she now needs the protection offered by Gang A more than ever. Hagedorn's (1988) Milwaukee gang study revealed that some of the gang members' gang identities were solidified initially by this process of overreaction by the Milwaukee police.

The third phase of this process, according to my own observations and the corpus of gang studies nationwide, is what I term *misidentification*. Misidentification has two connotations: (a) the misidentification of gang members, which occurs in the overreaction stage described above and in paramilitary tactics such as indiscriminate "gang sweeps" [3] that are not based on probable cause; and (b) the misidentification of the *causes* of gang problems. As Miller notes in Chapter 12, there is a tendency to base reactions to gangs on either conservative (individual pathology) or liberal (social injustice) intuitive explanations, without the painstaking work required to establish causal connections so that our policies can be guided by sound theories. There is nothing more efficient than good theory as the basis for sound public policy; conversely, there is nothing more inefficient and wasteful (of financial and human resources) than policies based on political perspectives and intuitive judgments. The realities of life suggest that complex socioeconomic phenomena such as gangs (or, for that matter, crime in general) usually defy simple intuitive explanations, and yet such explanations constitute the modal response.

This brings us to a final consideration of the public policy implications of extant gang research. I have outlined some of the things we've done wrong; now the question is what can we do that would represent an improvement? Elsewhere, I have discussed the diffusion of gangs and some of the policy implications for criminal justice system response (because I do believe that both "sticks" and "carrots" will be necessary) (Huff, 1988a, 1988b, 1989a, 1989b). Here, however, I want to concentrate on the most generic and parsimonious public policy responses that I see as necessary. A thorough review of the gang literature, including the provocative chapters in this volume, causes me to believe the following things about the gang problem in the United States:

(1) We need more research on gangs, especially studies of gangs in the context of their social and economic milieu.

(2) The research that we have suggests that gangs tend to be located in central cities and are composed primarily of poor, disadvantaged, culturally marginal youths. Many youths, however, who are ostensibly subject to the same living conditions do not become gang members.

(3) Whether researchers adopt an urban underclass perspective or a subcultural perspective, we tend to be discussing the same *ecological* areas of our cities.

(4) The solutions to the problems that cause gangs and the problems caused by gangs will require intervention strategies that involve community participants in efforts to counteract the decay of local institutions (families, churches, schools, recreational and job opportunities) by establishing the kind of functional communities described by Short in Chapter 10. Elitist, top-down policy formulation and implementation are doomed to failure because they are usually devoid of an understanding of the economic and sociocultural milieu of the target population and avoid establishing a sense of ownership or social investment on the part of those indigenous to the area.

(5) Finally (and perhaps surprisingly, given the focus of this volume on gangs), I do not believe that the optimal public policy response to gangs and gang violence is to identify the problem in those terms. Rather, I believe we should

view gangs as a manifestation of other problems endemic in our socioeconomic structure and in certain ecological areas of our cities. Whether one adopts a social disorganization (or other subcultural) perspective or an urban underclass (economic) perspective, it is likely that these ecological areas are generating the highest rates of crime, delinquency, incarceration, mental illness, public assistance, and other indicators of "social pathology."

Elsewhere I have proposed a methodology for documenting the "social costs" of these ecological areas by collecting data for all these indicators using zip code information that is collected routinely by all agencies (Huff, 1989a).[4] If the conditions in these ecological areas are so costly, in both human and fiscal terms, then shouldn't we invest in prevention and community-wide coordination efforts with the rationale that such efforts could generically address the conditions that contribute to a wide array of social problems? In an era of very limited federal funding for social programs, doesn't it make good sense to pursue policies and intervention programs that give us "more bang for the buck" by addressing underlying problems that contribute to the production of various types of deviance (crime, gangs, mental illness, and so on)?

As one illustration of such prevention-based approaches, consider the record of the 1962 Perry Preschool Project in Ypsilanti, Michigan (the forerunner of the national Head Start program). This project involved 123 Black youths of low socioeconomic status who were at risk of school failure. At ages 3-4, they attended a high-quality preschool program. The researchers collected longitudinal data for these children annually from ages 3 to 11, then again at ages 14, 15, and 19. Data also were collected for a control group of 65 children. The researchers assessed the involvement of these children with the legal system via interviews and an examination of police and court records. The findings: 69% of those who attended the preschool program had no reported offenses (compared with 49% of the control group), and 16% were arrested as juveniles, while 25% of the control group members experienced juvenile arrest (Berrueta-Clement et al., 1984).

Once again we learn that some of our best investments may be in those programs that have *indirect* effects on crime and delinquency. The significant beneficial effects of a program such as this are quite encouraging—especially if such affected ecological areas could offer other prevention programs and opportunities (job training, child care, nutrition counseling) in a coordinated, comprehensive effort to address the overall quality of life in these areas.

In the final analysis, the concepts of "criminal justice" or "juvenile justice" are anachronisms in the absence of fundamental social justice for all citizens. Whether one believes that gangs are a result of individual pathology or structural inequality, we should be able to agree that the provision of social justice, including an adequate quality of life, is the most efficient investment we can make. The Achilles heel of a free, democratic society is the breakdown of its socioeconomic institutions. If families, schools, and churches don't socialize children to act responsibly, and if the national and local economies don't provide adequate *legal* opportunity structures, then we as a society are in deep trouble. Gangs and gang-related crime represent important manifestations of these underlying failures, and it is my hope that this volume will add to our understanding of this important social problem.

Notes

1. An anecdote illustrates quite vividly the striking difference between the reality of gangs and the willingness to recognize them (a political decision). During the course of my research, I was meeting with a police chief and some of his top management staff, and we were discussing the gangs in that particular city. I shared with them some photos of gang graffiti in the parks and other nonconfidential data I had been collecting concerning gangs in that city. The chief then shared with me some of their "inside" information about gangs and gang activities. We had a very pleasant and useful exchange. As the meeting ended and I got up to walk to my car, the chief said, "Goodbye, Dr. Huff. Now remember, we don't have any gangs here!"

2. While participating in our 1988 conference on gangs and the urban underclass at Ohio State, Professor William Julius Wilson of the University of Chicago told me that although he still resides in Chicago (near the

University), many of his friends who have experienced success have moved out to the suburbs. He has a difficult time convincing them that their old neighborhoods in Chicago have changed and are experiencing much more intractable problems, more extensive poverty, and more violence. Likewise, the mayor of my own city, Columbus, initiated a program he calls "Beyond the Freeways." Beginning with the mayor's own cabinet members, this program has been exposing suburban residents to the soup kitchens, shelters for the homeless, jail overcrowding, and other aspects of urban life that they miss as they commute to work on the suburban freeway system.

3. This is not to suggest that such "sweeps" are never appropriate or that they cannot be properly carried out. However, they resemble a military operation more than civilian policing, and these roundups inevitably involve a great deal of discretion concerning who should be arrested. It is also likely that one of the unintended consequences of such sweeps is usually displacement of the illegal activities into surrounding neighborhoods, rather than total elimination of those activities.

4. John Hagedorn, who serves as Youth Program Coordinator for Milwaukee County's Department of Health and Human Services, is familiar with this approach and cautions that one must be careful that "the truly disadvantaged" (to borrow William Julius Wilson's term) are targeted for these intervention efforts, because the population residing in the zip code may in fact be quite heterogeneous, consisting of some residents who could be described as "underclass" and others who may be working class. Simply targeting a zip code area could result in services being provided only to those who are best able to advocate for themselves, a familiar outcome in programs that are not carefully targeted at the "truly disadvantaged" (Wilson, 1987). I believe that careful study of these zip code areas is needed in order to identify specific neighborhoods and to assess carefully the needs of the residents. Hagedorn reports that such neighborhood assessments have been carried out in Milwaukee (see Moore & Edari, 1990).

References

A cool and weary reception. (1975, May 12). *Time.*

Acosta-Belen, E., & Christenson, E. H. (1979). *The Puerto Rican woman.* New York: Praeger.

Acuna, R. (1981). *Occupied America* (2nd ed.). New York: Harper & Row.

Allen, G., & Thomas, L. (1987). Orphans of war. *Toronto Globe and Mail, 1*(12), 34-57.

Anderson, E. (1989). Moral leadership and transitions in the urban Black community. In H. J. Bershady (Ed.), *Social class and democratic leadership: Essays in honor of E. Digby Balzel* (pp. 123-146). Philadelphia: University of Pennsylvania Press.

Anderson, E. (in press). *Streetwise: Race, class, and change in an urban community.* Chicago: University of Chicago Press.

Anderson, N., & Rodriguez, O. (1984). Conceptual issues in the study of Hispanic delinquency. *Research Bulletin* (Hispanic Research Center, Fordham University), *7,* 2-5.

Arax, M. (1987a, April 5). Asian influx alters life in suburbia. *Los Angeles Times.*

Arax, M. (1987b, February 10). Refugees called victims and perpetrators of fraud. *Los Angeles Times.*

Asbury, H. (1927). *The gangs of New York.* New York: Capricorn.

Auletta, K. (1982). *The underclass.* New York: Random House.

Bach, R. L., & Bach, J. B. (1980). Employment patterns of Southeast Asian refugees. *Monthly Labor Review, 103,* 31-38.

Badey, J. R. (1988). *Dragons and tigers.* Loomis, CA: Palmer Enterprises.

Barber, D. (1987, October). Inside Asian gangs. *AsiAm.*

Beach, W. G. (1932). *Oriental crime in California.* Stanford, CA: Stanford University Press.

Becker, H. (1963). *Outsiders.* New York: Free Press.

Berkman, L. (1984, September 30). Banks catering to Asians facing a culture gap. *Los Angeles Times.*

Bernard, H. R. (1988). *Research methods in cultural anthropology.* Newbury Park, CA: Sage.

Bernard, W. (1949). *Jailbait.* New York: Greenberg.

Berrueta-Clement, J. R., et al. (1984). Preschool's effects on social responsibility. In *Changed Lives: The effects of the Perry Preschool Program on youths through age 19.* Ypsilanti, MI: High/Scope.

Biernacki, P., & Waldorf, D. (1981). Snowball sampling: Problems and techniques of chain referral sampling. *Sociological Methods and Research, 10,* 141-163.

Blauner, R., & Wellman, D. (1973). Toward the decolonization of social research. In J. A. Ladner (Ed.), *The death of white sociology.* New York: Vintage.

Block, C. B. (1985). *Lethal violence in Chicago over seventeen years: Homicides known to the police, 1965-1981.* Chicago: Illinois Criminal Justice Information Authority.

Block, J. H. (1978). Another look at sex differentiation in the socialization behaviors of mothers and fathers. In F. Wermarle & J. Sherman (Eds.), *Psychology of women: Future directions of research.* New York: Psychological Dimensions.

Bobrowski, L. J. (1988). *Collecting, organizing and reporting street gang crime.* Chicago: Chicago Police Department, Special Functions Group.

Bogardus, E. S. (1926). *The city boy and his problems.* Los Angeles: House of Ralston, Rotary Club of Los Angeles.

Bogardus, E. S. (1934). *The Mexican in the United States* (USC Social Science Series, No. 8.) Los Angeles: University of Southern California Press.

Bogdan, R., & Taylor, S. J. (1975). *Introduction to qualitative research methods.* New York: John Wiley.

Bookin-Weiner, H., & Horowitz, R. (1983). The end of the gang: Fad or fact? *Criminology, 21,* 585-602.

Bordua, D. (1961). Delinquent subcultures: Sociological interpretations of gang delinquency. *Annals of the American Academy of Political and Social Science, 338,* 120-136.

Bowker, L. H., & Klein, M. W. (1983). The etiology of female juvenile delinquency and gang membership: A test of psychological and social structural explanations. *Adolescence, 18,* 740-751.

Brake, M. (1980). *The sociology of youth culture and youth subcultures.* London: Routledge & Kegan Paul.

Brand, D. (1987, August 31). The new whiz kids. *Time.*

Bresler, F. (1981). *The Chinese mafia.* New York: Stein & Day.

Brown, W. (1983). *The other side of deliquency.* New Brunswick, NJ: Rutgers University Press.

Brown, W. K. (1977). Black female gangs in Philadelphia. *International Journal of Offender Therapy and Comparative Criminology, 21,* 221-228.

Bryant, D. (1989). *Communitywide responses crucial for dealing with youth gangs* (Juvenile Justice Bulletin). Washington, DC: Office of Juvenile Justice and Delinquency Prevention.

Buriel, R. (1984). Integration with traditional Mexican-American culture and sociocultural adjustment. In J. L. Martinez, Jr., & R. Mendoza (Eds.), *Chicano psychology* (2nd ed.). New York: Academic Press.

Burton, R. V., & Whiting, J. W. M. (1961). The absent father and cross-sex identity. *Merrill-Palmer Quarterly, 7*, 85-95.

Camp, G., & Camp, C. G. (1985). *Prison gangs: Their extent, nature, and impact on prisons.* Washington, DC: U.S. Department of Justice.

Campbell, A. (1980). Friendship as a factor in male and female delinquency. In H. C. Foot, A. J. Chapman, & J. R. Smith (Eds.), *Friendships and social relations in children.* New York: John Wiley.

Campbell, A. (1981). *Girl delinquents.* Oxford: Basil Blackwell.

Campbell, A. (1984). *The girls in the gang.* New York: Basil Blackwell.

Campbell, A. (1987). Self-definition by rejection: The case of gang girls. *Social Problems, 34*, 451-466.

Campbell, A. (in press). On the invisibility of the female delinquent peer group. *Women and Criminal Justice.*

Canter, R. J. (1982a). Family correlates of male and female delinquency. *Criminology, 20*, 149-167.

Canter, R. J. (1982b). Sex difference in self-report delinquency. *Criminology, 20*, 373-393.

Center for Successful Child Development. Unpublished project report. Chicago, IL: Author.

Cernkovich, S. A., & Giordano, P. C. (1979). A comparative analysis of male and female delinquency. *Sociological Quarterly, 20*, 131-145.

Cernkovich, S. A., & Giordano, P. C. (1987). Family relationships and delinquency. *Criminology, 25*, 295-319.

Chambers, E. (1985). *Applied anthropology.* Prospect Heights, IL: Waveland.

Chambliss, W. J. (1973). The saints and the roughnecks. *Society, 11*, 24-31.

Chang, H. (1972). Die today, die tomorrow: The rise and fall of Chinatown gangs. *Bridge Magazine, 2*, 10-15.

Chavez, L. R. (1988). Settlers and sojourners: The case of Mexicans in the United States. *Human Organization, 47*, 95-108.

Chesney-Lind, M. (1974). Juvenile delinquency: The sexualization of female crime. *Psychology Today, 8*, 43ff.

Chin, K. (1986). *Chinese triad societies, tongs, organized crime, and street gangs in Asia and the United States.* Unpublished doctoral dissertation, University of Pennsylvania.

Chin, K. (1990). *Chinese subculture and criminality: Non-traditional crime groups in America.* Westport, CT: Greenwood.

Chin, R. (1977). New York Chinatown today: Community in crisis. *Amerasia Journal, 1*(1), 1-32.

Cloward, R. A., & Ohlin, L. E. (1960). *Delinquency and opportunity: A theory of delinquent gangs.* New York: Free Press.

Cohen, A. K. (1955). *Delinquent boys: The culture of the gang.* Glencoe, IL: Free Press.

Cohen, A. K. (1990). Criminal actors: Natural persons and collectivities. In *New directions in the study of justice, law, and social control* (pp. 101-125). New York: Plenum.

Cohen, B. (1969). The delinquency of gangs and spontaneous groups. In T. Sellin & M. E. Wolfgang (Eds.), *Delinquency: Selected studies.* New York: John Wiley.

Cohen, P. (1972). *Sub-cultural conflict and working class community* (Working Papers in Cultural Studies, No. 2). Birmingham, England: University of Birmingham.

Cohen, S. (1985). *Visions of social control: Crime, punishment and classification.* Cambridge: Polity.

Coleman, J. S. (1988). Social capital in the creation of human capital. *American Journal of Sociology, 94* (Supplement), S95-S120.

Coleman, J. S., & Hoffer, T. (1987). *Public and private high schools: The impact of communities.* New York: Basic Books.

Conger, R. D. (1980). Juvenile delinquency: Behavior restraint or behavior facilitation? In T. Hirschi & M. Gottfredson (Eds.), *Understanding crime.* Beverly Hills, CA: Sage.

Corrigan, P. (1976). Doing nothing. In S. Hall & T. Jefferson (Eds.), *Resistance through rituals.* London: Hutchinson.

Cowie, J., Cowie, B., & Slater, E. (1968). *Delinquency in girls.* London: Heinemann.

Cuellar, J. B. (1987). *Cholismo: On the development and distribution of an international Mexican barrio subculture.* Paper presented at the annual meeting of the Society for Applied Anthropology.

Curry, G. D., & Spergel, I. A. (1988). Gang homicide, delinquency and community. *Criminology, 26*(3), 381-405.

Curtis, L. C. (Ed.). (1987, November). Policies to prevent crime: Neighborhood, family, and employment strategies. *Annals of the American Academy of Political and Social Science.*

Dahmann, J. (1981). *Operation Hardcore, a prosecutorial response to violent gang criminality: Interim evaluation report.* Washington, DC: Mitre Corporation.

Daly, M. (1983, February). The war for Chinatown. *New York Magazine,* pp. 31-38.

Date, K., & Foley, D. (1984, September 30). Vietnamese create their own Saigon. *Los Angeles Times.*

Delaney, J. L., & Miller, W. B. (1977). *Intercity variation in the seriousness of crime by youth gangs and youth groups.* Report to the Office of Juvenile Justice and Delinquency Prevention.

Dillon, R. H. (1962). *The hatchet men.* New York: Coward-McCann.

Dolan, E. F., & Finney, S. (1984). *Youth gangs.* New York: Simon & Schuster.

Dunford, F. W., & Elliott, D. S. (1984). Identifying career offenders using self-reported data. *Journal of Research in Crime and Delinquency, 21*(1), 57-86.

Eckland-Olsen, S. (1982). Deviance, social control, and social networks. *Research in Law, Deviance and Social Control, 4,* 271-299.

Elliott, D. S., Ageton, S., & Canter, R. (1979). An integrated perspective on delinquent behavior. *Journal of Research in Crime and Delinquency, 16,* 3-27.

Elliott, D. S., & Huizinga, D. (1984). *The relationship between delinquent behavior and ADM problems* (National Youth Survey Report No. 28). Boulder, CO: Behavioral Research Institute.

Elliott, D. S., Huizinga, D., & Ageton, S. (1985). *Explaining delinquency and drug abuse.* Beverly Hills, CA: Sage.

Emch, T. (1973, September 9). The Chinatown murders. *San Francisco Sunday Examiner & Chronicle.*

Emler, N., Reicher, S., & Ross, A. (1987). The social context of delinquent conduct. *Journal of Child Psychology and Psychiatry and Allied Disciplines, 28,* 99-109.

Emmons, S., & Reyes, D. (1989, February 5). Gangs, crime top fear of Vietnamese in Orange County. *Los Angeles Times.*

Erickson, M. L., & Jensen, G. F. (1977). Delinquency is still group behavior: Toward revitalizing the group premise in the sociology of deviance. *Journal of Criminal Law and Criminology, 68*(2), 262-273.

Erikson, E. H. (1956). Ego identity and the psychological moratorium. In H. L. Witmer & R. Kotinsky (Eds.), *New perspectives for research on juvenile delinquency* (Publication No. 356, pp. 1-23). Washington, DC: U.S. Children's Bureau.

Fagan, J. (1989). The social organization of drug use and drug dealing among urban gangs. *Criminology, 27*(4), 633-669.

Fagan, J., & Chin, K. (1989). Violence as regulation and social control in the distribution of crack. In M. de la Rosa, B. Gropper, & E. Lambert (Eds.), *Drugs and violence* (National Institute of Drug Abuse Research Monograph). Rockville, MD: U.S. Department of Health and Human Services.

Fagan, J., & Jones, S. J. (1984). Toward a theoretical model for intervention with violent juvenile offenders. In R. Mathias, P. DeMuro, & R. A. Allinson (Eds.), *Violent juvenile offenders: An anthology.* San Francisco: National Council on Crime and Delinquency.

Fagan, J., Piper, E. S., & Cheng, Y. T. (1987). Contributions of victimization to delinquency in inner cities. *Journal of Criminal Law and Criminology, 78*(3), 586-613.

Fagan, J., Piper, E., & Moore, M. (1986). Violent delinquents and urban youths. *Criminology, 23*(4), 439-466.

Fagan, J., Weis, J. G., & Cheng, Y. (1990). Drug use and delinquency among inner city students. *Journal of Drug Issues, 20*(3), 349-400.

Farrington, D. P., Berkowitz, L., & West, D. J. (1981). Differences between individual and group fights. *British Journal of Social Psychology, 20*(1), 163-171.

Feldman, H. W., Mandel, J., & Fields, A. (1985). In the neighborhood: A strategy for delivering early intervention services to young drug users in their natural environments. In A. S. Friedman & G. M. Beschner (Eds.), *Treatment services for adolescent substance abusers*. Rockville, MD: National Institute on Drug Abuse.

Fessler, L. W. (Ed.). (1983). *Chinese in America: Stereotyped past, changing present*. New York: Vantage.

Figueria-McDonough, J., Barton, W. H., & Sarri, R. C. (1981). Normal deviance: Gender similarities in adolescent subcultures. In M. Q. Warren (Ed.), *Comparing female and male offenders*. Beverly Hills, CA: Sage.

Fishman, L. (1988). *The Vice Queens: An ethnographic study of black female gang behavior*. Paper presented at the annual meeting of the American Society of Criminology, Chicago.

Fitzpatrick, J. (1971). *Puerto Rican Americans: The meaning of migration to the mainland*. Englewood Cliffs, NJ: Prentice-Hall.

Friedman, C. J., Mann, F., & Friedman, A. S. (1975). A profile of juvenile street gang members. *Adolescence, 10*, 563-607.

Galbraith, John K. (1983). *The anatomy of power*. Boston: Houghton Mifflin.

Gamio, M. (1969). *Mexican immigration to the United States*. New York: Arno.

Gans, H. (1962). *The urban villagers*. Glencoe, IL: Free Press.

Gastil, R. D. (1971). Homicide and a regional culture of violence. *American Sociological Review, 36*, 412-427.

Gibbs, J. P. (1981). *Norms, deviance and social control*. New York: Elsevier-North Holland.

Giordano, P. C. (1978). Girls, guys, and gangs: The changing social context of female delinquency. *Journal of Criminal Law and Criminology, 69*, 126-132.

Giordano, P. C., Cernkovich, S. A., & Pugh, M. D. (1986). Friendships and delinquency. *American Journal of Sociology, 91*, 1170-1202.

Glasgow, D. G. (1980). *The black underclass: Poverty, unemployment and entrapment of ghetto youth*. San Francisco: Jossey-Bass.

Gold, M., & Reimer, D. J. (1975). Changing patterns of delinquency behavior among Americans 13 through 16 years old. *Crime and Delinquency Literature, 7*, 483-517.

Goldstein, H. (1987). *Comments presented to the conference on policing: State of the art III*. Unpublished paper presented at a conference sponsored by the National Institute of Justice.

Gong, Y. E., & Grant, B. (1930). *Tong war!* New York: N. L. Brown.

Gonzalez, A. (1981). *Mexicano/Chicano gangs in Los Angeles: A sociohistorical case study*. Unpublished doctoral dissertation, University of California, Berkeley.

Goodman, P. (1960). *Growing up absurd: Problems of youth in the organized society*. New York: Random House.

Gouldner, A. (1968, May). The sociologist as partisan: Sociology and the welfare state. *American Sociologist*.

Grant, B. (1979). *The boat people*. Sydney, Australia: Penguin.

Hagan, J., Simpson, J., & Gillis, A. R. (1979). The sexual stratification of social control: A gender-based perspective on crime and delinquency. *British Journal of Sociology, 30,* 25-38.

Hagedorn, J. M. (1987). *Final report: Milwaukee Gang Research Project.* Milwaukee: University of Wisconsin—Milwaukee.

Hagedorn, J. M. (1988). *People and folks: Gangs, crime and the underclass in a rustbelt city.* Chicago: Lake View.

Hagedorn, J. M., & Moore, J. W. (1987). *Milwaukee and Los Angeles gangs compared.* Paper presented at the annual meeting of the American Anthropological Association, Oaxaca, Mexico.

Hagerty, E. A. (1980). *Vietnamese in Southern California.* Unpublished doctoral dissertation, United States International University.

Hall, S., & Jefferson, T. (1976). *Resistance through rituals.* London: Hutchinson.

Hamparian, D. M., Schuster, R., Dinitz, S., & Conrad, J. P. (1978). *The violent few.* Lexington, MA: Lexington.

Hanson, K. (1964). *Rebels in the streets: The story of New York's girl gangs.* Englewood Cliffs, NJ: Prentice-Hall.

Harris, M. (1988). *Culture, people, nature: An introduction to general anthropology* (5th ed.). New York: Harper & Row.

Harris, M. G. (1988). *Cholas: Latino girls and gangs.* New York: AMS.

Harrison, L. (1987, July 17). Van de Kamp's report on gangs irks Asians. *AsianWeek.*

Hechter, M. (1989). Rational choice foundation for social order. In J. H. Turner (Ed.), *Theory building in sociology.* Newbury Park, CA: Sage.

Hill, G. D., & Atkinson, M. P. (1988). Gender, familial control and delinquency. *Criminology, 26,* 127-149.

Hindelang, M. J. (1971). Age, sex and the versatility of delinquent involvements. *Social Problems, 18,* 522-535.

Hirschi, T. (1969). *Causes of delinquency.* Berkeley: University of California Press.

Hochschild, J. L. (1989). Equal opportunity and the estranged poor. *Annals of the American Academy of Political and Social Science, 501,* 143-155.

Hoffman, A. (1974). *Unwanted Mexican-Americans in the Great Depression.* Tucson: University of Arizona Press.

Hormell, S. (1990, January 11). Gang killings break city, county record. *United Press International* (Los Angeles Bureau).

Hornblower, M. (1987, February 14). Gangs fight Viet conflict of a different sort in U.S. *Washington Post.*

Horowitz, R. (1983). *Honor and the American dream: Culture and identity in a Chicano community.* New Brunswick, NJ: Rutgers University Press.

Horowitz, R. (1987). Community tolerance of gang violence. *Social Problems, 34,* 437-450.

Huang, K., & Pilisuk, M. (1977). At the threshold of the Golden Gate: Special problems of a neglected minority. *American Journal of Orthopsychiatry, 47,* 701-713.

Huff, C. R. (1988a). *Youth gangs and public policy in Ohio: Findings and recommendations.* Paper presented at the Ohio Conference on Youth Gangs and the Urban Underclass, Ohio State University, Columbus.

Huff, C. R. (1988b). *Youth gangs and police organizations: Rethinking structure and functions.* Paper presented at the annual meeting of the Academy of Criminal Justice Sciences, San Francisco.

Huff, C. R. (1989a). Youth gangs and public policy. *Crime and Delinquency, 35*(4), 524-537.

Huff, C. R. (1989b). Gangs, organized crime, and drug-related violence in Ohio. In Governor's Office of Criminal Justice Services, *Understanding the enemy: An informational overview of substance abuse in Ohio.* Columbus, OH: Governor's Office of Criminal Justice Services.

Irwin, J. (1970). *The felon.* Englewood Cliffs, NJ: Prentice-Hall.

Jackson, P. G. (1989). Theories and findings about youth gangs. *Criminal Justice Abstracts, 21*(2), 313-329.

Jacobs, J. B. (1977). *Stateville: The penitentiary in mass society.* Chicago: University of Chicago Press.

Jessor, R., & Jessor, S. L. (1977). *Problem behavior and psychosocial development: A longitudinal study of youth.* New York: Academic Press.

Johnson, B. D., Williams, T., Dei, K., & Sanabria, H. (1990). Drug abuse and the inner city: Impacts of hard drug use and sales on low income communities. In J. Q. Wilson & M. Tonry (Eds.), *Drugs and crime.* Chicago: University of Chicago Press.

Johnson, R. E., Marcos, A. C., & Bahr, S. J. (1987). The role of peers in the complex etiology of adolescent drug use. *Criminology, 25,* 323-340.

Johnston, L. D., O'Malley, P. M., & Bachman, J. G. (1988). *Use of licit and illicit drugs by American high school students: 1985-1987.* Rockville, MD: National Institute on Drug Abuse.

Kasarda, J. D. (1985). Urban change and minority opportunities. In P. E. Peterson (Ed.), *The new urban reality.* Washington, DC: Brookings Institution.

Katz, J. (1988). *Seductions of crime.* New York: Basic Books.

Keiser, R. L. (1969). *The Vice Lords: Warriors of the street.* New York: Holt, Rinehart & Winston.

Kelly, G. (1977). *From Vietnam to America: A chronicle of the Vietnamese immigration to the United States.* Boulder, CO: Westview.

Kids and cocaine. (1986, March 17). *Newsweek,* pp. 58-68.

Kirk, J., & Miller, M. L. (1986). *Reliability and validity in qualitative research.* Beverly Hills, CA: Sage.

Klein, M. W. (1971). *Street gangs and street workers.* Englewood Cliffs, NJ: Prentice-Hall.

Klein, M. W., & Crawford, L. Y. (1967). Groups, gangs and cohesiveness. *Journal of Research in Crime and Delinquency, 4*(1), 63-75.

Klein, M. W., Gordon, M. A., & Maxson, C. L. (1986). The impact of police investigation on police-reported rates of gang and nongang homicides. *Criminology, 24,* 489-512.

Klein, M. W., & Maxson, C. L. (1989). Street gang violence. In N. A. Weiner & M. E. Wolfgang (Eds.), *Violent crime, violent criminals*. Newbury Park, CA: Sage.

Klein, M. W., Maxson, C. L., & Cunningham, L. (1988). *Gang involvement in cocaine "rock" trafficking* (Final report to the National Institute of Justice, Grant 85-IF-CX-0057). Los Angeles: University of Southern California, Social Science Research Institute.

Klein, M. W., Maxson, C. L., & Gordon, M. A. (1984). *Evaluation in a gang violence deterrence program: Final report*. Los Angeles: University of Southern California, Social Science Research Institute.

Konopka, G. (1966). *The adolescent girl in conflict*. Englewood Cliffs, NJ: Prentice-Hall.

Kornhauser, R. R. (1978). *Social sources of delinquency*. Chicago: University of Chicago Press.

Kwong, P. (1987). *The new Chinatown*. New York: Hill & Wang.

Larson, D. (1988, October 23). Honor thy parents. *Los Angeles Times*.

Launer, H. M., & Palenski, J. E. (Eds.). (1989). *Crime and the new immigrants*. Springfield, IL: Charles C Thomas.

Lemert, E. M. (1951). *Social pathology*. New York: McGraw-Hill.

Lewis, O. (1965). *La vida*. New York: Random House.

Lieberson, S. (1980). *A piece of the pie: Black and white immigrants since 1880*. Berkeley: University of California Press.

Liebow, E. (1967). *Tally's corner*. Boston: Little, Brown.

Liu, W. T. (1979). *Transition to nowhere: Vietnamese refugees in America*. Nashville, TN: Charter House.

Loeber, R., & Stouthamer-Loeber, M. (1986). *Family factors as correlates and predictors of juvenile conduct problems and delinquency*. Unpublished manuscript.

Long, N. (1968). *Final report of the planning process in nine cities under the program of the President's Committee on Juvenile Delinquency*. Cambridge: MIT and Harvard University, Joint Center for Urban Studies.

Loo, C. K. (1976). *The emergence of San Francisco Chinese juvenile gangs from the 1950s to the present*. Unpublished master's thesis, San Jose State University.

Los Angeles County Sheriff's Department. (1984). *Asian criminal activities survey*. Los Angeles: Author.

Lynn, D. B. (1974). *The father: His role in child development*. Belmont, CA: Wadsworth.

Maccoby, E. E., & Jacklin, C. N. (1974). *The psychology of sex differences*. Stanford, CA: Stanford University Press.

MacGill, H. G. (1938). The Oriental delinquent in the Vancouver juvenile court. *Sociology and Social Research, 12*, 428-438.

MacLeod, J. (1987). *Ain't no makin' it: Leveled aspirations in a low-income neighborhood*. Boulder, CO: Westview.

Manning, P. K. (1989). On the phenomenology of violence. *Criminologist, 14*(4), 1-22.

Maris, P., & Rein, M. (1967). *Dilemmas of social reform: Poverty and community action in the United States.* New York: Atherton.

Marsh, P., Rosser, E., & Harre, R. (1978). *The rules of disorder.* London: Routledge & Kegan Paul.

Marsh, R. E. (1980). Socioeconomic status of Indochinese refugees in the United States: Progress and problems. *Social Security Bulletin, 43,* 11-12.

Maxson, C. L., Gordon, M. A., & Klein, M. W. (1985). Differences between gang and nongang homicides. *Criminology, 23,* 209-222.

Maxson, C. L., & Klein, M. W. (1986). *Street gangs selling cocaine "rock": The confluence of two social problems.* Unpublished manuscript, University of Southern California, Social Science Research Center.

Maxson, C. L., Klein, M. W., & Gordon, M. A. (1990). *Street gang violence as a generalizable pattern.* Unpublished manuscript, University of Southern California, Social Science Research Institute.

Mazon, M. (1985). *The zoot-suit riots: The psychology of symbolic annihilation.* Austin: University of Texas Press.

McRobbie, A. (1978). *Working class girls and the culture of femininity.* Unpublished master's thesis, University of Birmingham, England.

McWilliams, C. (1968). *North from Mexico: The Spanish-speaking people of the United States.* New York: Greenwood.

Merton, R. K. (1938). Social structure and anomie. *American Sociological Review, 3*(5), 672-682.

Meskil, P. (1989, February 5). In the eye of the storm. *New York Daily News Magazine,* pp. 10-16.

Miller, S. M. (1969). The participant observer and "over-rapport." In G. J. McCall & J. L. Simmons (Eds.), *Issues in participant observation.* Reading, MA: Addison-Wesley.

Miller, W. B. (1958). Lower class culture as a generating milieu of gang delinquency. *Journal of Social Issues, 14,* 5-19.

Miller, W. B. (1959). Implications of urban lower class culture for social work. *Social Service Review, 33*(3), 219-230.

Miller, W. B. (1966a). Violent crimes by city gangs. *Annals of the American Academy of Political and Social Science, 364,* 96-112.

Miller, W. B. (1966b). *Evaluative research and federal social change programs.* Cambridge: MIT and Harvard University, Joint Center for Urban Studies.

Miller, W. B. (1969a). White gangs. *Trans-Action, 6*(1).

Miller, W. B. (1969b). The elimination of the American lower class as a national policy. In D. P. Moynihan (Ed.), *On understanding poverty: Perspectives from the social sciences.* New York: Basic Books.

Miller, W. B. (1973). The molls. *Society, 11,* 32-35.

Miller, W. B. (1974). American youth gangs: Past and present. In A. Blumberg (Ed.), *Current perspectives on criminal behavior.* New York: Knopf.

Miller, W. B. (1975). *Violence by youth gangs and youth groups as a crime problem in major American cities.* Report to the National Institute for Juvenile Justice and Delinquency Prevention.

Miller, W. B. (1976). A proposal for a new federal role in dealing with collective youth crime. In *Serious youth crime: Hearings before the Subcommittee to Investigate Juvenile Delinquency, Committee on the Judiciary, United States Senate, Ninety-fifth Congress.* Washington, DC: Government Printing Office.

Miller, W. B. (1980). Gangs, groups and serious youth crime. In D. Shichor & D. Kelly (Eds.), *Critical issues in juvenile delinquency.* Lexington, MA: Lexington.

Miller, W. B. (1982). *Crime by youth gangs and youth groups in the United States* (report prepared for the National Youth Gang Survey). Washington, DC: Office of Juvenile Justice and Delinquency Prevention.

Miller, W. B. (1985). Historical review of programs and theories of work with youth gangs: 1920-1985. In D. Ingemunsen & G. Johnson, *Report on the Illinois Symposium on Gangs.* Springfield: Illinois Department of Children and Family Services.

Miller, W. B. (1989, September). *Recommendations for terms to be used for designating law violating youth groups.* Paper presented at the conference of the National Youth Gang Suppression and Intervention Project, Chicago.

Mills, C. W. (1959). *The sociological imagination.* London: Oxford University Press.

Molohon, K. T., Paton, R., & Lambert, M. (1979). An extension of Barth's concept on ethnic boundaries to include both other groups and developmental stages of ethnic groups. *Human Relations, 32*(1), 1-17.

Moore, J. W. (1977). The Chicano Pinto Research Project: A case study in collaboration. *Journal of Social Issues, 33*(4), 144-158.

Moore, J. W. (1978). *Homeboys: Gangs, drugs, and prison in the barrios of Los Angeles.* Philadelphia: Temple University Press.

Moore, J. W. (1979). *Research in minority communities: Collaborative and street ethnography models compared.* Milwaukee: University of Wisconsin—Milwaukee, Urban Research Center.

Moore, J. W. (1985). Isolation and stigmatization in the development of an underclass: The case of Chicano gangs in East Los Angeles. *Social Problems, 33*(1), 1-10.

Moore, J. W. (1988). Changing Chicano gangs: Acculturation, generational change, evolution of deviance or emerging underclass? In J. H. Johnson, Jr., & M. L. Oliver (Eds.), *Proceedings of the Conference on Comparative Ethnicity.* Los Angeles: Institute for Social Science Research, UCLA.

Moore, J. W. (1989a). Is there a Hispanic underclass? *Social Science Quarterly, 70*(2), 265-285.

Moore, J. W. (1989b). Gangs, drugs, and violence. In M. de la Rosa, B. Gropper, & E. Lambert (Eds.), *Drugs and violence* (National Institute of Drug Abuse Research Monograph). Rockville, MD: U.S. Department of Health and Human Services.

Moore, J. W. (1989c, May 2). *Gangs and gang violence: What we know and what we don't know.* Paper presented at California State University, Los Angeles.

Moore, J. W., & Edari, R. (1990). *Final report, Youth Initiative Needs Assessment Survey.* Milwaukee: University of Wisconsin.

Moore, J. W., & Long, J. M. (1987). *Youth culture vs. individual factors in adult drug use.* Los Angeles: Community Research Systems, Inc.

Moore, J. W., & Pachon, H. (1985). *Hispanics in the United States.* Englewood Cliffs, NJ: Prentice-Hall.

Moore, J. W., & Vigil, J. D. (1987). Chicano gangs: Group norms and individual factors related to adult criminality. *Aztlan, 18*(2).

Morash, M. (1983). Gangs, groups and delinquency. *British Journal of Criminology, 23*(3), 309-331.

Morash, M. (1990). Gangs and violence. In A. J. Reiss, Jr., N. Weiner, & J. Roth (Eds.), *Violent criminal behavior* (report of the Panel on the Understanding and Control of Violent Behavior, National Academy of Sciences). Washington, DC: National Academy Press.

Morganthau, T., Contreras, J., Lam, H., & Sandza, R. (1982, August 2). Vietnamese gangs in California. *Newsweek.*

Morris, R. (1964). Female delinquents and relational problems. *Social Forces, 43,* 82-89.

Moynihan, D. P. (1969). *Maximum feasible misunderstanding.* New York: Free Press.

National School Safety Center. (1988). *Gangs in schools: Breaking up is hard to do.* Malibu, CA: Pepperdine University Press.

New York City Police Department, Fifth Precinct. (1983). *Gang intelligence information.* New York: Author.

Nguyen, L. T., & Henkin, A. B. (1982). Vietnamese refugees in the United States: Adaptation and transitional status. *Journal of Ethnic Studies, 9*(4), 101-116.

Park, R. (1969). Human migration and the marginal man. In R. Sennett (Ed.), *Classic essays on the culture of cities.* Englewood Cliffs, NJ: Prentice-Hall.

Parsons, T. (1951). *Toward a general theory of action.* Cambridge, MA: Harvard University Press.

Patterson, G. R., & Dishion, T. (1985). Contributions of families and peers to delinquency. *Criminology, 23,* 63-80.

Peyser, N. (1932, October). What the schools are doing or what they should do to prevent delinquency. In *Proceedings of the National Conference of Juvenile Agencies* (29th annual conference, Indianapolis, IN).

Pike, K. (1954). *Language in relation to a unified theory of the structure of human behavior* (Vol. 1). Glendale, CA: Summer Institute of Linguistics.

Plant, J. S. (1937). *Personality and the cultural pattern.* New York: Commonwealth Fund.

Polsky, N. (1967). *Hustlers, beats, and others.* Chicago: University of Chicago Press.

Posner, G. (1988). *Warlords of crime.* New York: McGraw-Hill.

President's Commission on Organized Crime. (1984). *Organized crime of Asian origin: Record of hearing III—October 23-25, 1984, New York, New York.* Washington, DC: Government Printing Office.

Quicker, J. C. (1981). *Seven decades of gangs.* Sacramento: California Commission on Crime Control and Violence Prevention.

Quicker, J. C. (1983). *Homegirls: Characterizing Chicano gangs.* San Pedro, CA: International University Press.

Rand, A. (1988). Transitional life events and desistance from delinquency and crime. In M. E. Wolfgang, T. P. Thornberry, & R. F. Figlio (Eds.), *From boy to man, from delinquency to crime.* Chicago: University of Chicago Press.

Reiss, A. J., Jr. (1986). Co-offending influences on criminal careers. In A. Blumstein, J. Cohen, J. Roth, & C. Visher (Eds.), *Criminal careers and "career criminals"* (Vol. 2). Washington, DC: National Academy Press.

Reiss, A. J., Jr., & Tonry, M. (Eds.). (1986). *Communities and crime.* Chicago: University of Chicago Press.

Report: L.A.'s Asian gangs grow in power. (1987, October 16). *AsianWeek.*

Reuter, P. (1989). *Youth gangs and drug distribution: A preliminary enquiry.* Unpublished manuscript, RAND Corporation, Washington, DC.

Rice, R. (1963). A report at large: The Persian Queens. *New Yorker, 39,* 135ff.

Richardson, H. J. (1969). *Adolescent girls in approved schools.* London: Routledge & Kegan Paul.

Rittenhouse, R. (1963). *A theory and comparison of male and female delinquency.* Unpublished doctoral dissertation, University of Michigan, Ann Arbor.

Roache, F. M. (1988, January). Organized crime in Boston's Chinatown. *Police Chief,* pp. 48-51.

Robertson, F. (1977). *Triangle of death.* London: Routledge & Kegan Paul.

Robinson, N., & Joe, D. (1980). Gangs in Chinatown. *McGill Journal of Education, 15,* 149-162.

Rodman, H. (1963). The lower class value stretch. *Social Forces, 42,* 205-215.

Rubinow, L. B. (1954). Official agency participation in community programs. In *Group work and community organization: 1953-1954.* New York: Columbia University Press.

Sampson, R. J. (1987). Urban black violence: The effect of male joblessness and family disruption. *American Journal of Sociology, 93*(2), 348-382.

Sanchez-Jankowski, M. (in press). *Islands in the street: Gangs in American urban society.* Berkeley: University of California Press.

Sandhu, H. S., & Allen, D. E. (1969). Female delinquency, goal obstruction, and anomie. *Canadian Review of Sociology and Anthropology, 6,* 107-110.

Sawyer, E. (1973). Methodological problems in studying so-called "deviant" communities. In J. Ladner (Ed.), *The death of white sociology.* New York: Vintage.

Schwartz, G. S. (1987). *Beyond conformity or rebellion: Youth and authority in America.* Chicago: University of Chicago Press.

Schwendinger, H., & Schwendinger, J. (1985). *Adolescent subcultures and delinquency.* New York: Praeger.

Shaw, C. R. (1930). *The Jack-Roller: A delinquent boy's own story.* Chicago: University of Chicago Press.

Shaw, C. R., & McKay, H. D. (1942). *Juvenile delinquency and urban areas.* Chicago: University of Chicago Press.

Sherman, L. (1970). *Youth workers, police, and the gangs.* Unpublished master's thesis, University of Chicago.

Short, J. F. (1976). Gangs, politics, and the social order. In J. F. Short (Ed.), *Delinquency, crime, and society.* Chicago: University of Chicago Press.

Short, J. F. (1989). Exploring integration of theoretical levels of explanation: Notes on gang delinquency. In S. F. Messner, M. D. Krohn, & A. E. Liska (Eds.), *Theoretical integration in the study of deviance and crime: Problems and prospects* (pp. 243-259). Albany: State University of New York Press.

Short, J. F. (1990). *Delinquency and society.* Englewood Cliffs, NJ: Prentice-Hall.

Short, J. F., & Moland, J., Jr. (1976). *Politics and youth gangs: A follow-up study.* Sociological Quarterly, 17, 162-179.

Short, J. F., & Strodtbeck, F. (1965). *Group process and gang delinquency.* Chicago: University of Chicago Press.

Sifakis, C. (1987). *The mafia encyclopedia.* New York: Facts on File.

Singer, S. L., & Levine, M. (1988). Power-control theory, gender and delinquency: A partial replication with additional evidence on the effects of peers. *Criminology, 26,* 627-647.

Skinner, K. (1980). Vietnamese in America: Diversity in adaptation. *California Sociologist, 3*(2), 103-124.

Skolnick, J. H., Correl, T., Navarro, E., & Rabb, R. (1988). *The social structure of street drug dealing.* Sacramento: Office of the Attorney General of the State of California.

Smart, C., & Smart, B. (1978). *Women, sexuality and social control.* London: Routledge & Kegan Paul.

Snodgrass, J. (1982). *The Jack-Roller at seventy: A fifty year follow-up.* Lexington, MA: Lexington.

Speckart, G., & Anglin, M. D. (1988). Narcotics use and crime: A causal modeling approach. *Journal of Quantitative Criminology, 2*(1), 3-28.

Spergel, I. A. (1966). *Street gang work: Theory and practice.* Reading, MA: Addison-Wesley.

Spergel, I. A. (1969). *Problem solving: The delinquency example.* Chicago: University of Chicago Press.

Spergel, I. A. (1983). *Violent gangs in Chicago: Segmentation and integration.* Chicago: University of Chicago, School of Social Service Administration.

Spergel, I. A. (1984). Violent gangs in Chicago: In search of social policy. *Social Service Review, 58*(2), 199-226.

Spergel, I. A. (1985a). *The violent gang problem in Chicago.* Chicago: University of Chicago, School of Social Service Administration.

Spergel, I. A. (1985b). *Youth gang activity and the Chicago public schools.* Chicago: University of Chicago, School of Social Service Administration.

Spergel, I. A. (1989a). Youth gangs: Continuity and change. In N. Morris & M. Tonry (Eds.), *Crime and justice: An annual review of research* (Vol. 12). Chicago: University of Chicago Press.

Spergel, I. A. (1989b). *Youth gangs: Problem and response. A review of the literature* (Tech. Rep. No. 1, National Youth Gang Suppression and Intervention Project). Chicago: University of Chicago, School of Social Service Administration.

Spergel, I. A., Curry, G. D., Ross, R. A., & Chance, R. (1989). *Survey of youth gang problems and programs in 45 cities and 6 sites* (Tech. Rep. No. 2, National Youth Gang Suppression and Intervention Project). Chicago: University of Chicago, School of Social Service Administration.

Stein, B. N. (1979). Occupational adjustment of refugees: The Vietnamese in the United States. *International Migration Review, 13*, 25-45.

Stern, L. M. (1981). Response to Vietnamese refugees: Surveys of public opinion. *Social Work, 26*, 306-311.

Strasburg, P. A. (1978). *Violent deliquents: A report to the Ford Foundation from the Vera Institute of Justice.* New York: Monarche Press.

Stumphauzer, J. S., Veloz, E. V., & Aiken, T. W. (1981). Violence by street gangs: East side story? In R. B. Stuart (Ed.), *Violent behavior: Social learning approaches to prediction, management and treatment.* New York: Brunner-Mazel.

Sullivan, M. L. (1989). *Getting paid: Youth crime and work in the inner city.* Ithaca, NY: Cornell University Press.

Sung, B. L. (1977). *Gangs in New York's Chinatown* (Monograph No. 6). New York: City College of New York, Department of Asian Studies.

Sung, B. L. (1979). *Transplanted Chinese children.* New York: City College of New York, Department of Asian Studies.

Sutherland, E., & Cressey, D. R. (1978). *Principles of criminology* (10th ed.). New York: J. B. Lippincott.

Suttles, G. D. (1968). *The social order of the slum.* Chicago: University of Chicago Press.

Takagi, P., & Platt, T. (1978). Behind the gilded ghetto. *Crime and Social Justice, 9*, 2-25.

Takaki, R. (1989). *Strangers from a different shore.* Boston: Little, Brown.

Taylor, C. S. (1990). *Dangerous society.* East Lansing: Michigan State University Press.

Thio, A. (1983). *Deviant behavior* (2nd ed.). Boston: Houghton Mifflin.

Thomas, W. I. (1923). *The unadjusted girl.* New York: Little, Brown.

Thornberry, T. P. (1987). Toward an interactional theory of delinquency. *Criminology, 25*(4), 863-892.

Thornberry, T. P., & Christenson, R. L. (1984). Unemployment and criminal involvement: An investigation of reciprocal causal structures. *American Sociological Review, 49,* 398-411.

Thrasher, F. M. (1927). *The gang: A study of 1,313 gangs in Chicago.* Chicago: University of Chicago Press.

Tienda, M. (1989). Puerto Ricans and the underclass debate. *Annals of the American Academy of Political and Social Science, 501,* 105-119.

Tracy, C. A. (1980, Winter). Race, crime, and social policy. *Crime and Social Justice,* pp. 11-25.

Tracy, P. E. (1979). *Subcultural delinquency: A comparison of the incidence and seriousness of gang and nongang member offensivity.* Unpublished manuscript, University of Pennsylvania, Center for Studies in Criminology and Criminal Law.

Tracy, P. E. (1984, November). *Gang membership and violent offending: Preliminary results from the 1958 cohort study.* Paper presented at the annual meeting of the American Society of Criminology, Cincinnati, OH.

Tracy, P. E., & Piper, E. S. (1981). *Gang membership and violent offending: Preliminary results from the 1958 cohort study.* Philadelphia: University of Pennsylvania, Center for Studies in Criminology and Criminal Law.

U.S. Department of Justice. (1985). *Oriental organized crime: A report of a research project conducted by the Organized Crime Section* (Federal Bureau of Investigation, Criminal Investigative Division). Washington, DC: Government Printing Office.

U.S. Department of Justice. (1988). *Report on Asian organized crime* (Criminal Division). Washington, DC: Government Printing Office.

U.S. Department of Justice. (1989). *The INS enforcement approach to Chinese crime groups* (Immigration and Naturalization Service, Investigative Division). Washington, DC: Government Printing Office.

U.S. Department of State. (1988). *Hong Kong 1997: Its impact on Chinese organized crime in the United States* (Foreign Service Institute). Washington, DC: Government Printing Office.

U.S. Office of Management and Budget and U.S. General Services Administration. (1989). *Catalog of federal domestic assistance programs* (23rd ed.). Washington, DC: Government Printing Office.

U.S. Senate. (1986). *Emerging criminal groups* (Hearings before the Permanent Subcommittee on Investigations of the Committee on Governmental Affairs). Washington, DC: Government Printing Office.

Valentine, B. (1978). *Hustling and other hard work: Life styles in the ghetto.* New York: Free Press.

Vedder, C. B., & Somerville, D. B. (1975). *The delinquent girl.* Springfield, IL: Charles C Thomas.

Vigil, J. D. (1979). Adaptation strategies and cultural life styles of Mexican-American adolescents. *Hispanic Journal of Behavioral Sciences, 1*(4), 375-392.

Vigil, J. D. (1984). *From Indians to Chicano: The dynamics of Mexican-American culture.* Prospect Heights, IL: Waveland.

Vigil, J. D. (1987). Street socialization, locura behavior and violence among Chicano gang members. In J. Kraus et al. (Eds.), *Violence and homicide in Hispanic communities.* Washington, DC: National Institute of Mental Health, Office of Minority Health.

Vigil, J. D. (1988a). *Barrio gangs: Street life and identity in Southern California.* Austin: University of Texas Press.

Vigil, J. D. (1988b). Group processes and street identity: Adolescent Chicano gang members. *Ethos, 16*(4), 421-445.

Wacquant, L. D., & Wilson, W. J. (1989). The costs of racial and class exclusion in the inner city. *Annals of the American Academy of Political and Social Science, 501,* 8-25.

Weis, J. G. (1976). Liberation and crime: The invention of the new female criminal. *Crime and Social Justice, 6,* 17-27.

Weis, J. G., & Hawkins, J. D. (1981). *Preventing delinquency: The social development approach.* Washington, DC: Government Printing Office.

Welfare Council of New York City. (1950). *Working with teenage groups: A report on the Central Harlem Project.* New York: Author.

White, H. (1990). The drugs-delinquency connection in adolescence. In R. Weischeit (Ed.), *Drugs, crime and criminal justice.* Cincinnati, OH: Anderson.

White, H. R., Pandina, R. J., & LaGrange, R. (1987). Longitudinal predictors of serious drug abuse and delinquency. *Criminology, 25,* 715-740.

Whyte, W. F. (1943). *Street corner society: The social structure of an Italian slum.* Chicago: University of Chicago Press.

Whyte, W. F. (1969). How do you know if the informant is telling the truth? In G. J. McCall & J. L. Simmons (Eds.), *Issues in participant observation.* Reading, MA: Addison-Wesley.

Wiatrowski, M., Griswold, D. B., & Roberts, M. K. (1981). Social control theory and delinquency. *American Sociological Review, 46,* 525-541.

Williams, T. (1989). *The cocaine kids.* Reading, MA: Addison-Wesley.

Wilson, W. J. (1987). *The truly disadvantaged: The inner city, the underclass, and public policy.* Chicago: University of Chicago Press.

Wolfgang, M. E., & Ferracuti, F. (1967). *The subculture of violence.* London: Tavistock.

Woodson, R. (Ed.). (1981). *Youth crime and urban policy: A view from the inner city.* Washington, DC: American Enterprise Institute for Public Policy Research.

Wright, W. E., & Dixon, M. C. (1977). An evaluation of community prevention and treatment of juvenile delinquency. *Journal of Research in Crime and Delinquency, 14*(1), 35-67.

Yablonsky, L. (1959). The gang as a near-group. *Social Problems, 7,* 108-117.

Yablonsky, L. (1962). *The violent gang.* New York: Macmillan.

Yu, A. (1988, September 19). As the Asian-American experience tells us, average is hard to define. *Los Angeles Times.*

Zatz, M. (1985). Los cholos: Legal processing of Chicano gang members. *Social Problems, 33,* 11-30.

Zimring, F. E. (1981). Kids, groups and crimes: Some implications of a well-known secret. *Journal of Criminal Law, Criminology and Police Science, 72,* 867-885.

Author Index

Subject Index

About the Authors

Anne Campbell, formerly at the School of Criminal Justice at Rutgers University is presently Senior Lecturer at Teeside Polytechnic, England. After earning a doctorate in female delinquency at Oxford University, she studied community violence by members of youth subcultures in Britain. She spent two years as a participant observer with New York female gangs, reporting this research in her book *The Girls in the Gang* (Basil Blackwell, 1984). Her current research is concerned with women's and men's implicit theories of aggression, which mediate differences in the form and frequency of their aggressive behavior.

Ko-lin Chin is Senior Research Analyst at the New York City Criminal Justice Agency. He received his Ph.D. in sociology from the University of Pennsylvania. He has conducted research on college students' drug abuse, alcoholism among Chinese immigrants, and Chinese Triad societies and criminal organizations. His recent publications include *Chinese Subculture and Criminality: Non-Traditional Crime Groups in America* (Greenwood Press, 1990). He currently is working on two research projects, both of which are funded by the National Institute of Justice: one on "crack" cocaine use and changing patterns of criminality, and another on the victimization of Asian businesses.

Albert K. Cohen received his A.B. from Harvard University in 1939 and his master's degree from Indiana University in 1942.

He worked for a year at the Indiana Boys School (the state institution for male delinquents) and served in the U.S. Army during World War II. He returned to Harvard for a year of graduate study in 1946, then joined the sociology faculty at Indiana University in 1947. He received his Ph.D. in sociology from Harvard in 1951 and after 17 years at Indiana University he joined the faculty at the University of Connecticut, where he taught for 23 years until his retirement in 1988. His best-known work is *Delinquent Boys: The Culture of the Gang* (Free Press, 1955). Another book, *Deviance and Control* (Prentice-Hall, 1965) was one of the first comprehensive texts in the field of deviance. His published works have dealt mostly with issues in deviance theory. He has been a Visiting Professor at the University of California (Berkeley and Santa Cruz), Cambridge University, John Jay College of Criminal Justice, and the University of Haifa (Israel), and Visiting Scholar at Arizona State University and Kansai University in Osaka, Japan.

G. David Curry is Associate Professor in the Crime and Justice Program, Department of Sociology and Anthropology, at West Virginia University. He is the author of *Sunshine Patriots: Punishment and the Vietnam Offender* (Notre Dame University Press, 1985). His other recent publications include "Teaching Sociological Methodology with Limited Computer Resources" (*Teaching Sociology*, 1988) and "Gang Homicide, Delinquency, and Community" (with Irving A. Spergel; *Criminology*, August 1988). Curry and Spergel are continuing their collaborative research on youth gang delinquency, and Curry also is conducting research on women, violence, and crime.

Jeffrey Fagan is Associate Professor in the School of Criminal Justice at Rutgers University. His research interests and recent publications include drug-crime relationships, youth gangs, violence in families, and the jurisprudence of crimes by adolescents. He recently completed a study of drug use, drug selling, and other criminality among users of crack cocaine and other drugs in New York City. His current research, with Ko-lin Chin and Robert Kelly, involves patterns of extortion and victimization by Asian gangs in New York City. He is coauthor (with Joseph Weis) of *Drug Use and Delinquency Among Inner City Youths* (Springer-Verlag, forthcoming) and is editor of the *Journal of Research in Crime and Delinquency.*

John M. Hagedorn is Youth Program Coordinator in Milwaukee County's Department of Health and Human Services and is affiliated with the University of Wisconsin—Milwaukee Urban Research Center. A social scientist who has been a draft resister, community organizer, rubber worker, journalist, and gang program director, he is currently coordinating a reform of Milwaukee County's social welfare system while writing his Ph.D. dissertation on that topic. He is the author (with former gang leader Perry Macon) of *People and Folks: Gangs, Crime, and the Underclass in a Rustbelt City* (Lake View Press, 1988). His research interests include the relationship of gangs and the underclass to urban neighborhoods, changing public policy toward gangs and the underclass, organizational change in social welfare, and the influence of welfare on poor communities.

Ruth Horowitz is Associate Professor of Sociology at the University of Delaware. She received her Ph.D. from the University of Chicago and has written a number of articles on gangs in Chicano communities. Her book *Honor and the American Dream: Culture and Identity in a Chicano Community* was published by Rutgers University Press in 1983. She is currently working with James Inciardi and Anne Pottieger on a study of very seriously involved delinquent/drug-abusing youth and is completing a book on social service workers and teenage mothers.

C. Ronald Huff is Director of the Criminal Justice Research Center and Professor of Public Policy and Management at Ohio State University, where he has taught since 1979. Prior to joining the Ohio State faculty, he taught for five years at the University of California (Irvine) and Purdue University, where he coordinated the applied sociology program and designed the criminology and criminal justice major. In addition, he has held previous professional positions in correctional, mental health, and children's services agencies and institutions. His publications include more than 40 journal articles and book chapters, numerous research reports and monographs, and six books. He is currently completing a seventh book, *Convicted but Innocent: Wrongful Conviction and Public Policy* (with Arye Rattner and the late Edward Sagarin), to be published by Ohio State University Press in 1991, and is working on a policy simulation model of wrongful conviction (with Anand Desai).

Malcolm W. Klein is Professor of Sociology and Senior Research Associate in the Social Science Research Institute at the University of Southern California. From 1962 to 1968, he directed evaluation and basic research projects dealing with juvenile gangs. From 1969 to the present, his research has centered on comprehensive criminal justice planning, evaluation of deinstitutionalization programs, and assessment of legislative impacts. His current research involves police handling of juvenile offenders and police investigation of gang-related homicides.

John M. Long has taught anthropology for two decades, mostly at East Los Angeles College, with which he remains affiliated. He has a master's degree in anthropology from UCLA and, in addition to his teaching, he has been involved extensively in anthropological research and program evaluation at UCLA, the University of Southern California, and Community Systems Research, Inc. Most of the ethnographic and survey research projects on which he has worked focused on urban ethnic minority subcultures, especially the Chicano subculture of East Los Angeles, where he grew up. He has coauthored several publications with Joan Moore and with James Diego Vigil, and his most recent publication focuses on drug and alcohol use in Chicano gangs (in Moore and Glick, eds., *Drug Use in Hispanic Communities*, Rutgers University Press, forthcoming).

Cheryl L. Maxson is Research Assistant Professor of Sociology and Research Associate at the Social Science Research Institute, University of Southern California. Her current research and publication activity is concerned with the deinstitutionalization of status offenders, the nature of gang violence, and police identification and response to gang-related crime. Her previous research topics have included predicting legislative change and evaluation of legislative implementation and impact.

Walter B. Miller has been concerned with youth gang problems since 1954, when he joined the staff of the Special Youth Program (one of the early detached worker programs) in Roxbury, Massachusetts. In the succeeding years, he has published more than 40 papers and books on youth gangs, juvenile delinquency, and lower-class subcultures. One of his papers, "Lower Class Culture as a Generating Milieu of Gang Delinquency," published in 1958, was the single most frequently cited journal article in the criminological literature. He retired in 1982 from the Center for Criminal Justice of the Harvard Law School, and has continued to write, lecture, and consult on youth gangs and related issues.

James F. Short is Professor of Sociology at Washington State University, where he has also served as Dean of the Graduate School (1964-1968) and Director of the Social Research Center (1970-1985) since receiving his Ph.D. from the University of Chicago in 1951. His books include *Suicide and Homicide* (with A. F. Henry, 1951), *Group Process and Gang Delinquency* (with Fred L. Strodtbeck, 1965, 1974), and *Delinquency and Society* (Prentice-Hall, 1990). He is a former Editor of the *American Sociological Review* and Associate Editor of the *Annual Review of Sociology*. A former President of the Pacific and American Sociological Associations, he has been a Fellow at the Center for Advanced Study in the Behavior Sciences, the Institute of Criminology at Cambridge University, the Rockefeller Center in Bellagio, and the Centre for Socio-Legal Studies at Oxford. He has received numerous honors, including the NIMH and Guggenheim Fellowships, the Edwin H. Sutherland Award from the American Society of Criminology, and the Bruce Smith Award from the Academy of Criminal Justice Sciences. He is the 1990 Beto Chair Professor of Criminal Justice at Sam Houston State University.

Irving A. Spergel is Professor in the School of Social Service Administration at the University of Chicago. His major research interests have been youth gangs, community organization, and youth services evaluation. He is currently principal investigator of the National Youth Gang Suppression and Intervention Research and Development Program, funded by the Office of Juvenile Justice and Delinquency Prevention, U.S. Department of Justice. He also is completing a statewide evaluation of the Comprehensive Community Based Youth Services program of the Illinois Department of Children and Family Services, a program designed to divert status offenders from both the juvenile justice and the child welfare systems. His most recent publication is "Youth Gangs: Continuity and Change" (*Crime and Justice: An Annual Review of Research*, 1989).

Carl S. Taylor is Director of Criminal Justice Programs at Jackson Community College in Michigan and Adjunct Professor in the School of Criminal Justice at Michigan State University, where he received his Ph.D. in the administration of higher education. For the last 10 years, he has conducted extensive research on the subculture of gangs and their impact on society. He has lectured throughout the United States and has appeared on national television on such topics as urban gangs and prisons, gangs and school environments, youth gangs and law enforcement, and drug abuse and gang imperialism. He has just completed a book, *Dangerous Society* (Michigan State University Press, 1990), based on a study of Detroit youth.

James Diego Vigil is Associate Professor of Anthropology and Director of the Center for Urban Policy and Ethnicity at the University of Southern California. He received his Ph.D. in anthropology from UCLA in 1976. In addition to his present appointment, he also held positions at the University of Wisconsin at Madison (where he was Chair of Chicano Studies), UCLA, and Chaffey Community College, and has taught part-time at Whittier College, California State University at Sacramento, and California State University at Los Angeles. He is primarily an urban anthropologist, and his interest in youth issues stems from his experiences as an educator and counselor. He has linked this background with research on street gangs, especially the role of street socialization. His fieldwork in various urban, rural, and suburban barrios culminated in a recent book, *Barrio Gangs* (University of Texas Press, 1988). Among his other publications are *From Indians to Chicanos: The Dynamics of Mexican American Culture* (Waveland Press, 1984) and articles in such journals as *Social Problems, Human Organization, Aztlan,* and *Ethos.*

Steve Chong Yun is an undergraduate student in the Department of Anthropology at the University of Wisconsin at Madison. He is a member of the Asian American Studies Association. As a member of the Medical Scholars Program, he currently is preparing to enter medical school at the University of Wisconsin at Madison. He is also continuing his work with James Diego Vigil, which began when Vigil was teaching anthropology at the University of Wisconsin at Madison.